The Book of the STANIER 8F 2-8-0s

Part One: Pre-War Engines 48000-48125

Ian Sixsmith

Richard Derry

Irwell Press Ltd.

ISBN 978-1-911262-15-2

First published in the United Kingdom in 2018.
by Irwell Press Limited, 59A, High Street, Clophill,
Bedfordshire MK45 4BE
Printed by Akcent Media, UK

Contents

Acknowledgements

Thanks in especial to Allan Baker, who must have been reluctant to open his email account at times, in dread of yet another 8F query (or several, more likely). Eric Youldon pored over the notes as usual, expending his red ink to good effect. Peter Groom was immensely helpful, and Tony Sheffield, Tony Wright too; also Mike Fell, Barry Taylor, Nick Deacon, Tony Sheffield and Paul Chancellor.

This book would not have been possible without the kind help of John Jennison of 'Brassmasters', celebrated purveyors of exquisite etched brass kits n' bits of (mainly) LMS prototypes:

PO Box 1137, Sutton Coldfield,
West Midlands, B76 1FU
www.brassmasters.co.uk

Without his collection of photographs and Engine Records, the book would have been impossible.

Books consulted/ransacked include (first and foremost): *Heavy Goods Engines of the War Department* Volume 2 by J.W.P. Rowledge (Springhead Railway Books 1977). There is also R. Tourret's *Allied Locomotives of the Second World War*, published by the author in 1976 and the Wild Swan Publications *LMS Locomotive Profiles* No.8 by various authors, including the aforementioned John Jennison.

Later pages will testify to the glittering condition of the new engines but of course it didn't take long before these pristine examples were indistinguishable from the common herd. 8061 went to the new MPD at Royston in 1936 and (highly unusually for a freight loco) was apparently receiving the attentions of the shed cleaning gang there on 6 February 1937. There is, however, the strong whiff of 'posing' about this picture. 8061 later passed to the WD and only returned in 1949.

8000 arrayed in the traditional 'photographic grey' with various parts painted white, the more to highlight them on subsequent prints made for the record. All the engines were equipped with the steam brake but 8000-8011 did not have provision for working vacuum braked trains – hence there is no ejector pipe running along the left-hand side of the boiler. 7F power class above number, close under the window.

8000 under erection at Crewe.

Introductory Notes

The Stanier 8F 2-8-0 is one of the most familiar engine types to us today. There they were, at the very end in 1968: *Sixty-three of the eighty remaining standard-gauge steam locomotives were withdrawn from service on 3 August. The seventeen survivors included twelve Stanier Class 5s and 73069, three Cl.8Fs and 70013 OLIVER CROMWELL. The Cl.4 Standard 4-6-0s became extinct. The following week a further twelve were withdrawn, leaving in stock 70013 OLIVER CROMWELL, Cl.5s 44781, 44871, 45110 and Cl.8F 48448.*

This was the end of a thirty year story, of a class that had sprung from the drawing board, the 2-8-0 being one half of what E.S. Cox called 'the centre piece' of the new Stanier standard series. This centre piece was the 'two cylinder 4-6-0/2-8-0 group' which by the end of the LMS accounted for 60% of the locomotives produced under Stanier and Ivatt.

The first thoughts on these 4-6-0s/2-8-0s envisaged three cylinders, though this was soon abandoned. The locos owed 'a good deal in their conception' to the GWR Hall and 2800 classes: *At Crewe Coleman, to whom the production*

8015, from the third Crewe order, under construction at Crewe in 1936. The place is No.10 Erecting Shop on what was known as the New Work Belt. The men, probably still recovering from their Christmas break, are in the process of fitting the boiler into the frames, which would then be securely located on the smokebox saddle, which is already in position. The other end of the boiler will not be secured; rather, it will rest via the angle brackets visible on the side of the firebox, on matching brackets located on the frames and will thus be free to expand and contract when under steam pressure. Notice that the boiler has been lagged, apart from one ring where the lifting sling has been carefully positioned, such that the boiler is completely balanced. Boilers were generally slung this way rather than by attaching slings at both ends and using two cranes, as it allowed free movement when guiding the boiler into position. The boiler is of the sloping throatplate variety, derived from experience with the 5XP three-cylinder Jubilees and used on these locomotives from 8012 onwards. At the same time, the smokebox regulators combined with the superheater header were replaced by the sliding gate design mounted horizontally in the dome. With the boiler in position and secured, one of the next jobs would be lifting the locomotive on to its driving wheels. Behind the locomotive on the shop wall about midway along its length, is the clock face used to tell the team working on the locomotive when the next movement along the belt was due. This method of operation had been introduced when the Erecting Shop was first commissioned in 1926, part of a wholesale rearrangement of how locomotives were built and overhauled – hence the term *belt system*. At the appropriate time, all the locomotives on the belt would move along one berth; the one at the extreme end, being complete, would move out of the shop, while a new set of frames would be placed at the other end in the vacated place. This system kept the teams confined to a particular range of tasks, the idea being that by doing so, they would become more competent and therefore, more efficient. On the floor alongside the cylinder is an upturned piston complete with its rod, along with two rear valve chest covers, the design being integral with the bottom part of the valve crossheads. The rear end of the locomotive on the right is 8014, the three cranks just under the framing forming part of the gear for operating the ashpan doors. The other ends would be connected to the operating handles on the footplate. The holes in the frame are for lightening purposes. Notice that the horn gap in the frame plates to take the axlebox is unsupported at the top. This was a weak point in the design as, despite the small radius in the top corners, this is where fatigue cracks would develop. It was not helped by the horn stays being attached to the axlebox guides, rather than the frames plates. However, probably due to lower accumulating mileages, these locomotives did not suffer as badly in this respect as some of the other contemporary Stanier designs.

design was entrusted, at once imposed his own individuality upon these projects and reassembled them in a manner which produced much more balanced designs, adjusting the boiler heights and bringing the centre of gravity forward.

Details were announced as follows in 1935: *NEW SUPERHEATER 2-8-0. The first engine of a new design of 2-8-0 was completed at Crewe Works last month. These engines, which will be numbered 8000-8011, have been designed to meet heavy freight requirements over the whole of the LMS main line routes. Leading dimensions are as follows: Coupled wheels 4ft 8½in diameter, leading truck 3ft 3½in diameter, cylinders (2) 18½ x 28in, heating surface tubes 1,308 sq.ft., firebox 155 sq.ft., superheater 235 sq.ft., grate area 27.8 sq.ft., boiler pressure 225lb/sq.in., boiler barrel 12ft $10^{1}/_{16}$ inches long, 5ft $8^{3}/_{8}$ inches diameter tapering to 5ft 0in, weight in working order engine 70tons 10cwt., tender (4,000 gals. water, 9 tons coal) 54tons 2cwt., tractive effort 32,438lb, power classification 7F. Continuous brake is not fitted, but steam brake acting on all tender wheels, as well as the coupled wheels, is provided.*

The new 2-8-0s entered traffic quietly and barely noticed, at sheds like Toton, Wellingborough and Willesden, for the coal traffic, as might be expected. Power class 7F at first, they were officially reclassified 8F in November 1935. That only 126 had been built by the end of the 1930s is surprising but serves to highlight even more the wasteful dead end that was the 7F 0-8-0 class. So it was that a class we think of as ubiquitous (the 8F came to be the most numerous of Stanier's designs, though not the most numerous in Britain) was in fact barely seen across large tracts of the LMS – until after the War at least. The Midland coal workings were an exception with the new 2-8-0s to an extent concentrated thereon. The loser from this was the Central Section, the Fowler 0-8-0s displaced from the MR going to the former L&Y lines, inflicting misery on fitters until their hasty liquidation began in 1949 before a tide of repatriated 8Fs and WDs. The great majority of these were gone by 1951 but oddly a few survivors lasted until the 1960s.

The story of the 8Fs is complicated by the adoption of the design as a War Department locomotive, so that they could be said to have had different 'origins':

Those built by the LMS for its own use pre-War, 126 engines produced under ordinary peacetime conditions at a leisurely pace which became BR 48000-48125. A number of these, after working from various sheds in the normal course of things, were requisitioned and sent abroad, many never to return.

Engines ordered with some urgency in 1939 with the Stanier 8F declared the country's preferred 'War Locomotive'. Many detail alterations made for service on French metals but orders curtailed with the evacuation of the BEF and the Fall of France. Locomotives then made available for work at home.

Subsequent engines, built by the LMS at Crewe and by NBL, as directed by Government (Railway Executive Committee) and then put to use on the LMS.

8013 at the extreme east end of the No.10 Erecting Shop at Crewe in late 1936. The locomotive is just about complete with a few odd jobs to be undertaken prior to being winched out using the capstans provided for the purpose a short distance outside. The fitter who appears to be securing the smokebox door cross-bar is probably posed, but spot the joker popping out of the chimney! It's likely the photographer, doubtless using a tripod for a time exposure, did not realise he was there until some time later in the darkroom! Several onlookers on the right enjoy the proceedings, standing in one of the entrances to the adjacent Nine Shop. After pairing with its tender, the engine would be steam tested prior to finish painting. On the foot-framing alongside the boiler are the twin Silvertown mechanical lubricators, the front one for the valves and cylinders, piston and valve rod packing etc., and the rear one for the axleboxes. There is a brake block lying on the floor by the cylinder which tends to draw attention the three cylinder drain cocks below the cylinder, along with the cylinder pressure relief valve at the bottom of the cylinder. The locomotive behind, attached to the overhead travelling cranes, is probably 8014 in the process of being fitted with its driving wheels.

A shimmery black 8000, still with a few hints of that burnished metal. Riveted tender.

8001 begins life at Crewe around June 1935, standing outside the Iron Foundry by the look of it. The engine in front has already been paired with its tender, unless it is a tender on its own which, incidentally, is 'finish painted'. Engines that were not lined were not varnished, and were usually finish painted in the Erecting Shop – though not always so in the case of brand new engines receiving the photographic grey treatment – see 8000 pictured elsewhere for instance. The fellow is using oxy kit (you can see the trolley with the cylinders) and maybe he is heating something to make it fit rather than welding, though he does have an electric welding mask. The curious antique wooden drum is for that hosepipe, which looks like something to do with washing out. As a general rule the ONLY engines (post-War at least) that went in the Paint Shop were those that were lined and only those that were lined were varnished. Plain black goods engines were not varnished. The lining was all done by hand, only the numbers and the crests were transfers. Engines going into the Paint Shop were steam tested first, but those painted in the Erecting Shop were not. The Paint Shop was quite a place: HARDWICK, CORNWALL, 1439, PET, LION and the replica (wooden) ROCKET were there, later joined by the Super D 9395. In the Foreman's Office were the plaques of the front ends of a maroon and blue streamliner and the bell off The ROYAL SCOT. Outside was the Ince tram engine. Quite a display!

8011 in course of erection. The air-operated equipment to move the wheel for valve setting is in position under the solitary driving wheel. Obviously the plan is to set valves prior to putting the other coupled wheelsets in. The open strip at the base of the firebox is the expansion bracket, which has a distinctive oblong cover when the engine is in working condition. Thus the boiler can move back and forth, free of the cab also, which is not fixed at the front. The upright rod to the right of the right-hand cylinder is a piston and its rod; a valve chest cover sits just behind the buffer beam by the framing and a crosshead is placed on end on the floor.

More locos for similar purpose, for work at home and abroad, built in the workshops of the other home railways; thus, among other unlooked for developments, Brighton built locos for the LNER!

A grand total of 852 – ten more than the Black 5s.

It was thus the Second World War that catapulted the 8F to the forefront of freight working across the Nation, though many sent abroad never returned to these shores. Some of the original pre-War 8Fs 8000-8125 were requisitioned by the War Department as mentioned above.

It was not foreseen, or at least it was not part of a plan, that those 8Fs requisitioned for overseas service (of the pre-War 8000-8125 series) or those subsequently built with service abroad their main purpose should be returned to Britain but a number did. All this accounts for the puzzling gaps perceived in a childhood 1960 Ian Allan *London Midland abc* (2/6d, never forgotten). Just where *were* they? With all the stragglers in, a maximum of 666 were running on BR by 1957; it is those that we'll deal with in these books, in BR numerical order of course, as with all the other 'Books Of' but the 'missing' 8Fs have been interleaved in the places they would have occupied had they *all* returned to the UK, so the origin, life and times and fate of every one can be ascertained by looking at each loco entry – though some will be thin, by definition.

It is difficult to make sense of the 8Fs, both 'home' and 'abroad' engines without recourse to a series of cross-referenced tables. Which of course is what Peter Rowledge has done (see *Heavy Goods Engines of the War Department* below). Take LMS 8226. It appears first (this is not a criticism, for the work is phenomenal) as WD 300 under *Locomotives Built to Ministry of Supply Orders 1940-42*, then under *Locomotives Lent to LMS and GWR 1940-41* in both guises, and then as 300 again and finally 48246 under *Locomotives Sent to Middle East Forces 1941-42*. In an effort to avoid this, which would only mean transcribing his tables more or less verbatim in any event, there is a brief entry, in numerical sequence with photograph where possible of each engine which remained abroad. A number worked for years and others were soon rusting away forgotten in some desert (most of the places they ended up were deserts) while one or two now entertain amateur divers in the Red Sea.

Sent Abroad, Lost at Sea, Repatriated

The Stanier 8F was distinguished by being selected as the standard for locomotive building for service in Europe, at least until Riddles had the design transmuted into the WD 'Austerity' (also termed 'Utility' at the time) 2-8-0 from January 1943. R.A. Riddles had been the LMS Vice President responsible for Mechanical Engineering on the LMS and was seconded to the Ministry of Supply as Director of Transport Equipment. In the circumstances it would have been truly startling had he *not* selected the LMS 8F though it was surely the correct choice. The 8F design was the most recent, the most modern and the most widely available in terms of route availability. The other contenders had age, complexity, accessibility and availability against them – sometimes all four!

The LMS had completed only 125 8Fs by the outbreak of the Second World War, as noted earlier. This was not very many, seeing how many others of diverse types had been built and although there were many ex-LNW 0-8-0s being given a modest new lease of life, the home-grown 7F 0-8-0s had proved duds (another point already laboured above). There had been a number of other false dawns – Fowler and Stanier between them cooked up *over 200* disappointing 2-6-2Ts for instance. The LMS remained largely an 0-6-0 railway in terms of freight – there were thousands of them.

It is not easy or straightforward to describe what happened to the 8Fs; a

8011 is seen to be sitting at the east end of 'The Belt' – somewhat unusually – by the doors. There is a better view of the crosshead on the floor, with the piston and rod beyond. The open pipe to the left under the footplate is the injector, the one to the right behind the steps the exhaust injector.

8000 in the Paint Shop ready for its grey 'photographic' paint. The handle seen through the cab side window is the independent steam brake valve. The steam brake on the engine was applied proportionally with the train vacuum. It meant you had to create vacuum even if working a loose coupled train. 8000 and 8001 had the steam brake only at first. The pipe under the rear drag box beam, with the chain, is the steam supply to the tender brake. They were renewed at the 7-9 week exam.

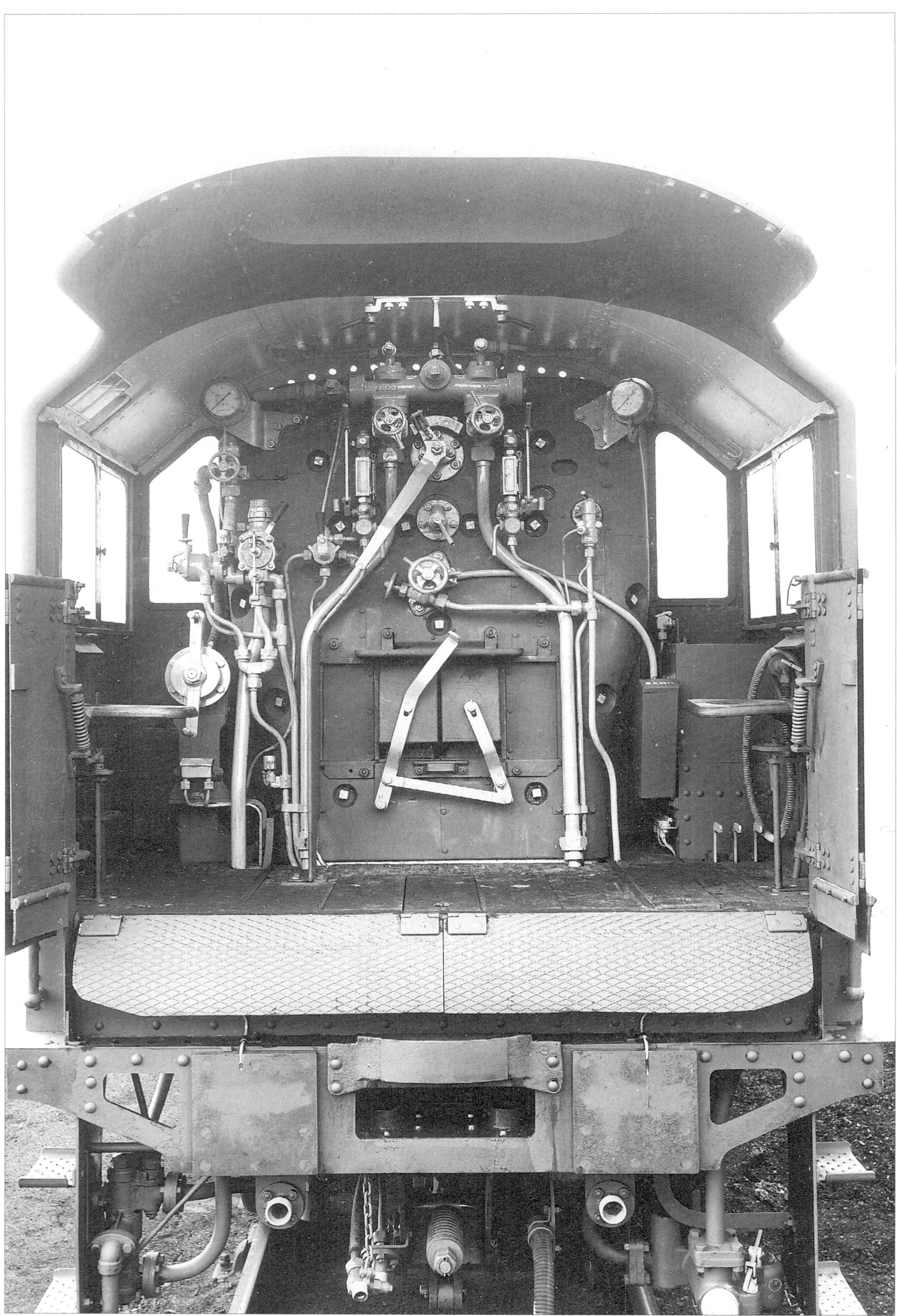

Where pictures are available of 8Fs in the 8000-8125 series working as WD locos, they are included at the appropriate point in 'The Record'. Here, though, is a flavour of the engines (not the 8000-8125 ones) working so far away some seventy years ago. This is Tehran MPD, a better appointed establishment than many at home, it looks like...

written account is particularly difficult through the need to constantly cross reference ('all things are always on the move simultaneously' as Churchill said of the War and though he wasn't talking of war locomotives, he might as well have been) and it is not possible to draw up a single Explanatory Table – well, not by me at least. It was as early as December 1939 that the Ministry of Supply placed its first order, for a standard freight loco for service in Europe – a measure it had adopted in the Great War, probably dusting down the earlier paperwork. The Stanier 8F was simple, robust, proven and modern and was a fairly obvious choice as we've seen. The Ministry's 1939 order was for 240 of them, of which 208 were built. These wartime matters have been laid out in remarkable detail in published accounts before and the brief notes that follow here are derived entirely from R. Tourret's *Allied Locomotives of the Second World War*, published by the author in 1976 and the equally remarkable efforts of J.W.P. Rowledge, in his *Heavy Goods Engines of the War Department* Volume 2 (Springhead Railway Books 1977). These are truly works to marvel at, the like of which we will not see again.

The Ministry for this order specified various modifications, to make them easier to operate and repair under difficult conditions and to avoid material, insofar as it was possible, that would be better used elsewhere in the war effort, in tanks and ships, for instance. So it was that the frames were thickened by a sixteenth of an inch and made of mild steel rather than the scarcer high grade stuff – coupling and connecting rods too. In addition to this Tourret notes that the connecting rods were shortened by five inches and the slidebars and piston rods lengthened accordingly to render piston ring changes easier, (it allowed the piston head to come forward enough to leave the cylinder without splitting the

Left. **Footplate view of 8111 when new. From left to right, by the driver's tip-up seat, is the reversing handle for the screw reverse and immediately above it, the engine steam brake valve and to its right, the train vacuum brake valve – the one with all the holes to let the air in when the brake is applied. The valve above is for the single-stage vacuum ejector and the gauge, the train pipe vacuum. The two valves on the manifold at the top, are the injector steam valves with the regular handle below, flanked by the twin water level gauges. Immediately below the regulator is the blower and below that the controls for the sand-gun, with the sand hopper on the right, by the fireman's tip-up seat. To the left of the regulator is the steam sanding valve. The gauge on the right is for the steam pressure and the valve below it, the automatic continuous blowdown – this discharges a small amount of water while either the regulator is open or an injector is working to help in removing undesirable elements from the feed water. Initially these valves discharged onto the track, after passing the discharge pipe through the tender to recover any heat. However, complaints from the Civil Engineers regarding its effect on the permanent way, culminating in an accident partly blamed on this contamination at Watford in February 1954, led to a modification to discharge into the engine's ashpan. Underneath the fireman's seat are the three levers for the ashpan dampers, while the wheel valve is the water regulator for the exhaust steam injector. The water valve for the live steam injector is in a similar position under the driver's seat, with the cylinder cock control to its left. The hose pipe on the right is the slacker pipe, for hosing down the footplate and dampening any coal dust. The square ended plugs dotted around the boiler backhead are washout plugs. Various oil reservoirs are in evidence. Underneath each cab sliding window is a hinged flap with a timber top, which can be moved into position on the window ledge when the window is open, for the crews' comfort. Below the footplate from left to right, the live steam injector and its water supply connection to the tender, duplicated on the other side for the exhaust steam injector. The hose with the chain is the steam supply for the tender brake, while the other pipe is the vacuum train pipe. Although it cannot be discerned, the whistle valve handle, which can be operated by either crew member, it right at the top above the steam manifold.**

THERE AND BACK AGAIN.
Original pre-War 8Fs Requisitioned from LMS Sept-Nov 1941 and given WD Numbers

WD Nor	*Date WD No.*	*Date LMS No.*	*Fate*
572	Sep-41	8041	Israel
573	Sep-41	8045	Bought by BR Jul 49 becoming 48045
574	Sep-41	8019	Scrapped by WD c1954
575	Sep-41	8021	Returned to Britain in 1952 scrapped1959
576	Sep-41	8015	Egypt
577	Sep-41	8012	Bought by BR Dec 49 becoming 48012
578	Sep-41	8013	Persia
579	Sep-41	8020	Bought by BR Dec 49 becoming 48020
580	Sep-41	8022	Persia
581	Sep-41	8030	Persia
582	Sep-41	8018	Bought by BR Dec 49 becoming 48018
583	Sep-41	8025	Returned UK 1952. Bought BR Jul 57 becoming 48775
584	Sep-41	8031	Persia
585	Sep-41	8032	Italy
586	Sep-41	8047	Israel
587	Sep-41	8023	Persia
588	Sep-41	8039	Bought by BR 10/49 becoming 48039
589	Sep-41	8091	Italy
590	Sep-41	8014	Persia
591	Sep-41	8016	Bought by BR 10/49 becoming 48016
592	Oct-41	8028	Persia
593	Oct-41	8034	Egypt
594	Oct-41	8038	Italy
595	Oct-41	8040	Italy
596	Oct-41	8042	Israel
597	Oct-41	8043	Persia
598	Oct-41	8044	Italy
599	Oct-41	8046	Bought by BR Aug 49 becoming 48046
600	Oct-41	8048	Persia
601	Oct-41	8052	Persia
602	*Nov-41*	*8079***	*Reverted to 8079*
603	*Nov-41*	*8024***	*Reverted to 8024*
604	*Nov-41*	*8080***	*Reverted to 8080*
605	Oct-41	8086	Israel
606	Oct-41	8094	Bought by BR Dec 49 becoming 48094
607	Oct-41	8051	Egypt
608	Oct-41	8066*	Lost at sea
609	Oct-41	8072	Italy
610	Oct-41	8049	Persia
611	Oct-41	8077	Bought by BR Dec 49 becoming 48077
612	Nov-41	8058	Italy
613	Nov-41	8059	Egypt
614	Nov-41	8061	Bought by BR Sep 49 becoming 48061
615	*Nov-41*	*8069***	*Reverted to 8069*
616	*Oct-41*	*8078***	*Reverted to 8078*
617	Nov-41	8071*	Lost at sea
618	*Nov-41*	*8085***	*Reverted to 8085*
619	Nov-41	8087*	Lost at sea
620	*Nov-41*	*8088***	*Reverted to 8088*
621	*Nov-41*	*8093***	*Reverted to 8093*
622	Nov-41	8068*	Lost at sea

**Four jettisoned from SS PENTRIDGE HALL*
*** Eight returned with SS PENTRIDGE HALL. Put to work, bought by LMS, May 1943, despatches overseas having ceased.*

crosshead). The water scoop was dispensed with and various other items such as springs, bearings, executed in more easily available material. Two live steam injectors were specified, and the tyres turned to a European profile. The engines were fitted with Westinghouse air brakes.

Of the total of 240 8Fs ordered, there were 100 each from North British and Beyer Peacock (WD 300-399, 400-499) and forty from Vulcan Foundry, WD 500-539. The first one, WD 300, was handed over in a ceremony to the Ministry of Supply on 24 May 1940. The British Expeditionary Force however was beset and its evacuation from Dunkirk was underway within days. The Fall of France came soon after. So it was that none could be sent to Europe; they would be staying in the country for the foreseeable future so those that were ready, 'Europe-tailored' as it were, went into Crewe to be 'de-Europed' for work on the LMS and (later) GWR 'on loan'. As more were being completed, they went straight into home service but it was obvious that the numbers now would not be needed so the orders were curtailed. No engines resulted from the Vulcan order for instance, though boilers were completed.

Hostilities began in North Africa, in the words of Mark Arnold-Foster, 'simply because soldiers were there'. British forces were guarding Suez, Italians occupied the East and the two first came to blows in June 1940 after Mussolini's Declaration of War on the UK. Opposing forces spent the best part of the next three years contesting the Western Desert. At the end of 1940 more 8Fs were supplied by North British and Beyer Peacock and this time the engines did begin to be shipped abroad. At the same time the engines released on loan to the GW and LMS were taken back. The first to go abroad were a number sent to Turkey, a gesture of appreciation at its continued neutrality, though in fact there were pre-war orders to fulfil. The journey to Turkey saw the first 8Fs lost at sea. The locos began to be shipped to Egypt soon after, involving further losses. The Soviet Union became an ally in June 1941 and locos were needed for Persia and its 'back door' route to the USSR. Over 150 went to Persia (Iran) with twelve lost on the way. The tangled tale of the 8Fs sent to work abroad has been unpicked through the work of Peter Rowledge. All that we know flows from this international detective work. Those that came back and those that didn't are handily brought together from all this in a relatively straightforward table (no mean feat in itself, be assured) in the Wild Swan Publications *LMS Locomotive Profiles* No.8. Made available through the good offices of one of the authors, John Jennison, a version with minor tweakings follows herewith:

The engines in this volume, 8000-8125, were those which were 'purely' LMS; that is, built by the company for its own use. Of those, some were requisitioned and not all by any means, returned; the fate of each engine is given in the individual entry. What follows in subsequent volumes is the remainder of the 8Fs in BR numerical order.

Balarood in Persia with two oil burning 8Fs on what notes describe as a 'Poles Special' for Tehran. These would be Polish servicemen imprisoned in the USSR since that state's brutal annexation of eastern Poland in 1939. They would eventually end up fighting as part of the Allied Forces in places like Italy, later settling in the West. Clearly some brake vans were shipped abroad too!

One of the 8Fs in the pre-War 8000-8125 series to go abroad and come home was 8018, standing here as 70582 in what looks like Suez or some such place on 3 March 1948. It can be seen back home awaiting repair on page 91. It was the sand-laden desert winds it would seem, that gave the engines this 'scoured' look. The bracket on the smokebox side would have been for the Westinghouse pump. Peter W. Gray.

70332 being shipped aboard the SS BELNOR at Port Said on 26 March 1948. WD 332, it ended up as BR 48251. The one on the dockside will be next; WD 506, it became 48263 in Britain.

A pre-War 8F, 8006 at Rugby MPD in May 1936. The prominent strip at the base of the firebox covers the expansion bracket – see 8011 on page 8. The said bracket enables the boiler to move back and forth, free of the cab also, which is not fixed at the front.

A Wartime 8F on the Home Front, 8017 with the Lady Cleaning Gang at Grimesthorpe shed, Sheffield.

A Wartime 8F on the supply route to the Soviet Union, WD 547. It is being unloaded at Ahwaz in Persia on 7 June 1942; according to Rowledge, the operation of the crane absorbed the entire electricity supply to the town, which had to be cut off during the work. Built by North British and despatched abroad immediately after steaming in February 1942. It ended up in Iraq from about 1946. It never came back to Britain.

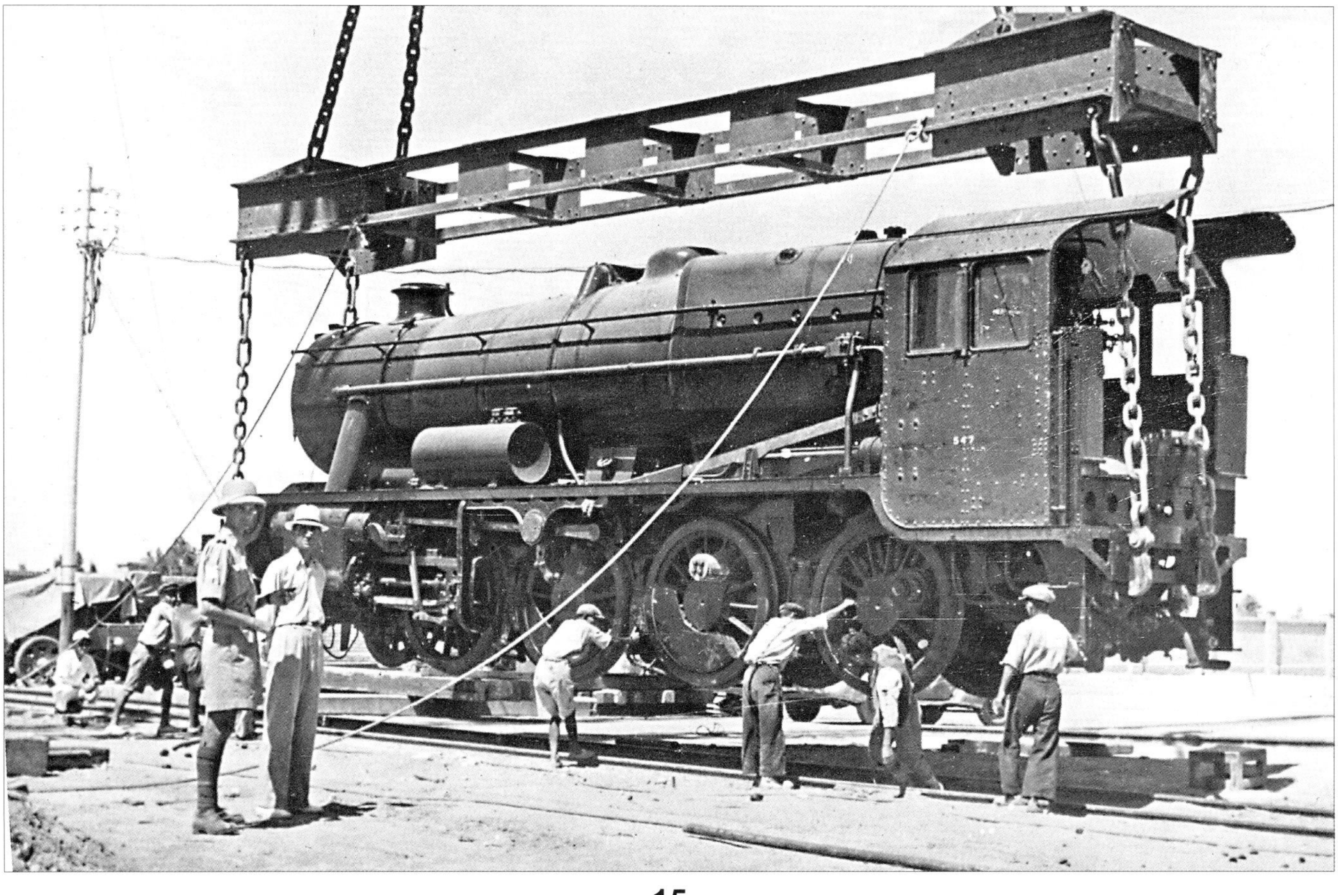

8000 (wearing its 18A Toton shed plate) at Rugby with a Toton-Willesden coal working, 6 August 1935. The new 8Fs were allotted more or less *en masse*, in eminently sensible fashion, to the coal trade East Midlands-London. To this end most of the first dozen, the straight throatplate 8000-8011, went to Willesden with others then going to sheds such as Toton and Wellingborough. This is a 'domeless' boiler; what looks very much like a dome is the top feed – the regulator on 8000-8011 being housed in the smokebox, in the superheater header. The injector feed water pipes to the said top feed run vertically upwards and are recessed in the boiler cladding sheets and covered by a strip, in the finest British tradition of neatness. From 8012 this was 'partly recessed' though they look very much the same in many photographs. Smokebox cock for the steam lance (to blow out tubes) low down, in line with lower smokebox door hinge; lubricating oil box on inside of frame at front.

8000 at Derby on 21 August 1938. 'Dart' cover for oil atomiser cock prominent on smokebox, hollow axles, small circular access plate on cylinders. This gave access to the oil pipe connection to the cylinder. The 45 degree angle of the sand pipes indicate 'trickle' or gravity sanding; the steeper the angle, the more gravity is on your side. Later steam sand pipes had a lower angle. With steam brakes, there is NO ejector piping on this left-hand side. Note the curious non-alignment of the number and tender lettering typical of these years.

1. Parts and Service

Boilers

The 'Devil in the Detail' so far as the 8Fs are concerned, is not nearly so devilish as other classes, though they make up for that with the fiendish complications of their distribution, here and abroad. It was originally intended that the 8F should share a boiler (the 3B) with the Class 5 but various alterations were found necessary, so that a closely similar 3C boiler was devised instead. The three boilers 3A (Jubilee), 3B (Class 5) and 3C (8F) started life with vertical throatplates (that is, the plates at the front of the inner and outer firebox, uniting it to the boiler barrel). This was an arrangement Stanier had brought with him from Swindon but early on (initially with the Jubilees) he determined on a sloping throatplate instead. There were thermal, combustion, steaming etc., advantages to be derived there from. There was accordingly a switch to these during the production of the Class 5s too; the 8Fs, coming last of the three engine types, had hardly got underway before the change was made. So it was that only a dozen 8Fs had the original vertical throatplate (one, 8003, got a sloping throatplate boiler in March 1938 to provide a spare vertical throatplate boiler – it was easier and cheaper than building a new vertical throatplate boiler). The remaining eleven vertical throatplate engines kept this type of boiler throughout their lives.

Between the two forms of boiler there was no external difference at the 'join' as it were, between the boiler barrel and the front of the firebox but the twelve, then eleven vertical throatplate engines 8000-8002, 8004-8011 were instantly identifiable, having a combined dome and top feed whereas the remainder from 8012 onwards had a separate dome cover for the regulator behind the top feed.

The reason was the first dozen had a regulator in the smokebox, GWR fashion, not under the dome, with the steam collected in a form of an oblong tube, wide at the back and narrower at the front, leading to the pipe to the superheater header where the regulator was. One of the problems was, if the water level was allowed to get too high and there was then a surge, due to heavy braking or whatever, it could get in there and when steam was applied again, the engine would prime.

There are immensely detailed expositions of what was involved in the design and construction of these boilers, some of it venturing into materials science and all of it complicated, in various publications, starting with the RCTS *Raising Steam on the LMS* (A.F. Cook, 1999) and explored in various individual *LMS Locomotive Profiles* (Wild Swan Publications) most relevantly No.8 which deals with the 8Fs.

So it will come as no surprise that minor detail differences in the boiler/firebox manifested themselves very early on. On the sloping throatplate boilered engines, post-8011 for instance, there were six washout plugs in a row on the right-hand side instead of five. Washout plugs were just that, a plug, with a tapered BSP thread and a square end for the spanner. The hole in the boiler/firebox has a tapered thread to suit. It was relatively important that, after washouts, the plugs went back in the same holes they came out of. The larger ones are usually referred to as hand-holes or inspection doors. They are bigger and oval so that the door will fit inside the firebox as the mating face of the firebox is on the inside. They have a long stud from the centre and are retained in place by a bridge piece with a hole in the middle to take the stud and a nut. They have the characteristic

A brand new 8003 on 29 June 1935. The taper boiler was emblematic of what H.A.V. Bulleid called 'Stanier's Mighty Re-stocking of the LMS' (*Master Builders of Steam*, Ian Allan, 1963) and even freight locos like 8003 certainly had that 'shock of the new' quality – certainly when one appeared in a shed yard full of 3F and 4F 0-6-0s, which looked antediluvian in comparison. E.S. Cox (*Locomotive Panorama* Volume 1, Ian Allan, 1965) surveyed Stanier's early essays in the craft of locomotive building concluding, reasonably enough, that some went well and some didn't. He noted that some boilers at first were domeless, as on our first twelve vertical throatplate engines, 8000-8011 (soon to be eleven 8000-8002, 8004-8011). These had *...a steam collector pipe leading to a regulator combined with the superheater header in the smokebox. This arrangement not only demanded separate means of lubrication but with the mixtures of waters encountered on the LMS, including a proportion of softened water, priming occurred against which the low level of the steam intake did not offer much protection. Domes with sliding regulators set horizontally at the highest practicable point within the loading gauge soon joined the larger superheater as a 'must' for all further construction.* And from 8012 onwards, they did.

Left. 8001, bound for 18A Toton – oddly with a three link coupling at the front rather than the screw coupling found on just about every other 8F.

Below. Lovely new 8003 at Crewe South, 29 June 1935. It was on that very day that its official allocation to Willesden was made, though it wouldn't get the 1A plate till it arrived there. A similar, somewhat closer view, is at page 64.

8003 a few years later, at Derby shed on 16 July 1938 having swiftly attained the state of grace associated with all 8Fs. Coal has been neatly delivered in two chute loads from the new mechanical coaling plant. This was the straight throatplate engine that was converted to sloping throatplate in order to provide a spare boiler for the remainder of its straight throatplate ilk, 8000-8002, 8004-8011. At the same time opportunity was taken to provide 8003 with a drop grate and hopper ashpan. The tip of the spindle to operate it (using a hefty lever) is *barely* visible, as a dot, immediately to the rear of the rearmost driving wheel, together with the supporting bracket. It appears to have gone out of use (probably staff at 'foreign' sheds were not even aware of its existence) during the War and the provision of drop grates was not taken seriously until Ivatt's time.

8Fs at war 1. *Chez* Casserley at Berkhamsted has provided many intimate peeks at the LNW main line over the years, most notably during wartime – when such photography was illegal! See, for instance the recent *Book of the Crab 2-6-0s*. 8096 drifts south in the last weeks of peace in 1939, on 8 June, its axles visibly hollow even at this distance. H.C. Casserley, courtesy R.M. Casserley.

8Fs at war 2. Now with blackout tarpaulin, 8114 comes by on 11 May 1940. H.C. Casserley, courtesy R.M. Casserley.

8Fs at war 3. It is now 1944, a month after D Day, on 7 July as 8119 makes its way up to London. H.C. Casserley, courtesy R.M. Casserley.

8002 at Nottingham shed, 9 April 1939 with the original 14in LMS in gold, shaded black serif and the 12 inch cabside number in similar style. The shaded black was more or less invisible in normal service – to the extent that we can forget it was there in fact. The 8Fs had screw reverse. A screw handle in the cab (see the cab description earlier) moves the prominent reversing reach rod, running at a slope on the left-hand side from the cab to the motion bracket just below the sandbox filler (with the circular cover on the end of its trunnion). This moves the lifting arm, mounted on the end of the weighbar shaft, which in turn moves the die up and down the link, to effect forward and reverse movement and adjusts the cut-off. The weighbar shaft is mounted transversely across the main frames, transferring the movement of the reversing rod to the valve gear on the other side of the locomotive. The support for the slide bars and the housing for the link are in effect, all part of the same – generally referred to as the motion bracket. The weighbar shaft sits behind, with the lifting arms connected to the radius rod via it slotted end. The shaft runs across the engine to effect the same movement on the other side.

Original serif 12 inch 'low slung' numbers with a hint (if you stand back and squint) of the black shading to the gold numerals.

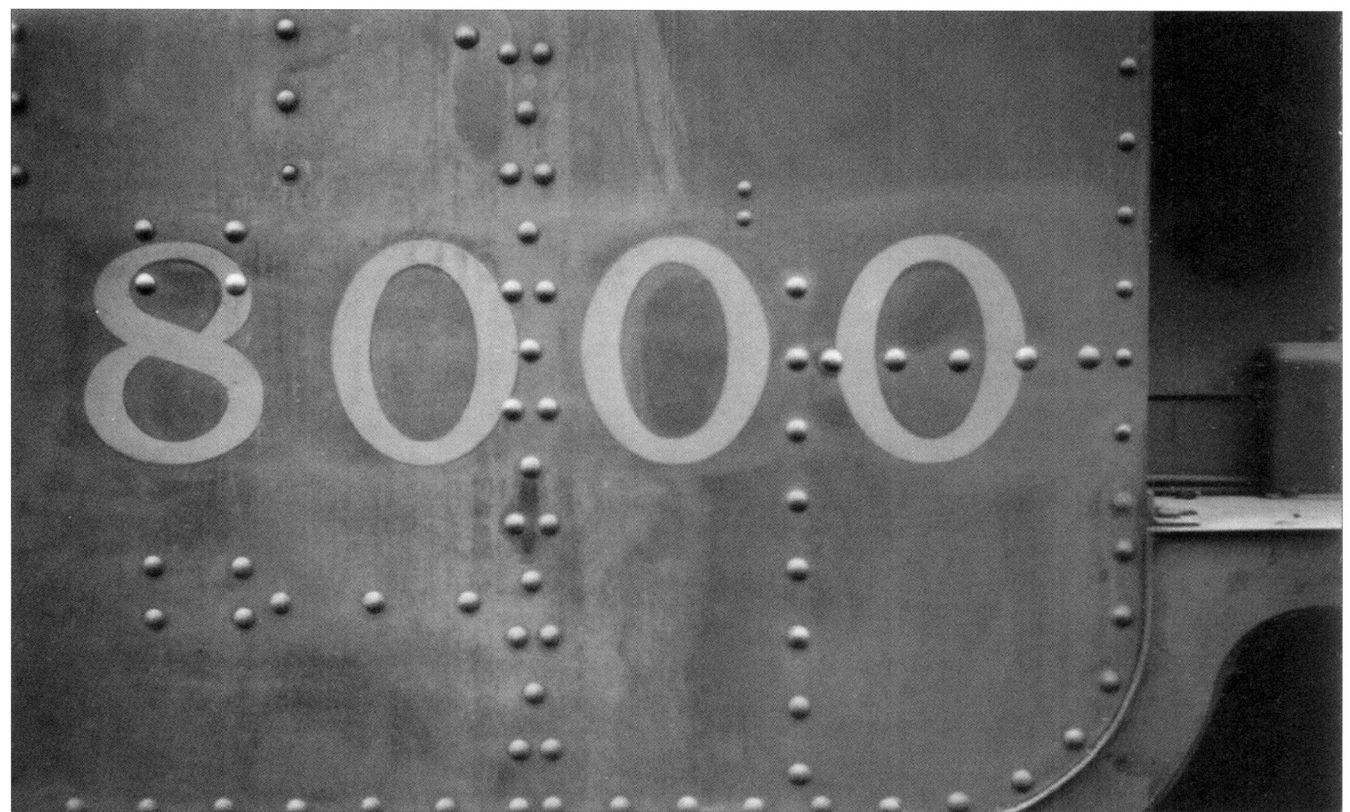

dome shaped metal cover. The plugs by the top feed allow the boiler washer to clear any scale from the top feed tray. The plugs allow little more than somewhere for the boilerwasher to put the nozzle of his hose; the hand holes are where he can poke around with a long rod to remove scale and for the boilersmith to make his inspection of as much of the innards as he can see. There were other plugs on the backhead and in the smokebox, as well as lower down on the firebox side. Boiler washers were a confounded nuisance so far as fitters were concerned, if they were doing their work at the same time! While boilerwashers took *out* all the plugs, a boilersmith had to be called to put them back.

Two more washout plugs appeared by the dome on top of the boiler, ahead of the firebox, then two more, similar, along the boiler by the smokebox.

A dart-like cover for the atomiser cock was positioned high up on the left-hand side of the smokebox. From 8012, this was markedly smaller. The purpose of atomising the oil on a superheated locomotive was to break it up (the oil that is) and mix it with the steam as the high temperature would otherwise affect its lubrication properties. So there is a need to atomise where the oil is on its way to valves, pistons and anywhere else it comes in to contact with superheated steam – reducing the carbonisation which would otherwise occur.

The tube cleaning steam cock on the right-hand side was positioned low down on the early engines and was placed much higher up from 8012. After that they could move about a bit, a result it is assumed, of exchanging smokeboxes.

Lubricating oil boxes with delivery pipes to the pony truck were on the INSIDE of frames at front on the early engines. From 8012 they were repositioned on the OUTSIDE, though the pipes ran through new holes in the frames along the inside of the frames, as before.

On the early engines, in classic British tradition of neatness the feed water pipes from the injector to the clacks were recessed neatly out of sight in the boiler cladding. From 8012 with the regulator placed in a dome the pipes served instead a top feed with its separate, elongated cover. The pipes now were only partly recessed. The top feed was left in its original position so that alterations to the boiler were unnecessary – the dome housing the new regulator was positioned a short distance behind.

Extra rivets appeared at the smokebox front on the engines after 8011; two horizontal rows of three at the centre line and more at the smokebox front rim. These signalled the presence of a hinged crossbar for the smokebox dart to engage in. The earlier ones were fixed and a hinged one allowed it to be got out of the way during maintenance. Any 'hinged' mechanism in the forbidding environment of a smokebox was soon rendered somewhat intractable so in day to day cleaning and most maintenance the crossbar stayed in place in traditional fashion. As was more or less universal in Britain, it was placed horizontally, not vertically, though it could of course be placed at any point of the compass.

A Question of Balance

A barely noticed variation in the 8Fs concerned the balance weights, a matter of impossible complexity. Throughout the construction period of our first 126 pre-War 8Fs they were conventional 'built-up' flush-riveted plates either side of the wheels, filled with lead. Wartime brought variations; Doncaster used prominent rivets on its 8510-8539 batch while a shortage of lead meant many other examples had weights that were cast to fit. These were rather different in size you'd need the eye of faith to differentiate them in any particular photograph; wheelsets were swapped around willy-nilly which also resulted in an unpredictable combination underneath any one loco, of hollow and solid axles, too.

The 'masses' exerted on a moving steam locomotive took two forms, rotational and reciprocal. Without these being properly balanced, a locomotive could not make an assured progress along the track. Rotating masses derived from crank pins, eccentrics, coupling rods and

Continues at page 34.

The Vulcan locomotives from 8027 had the 'new style' in block introduced in 1936 and so did those coming out from Crewe concurrently, in a switch from the serif in mid-stream as it were; e.g. 8012 being shunted by a works 4F at Crewe in 1936. The move includes new 5XP 5740 MUNSTER.

8093 at the end of the War, with serif number now high up under the window, above the tender lettering. Was not the obvious place *in line* with the tender LMS? Find a (reliably) dated picture if modelling a particular loco at a particular time... The atomiser cock on the smokebox side (oddly without a cover) is low down but was later moved to the conventional place higher up; see 48093 later, in *The Record,* for instance. R.K. Blencowe Collection.

New 8016 with welded tender, at Normanton MPD on 6 February 1937.

The Vulcan engines with their exquisite finish mellowed pleasingly – or at least the light flooding through at Toton was kind to 8027 in 1937. The loco had gone there new and stayed on the Midland Division for the great part of its life. The allotting of the new 2-8-0s was planned and deliberate; they were concentrated on the Midland where the coal working had long been in needless difficulty because of the failure to come up with something better, overall, than 3F and 4F 0-6-0s. The 8Fs must have been both revelatory and revolutionary.

8031, steamed probably for the first time on LMS metals, at Basford Hall Sidings Crewe in 1936. It would end its days in the sands of the Middle East.

The first Crewe series ran from 8000-8026, carrying first the serif, then block style (from 8012). The Vulcans 8027-8095 had the block style and then the next Crewe series from 8096 reverted to serif, 12 inch yellow shaded in vermillion. It is just possible (with the eye of faith) to see the shading on new 8105 at Crewe South in February 1939 on the original print, using a magnifying glass and hopefully an impression at least is possible from this view. Crewe did not trouble with burnished metal surfaces like Vulcan did! 8105 has a welded tender and the cab number is still determinedly low down.

Right. A haul of 8Fs has arrived at Derby, including 8038, minus connecting rods as usual, in August 1936. Brand new 8Fs were a daily sight here by now; no less than eight, 8032-8039 arrived in the three weeks up to 5 September 1936 alone. 8038 was sent to Kirkby in Ashfield but was claimed by the Government in 1941. After various adventures it was withdrawn by the Italian State Railways in 1953. It is safe to say that in no subsequent moment in its life did it look as good as this.

Below. And here's another, doubtless in the same delivery, 8036 the same day. It went on to spend several years at Wellingborough. On all these 'delivered' locos substantial planks of wood were tied to the bottom slidebar for protection in transit. The idea was to wedge the crosshead so the piston would not move backwards and forwards. However, in this case it looks as if it has tried to move as the timber appears to be split. Notice the big end bush has been removed from the connecting rod, put back on its journal and the return arm put back to retain it all. This was usual practice too, if the side rods were left on. For any movement over 25 miles, the connecting rods had to come off 'by order'. It was a good idea also, if they were left on, to pour a gallon or so of cylinder oil down the blast pipe! The link has been tied up too, to stop it swinging. Vacuum ejector just in front of the cab, exhaust pipe to smokebox, drain pipe downwards. Lovely finish, all those bright parts, even the smokebox numberplate – it couldn't have rained on its was south! They would not stay like that for very long. One wonders why some of the engines went to Derby and not Crewe?

Bottom right. And a third at Derby that day in August 1936, 8035. It was yet another 8F that, sorely needed, went to Wellingborough for the London coal traffic. Flawless and glittering in their newness, it is easy to appreciate that Stanier at one point thought to convert much of the existing LMS fleet to taper boilers and an early scheme indeed envisaged a relatively simple combination of flanging blocks, tube and firebox length that could see over 4,000 locomotives converted. This would include even the 0-8-0s (LMS and LNW) and the Midland Compounds! (Cox, *Locomotive Panorama* Vol.1, Ian Allan, 1965).

8035
8035
L M S

8065 on arrival from Vulcan, at Derby on 8 November 1936. It has been delivered with the burnished metal surfaces, including hand rail, that combine to such markedly impressive effect with the brilliant black paint. The dart atomiser cover is now smaller, it is a domed boiler (housing the regulator) with a top feed in front with feed pipes very much not recessed and inclined at a slope from the running plate rather than running vertically upwards. Vacuum ejector pipe (single cone – one pipe emerging from cab front) prominent with concomitant stand pipe on buffer. Connecting rod removed for the journey, timber on slidebar.

On the right-hand side 8065 reveals (now) six rather than five washout plugs on the firebox side on 8 November 1936. There are two more washout plugs, on the boiler top between the firebox 'shoulder' and the dome. The number and LMS are in the 'new style' of that year, a block version which actually had black shading to it, though it is barely ever visible. Hollow axles, exhaust steam injector arrangement beneath cab this side. New engines 8061-8065 seem to have arrived together in one train. Note that the right-hand eccentric rod is still in place (not like the other side, above) attached to the return crank so that the mechanical lubricators will still work, feeding the axleboxes.

8063 in the same consignment, at Derby on 8 November 1936. The little oil boxes on the frames at the front are now on the outside of the said frames. Connecting rods yet to be fitted – they were most likely safely and securely stowed in that carefully tarpaulined wagon, just visible at left and, below, to the right.

8063 from the other side. Steam lance cock at front now much higher. The two new washout plugs high up by the dome more noticeable at this angle.

48002 waits the next job north at Barnwood, the old Midland Gloucester shed, about 1962. The copper pipe looping somewhat untidily down the smokebox side is an external steam source for the tube cleaning cock lower down. Norman Preedy.

48002 awaiting repair (presumably at Crewe) in the period 1950-1952 when it was a Toton engine. Compare with the previous picture of the engine with the external feed to the steam cleaning (lower) cock. As related, the first straight throatplate engines 8000-8012 had the steam cleaning cock low down but here it is high up – which presumably points to a smokebox exchanged with a later engine.

8111 picked out in the photographic grey when new. At least it appears so; the LMS had a habit of doing up engines in other than their own identities, for the record. The little oil boxes on the front were moved from the inside of the frames to the outside, as we've seen, though the delivery pipes still ran down the inside (through holes newly drilled) to their original sites serving the pony truck. Later serif; shading stands out for once because of the grey painting.

48001 had a series of repairs at Derby throughout the 1950s and only ever worked from ex-Midland sheds. It keeps company here with North London 0-6-0T 58850 which doesn't really help to pin down the period to any meaningful degree; it was one of the High Peak locos and was not withdrawn till 1960.

Left. Serif work at Wellingborough, post-war; the numerals had been block, and would soon be Gill sans. transporttreasury

Below. The smokebox-mounted atomiser cock cover could take various guises; early on, on 8005 (at Toton in June 1939) it was the conventional 'dart'.

By 30 April 1960 (at Derby) it was more or less a bowl shape. D. Forsyth, ColourRail

Later on in the 1960s (the top lamp has been moved down to the smokebox door) it is a bulbous oblong, leaking a lot of water too. The coal stage in the background belongs to Mirfield MPD.

in part, the weight of the connecting rods. The aforementioned balance masses in the wheels literally 'balance' these out, simply and straightforwardly. Antimony is alloyed to the lead in the balance weight to prevent the latter becoming pulverised and therefore lost with prolonged working of the locomotive.

Reciprocal masses are much more difficult to balance and this proved problematic on the 8Fs. They derive from the functioning of the pistons, piston rods, crossheads, and part of the weight of the connecting rod. Put very simply, it is not practicable to completely balance reciprocating parts and the common compromise in order to avoid bad surging and excessive hammer blow is to balance a *proportion* of the reciprocating masses, up to two thirds – apparently it was 50% in the case of the 8Fs with built up balance weights. This was one thing, but lead/antimony shortages, different specifications for Government-ordered 8Fs and alterations at Crewe and Horwich resulted in engines of differing reciprocating balance. With wheelsets routinely and indiscriminately swapped between locos the balance was entirely unknown for a given locomotive at any point. This did not matter overmuch for slow plodding minerals but with increasing speed it could be problematic. At its most inconvenient, riding might be terrible for the crews and track damage inevitable.

So it was that each 8F had to be individually examined and 'passed' for speedier running if its reciprocating balance was found to be 50%. This only began in 1958, resulting in 'starred' engines for faster running – a star was painted on the cab side. It is said that wheelsets might be changed promiscuously at overhaul, rendering an engine's 'star' status no more but this seems unlikely. Doubtless MPDs got to know which 'starred' engines really were useful for faster work and which ones weren't – though that would only concern their 'own' engines.

Which is a lot to say to explain one tiny visual detail – the 'star' on the cabside.

Sanding

Either side, there were two sand fillers on the running plate, conventional ones with an angled plate supporting a filler tube, and a third one below the running plate, between the rear and second pair of driving wheels. The boxes for the former four were inside the frames, the boxes for the latter outside, and clearly visible under the firebox.

Ejector

Prominent on the left-hand (exhaust) side of the boiler is the ejector pipe, below the hand rail running from the front of the cab to the smokebox on the left-hand side. The ejector creates a vacuum for working the vacuum brake and most have large and small cones, the former ('large ejector') creates the vacuum initially or for releasing the brake after an application. The latter, 'small ejector' is used continuously to maintain vacuum which is always slightly leaking or, more exactly, air is leaking in. The first six 8Fs, 8000-8005, had steam brakes only; this utilises a cylinder under the footplate, its piston connected to the brake levers so at first there was no prominent ejector pipe on the left-hand side. The rest of the vertical throatplate ones, 8006-8011, had the same loco steam brake and vacuum for train brakes; accordingly, the 'large' and 'small' ejector and its distinctive piping appeared on the left-hand side. This was normal for railways where it was usual to work vacuum braked trains with locomotives fitted with steam brakes; a vacuum-operated steam brake valve controlled the application of the brake on the locomotive as the vacuum brake was applied on the train.

From 8012 the sloping throatplate locos came out with a single cone vacuum ejector, more or less indistinguishable from those that had gone before and this was so for the entirety of the engines in this volume, the pre-War 8Fs up to 8125 and indeed beyond.

In 1938 a start was made on equipping all the engines with large/small cone ejectors. The external manifestation of this (what we are really concerned with in this volume) is that a single cone ejector had one pipe from the cab front to the pipe while there were two pipes for the combined large/small cone ejector.

Boiler off 48046 on trolley at Crewe, almost certainly destined for another engine. Boilers were almost always changed at Heavy Generals as they generally took longer to repair than the engines. It looks as if the ensemble is standing outside Nine Shop and, judging by the temporary chimney and ladder by the firebox, may have been or is being, steam tested there in which case it would only have had minor repairs and not been to the Boiler Shop, which was in the Old Works. Hence much of lagging still in situ, patch on smokebox, steam pipe holes in smokebox covered up with old rags etc.

48113 has just arrived at Bolton shed on 9 August 1953, after a Light Intermediate at nearby Horwich, where someone forgot to remove the stencilled number on the motion parts, put on before the 8F entered works to make sure they went back on the same engine. All the surfaces not requiring any attention retain the coat of grime from before the engines' works visit. See the same engine in The Record. A.G. Ellis, transporttreasury

8019, a Crewe engine coming out in the 'new style' in block introduced in 1936 and characteristic of the Vulcan engines. 8019 was scrapped while still in the possession of the War Department out in the Middle East and never returned to Britain.

X marks the spot on Toton's 48075 at Crewe South MPD – 5B. It is of course way out of its specified sphere of working (see *X Marks the Spot*) and this would be following its early 1949 Heavy General at Crewe. It is on its way back to Toton, now with the 8F under its new BR number, tender left blank in this period of uncertainty. Chalked on the latter, inexplicably, is *5B 48075...*

Manual blowdown experiment 8F 48117 at Toton during the rebuilding of the roundhouses, 8 July 1948. Number in that curious block style, higher up than 48075 for instance, 8F still in 'old' position. Note further set of washout plugs near the front of the boiler close to the smokebox. H.C. Casserley, courtesy R.M. Casserley.

Transition. Burton shed, 19 September 1948. H.C. Casserley, courtesy R.M. Casserley.

Hybrid lettering/numbering on 48121 at Derby on 22 May 1948. The steam cleaning cock has a steady leak. H.C. Casserley, courtesy R.M. Casserley.

X Marks the Spot

Caustic embrittlement. It sounds terrible and it was, wasting and enfeebling plates and tubes. Yet it was but one of the ills of feed water which, depending on its origin might form hard scale or, alternatively might make for corrosive foaming, let alone the aforesaid caustic embrittlement. It was never possible in Britain to soften/treat all feed water and continuous blowdown on locos allowed a constant, definite but limited amount of sludge-laden water to be dumped on the track/ballast. This was through a coil in the tender tank; it cooled the sludge but the main purpose was to warm the tender water. It worked whenever an injector or regulator was open, discharging on to the track below behind the tender trailing wheelset. It was considered to cause track damage and was reputedly the cause of the Watford derailment (in the tunnel) in the early 1950s. Later, the discharge was channelled via the ashpan. Earlier, Midland coal traffic 8Fs had been equipped with a manual blowdown, with drivers specially instructed in its use. Fifty 8Fs, 22 at Toton and 28 at Wellingborough were involved and the staff enjoined to see that they were confined to coal trains to Willesden and Brent, with a view to assessing the results. The fifty 8Fs had to be marked accordingly and this is the explanation for the large X which appeared on the cabs of some 8Fs in 1946-47. The study petered out by 1953, largely ignored, you suspect, with incidences of the X wrongly applied and so on. *Profile No.8* helpfully lists those 8Fs involved – see table right.

8024	1/47
8033	10/46
8037	10/46
8050	10/46
8075	1/47
8082	11/46
8112	1/47
8117	2/47
8178	1/47
8180	10/46
8181	10/46
8194	10/46
8198	10/46
8204	12/46
8221	6/47
8222	9/46
8264	9/46
8281	7/47
8304	12/46
8305	12/46
8334	11/46
8338	6/46
8359	12/46
8360	7/47
8361	10/46
8362	2/47
8363	1/47
8364	11/46
8365	5/47
8371	6/47
8374	7/47
8384	2/47
8492	1/47
8617	9/46
8618	12/46
8636	10/46
8638	11/46
8644	11/46
8651	10/46
8662	2/47
8671	12/46
8672	11/46
8678	11/46
8681	12/46
8685	10/46
8692	11/46
8694	12/46
8695	2/47
8699	10/46

Some 8Fs, the earliest being 8003 in 1938, are recorded as getting 'manually operated blowdown valves'; this work predates the 'Toton-Brent' scheme.

Tenders

The ubiquitous standard LMS 4,000 gallon tender was attached to all 8Fs. These were either riveted or welded and as the first overhauls were enacted, they were inevitably further mixed up. Nothing could stay the same for long, particularly in a class this big with so many having different origins. The high-sided 3,500 gallon tenders also appeared on 8Fs – see later volumes.

Most unexpectedly, the distinctive straight sided WD tenders appeared in April 1948, attached to five engines to enable their own scoop-equipped tenders to be fixed to Southern Bulleid Pacifics taking part in the Locomotive Exchanges.

Some Stanier 3,500 gallon tenders (ten or so – impossible to clearly identify in most photographs – from 1953 all the way through to 1967) were taken off Jubilees and put on 8Fs. The obvious reason was to make Jubilee working more convenient. An 8F could take water at any number of wayside columns in the course of a working day while a Jubilee usually could not.

The Jubilees were indeed badly off with respect to tenders, many running with the 'Fowler' straight sided version which looked fine with a Crab or a 4F but not with a '5XP'. Late on, in 1957, it was ordered that forty or so should be swapped with 8F 4,000 gallon example and so late in the day as to be barely sensible, 42 were exchanged, in a process not coming to an end until 1960. Later on, as passenger engines fell like nine pins, some of these 8Fs regained surplus standard 4,000 gallon tenders, enabling them to look 'right' again.

Oil Burning

The overseas 8Fs went there as oil burners or were converted over there, in the main. The first few ordered by the Ministry of Supply were coal burners as they were of course intended for France, though that obviously was overtaken by well-known events. Once engines were being made ready for Egypt and more especially Persia, oil firing was deemed highly desirable. Some were converted over here, others were sent with a kit of parts to be

Continues at page 47.

Filling a riveted 4,000 gallon tender; Gloucester Central, 2 October 1963. This was the tender always associated with the 8Fs of course. The welded version ('Mk.2', if we term the riveted one 'Mk.1') looked the same at a glance, especially when covered in grime.

Welded tender – the essential point being the absence of rivets – on 48118, at Mangotsfield on 18 May 1961. The loco also carries the cabside star indicating it was balanced for 50% reciprocal masses, meaning it could run faster without damaging the track. D. Preston, ColourRail

Welded tender on 48114, at Westhouses on 14 May 1961. Riveted or welded, the tenders appeared with various batches of locos, riveted with the first vertical throatplate ones 8000-8011, welded with the Vulcans 8027-8095 and so on. Naturally enough virtually from the outset they began to be mixed up randomly. RailOnline

Riveted tender with the early BRITISH RAILWAYS, on 48001 at Hellifield in June 1949. Norman Preedy.

BRITISH RAILWAYS on 48096 at Belle Vue, 23 July 1949. The separate letters of LMS had been erased and the new lettering substituted. The lengthy gap between the two words was intended for an emblem.

Leeds Holbeck in May 1961 with its 8F 48067, still with its miniature snow plough fitted, along with one of the shed's independent snow-ploughs to the extreme right. The 9F on the left, 92103, belonged at the time to Leicester Midland. ColourRail

What we usually call 'Fowler' 3,500 gallon tenders came to be put to work with 8Fs, an unhappy aesthetic outcome, you'd have to think. Here is one (with water vents in the coal space) running with 48045 at Kirkby in Ashfield on 1 November 1965. The order was made in 1957 and over forty 8Fs were so affected between 1958 and 1960. The version with 48045 was 'beaded' – that horizontal strip which covers the join between the tank and the coal space. Others had a riveted join. This view shows how the cab hand rail reverted to the original arrangement, the cab edge beading being bent up to form the top support. K. Fairey, ColourRail

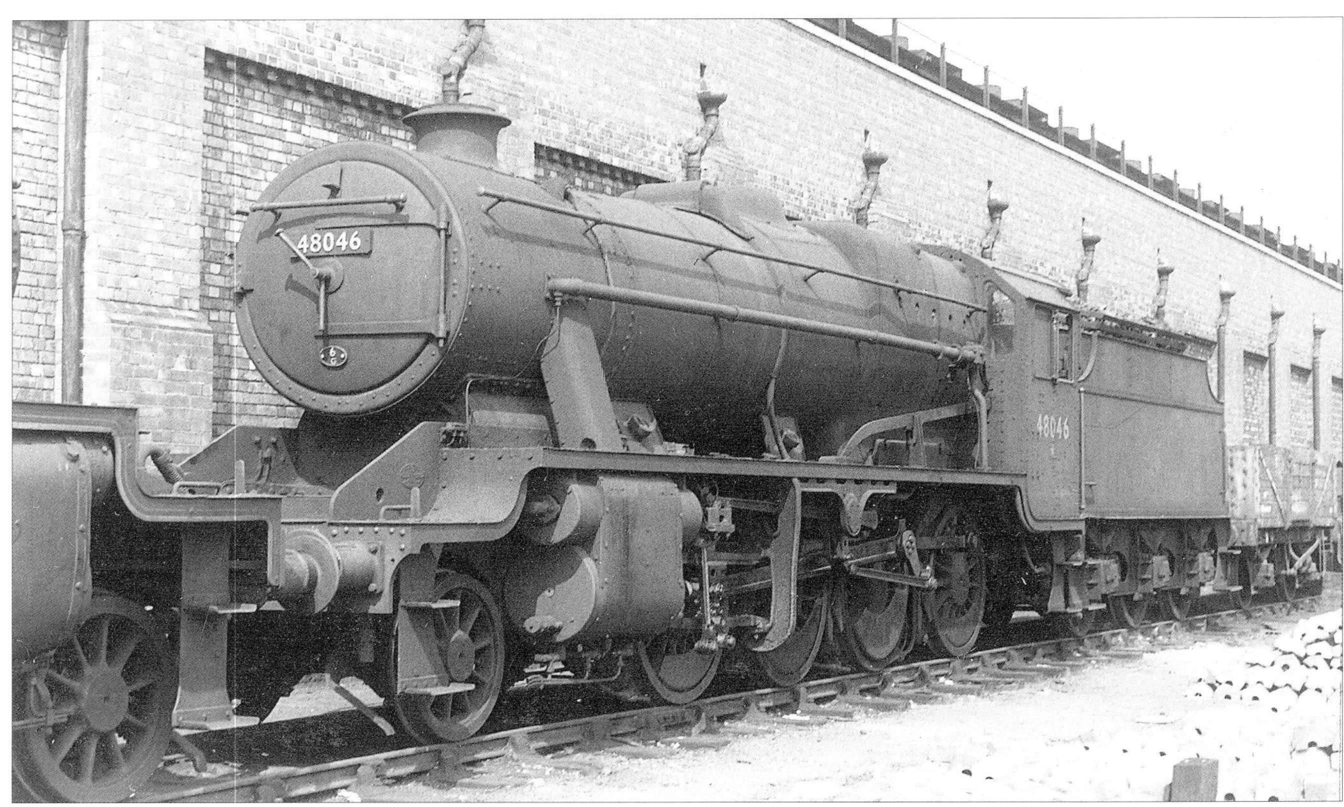

48046 at Llandudno Junction MPD on 5 June 1960. The 3,500 gallon tenders no more suited the 8Fs than they had the Jubilee 'donors' – though apparently in four cases they had come from Patriots. K. Fairey, ColourRail

Standard riveted tender on 48077 at Farington, 23 June 1967. RailOnline

Aesthetically challenged, 48045 with its new tender at Cheadle Heath, 31 May 1960. D. Forsyth, ColourRail

Tender on 70573, converted by the WD in standard fashion to carry oil. The engine is awaiting attention in the old Carriage Works south of the Chester line at Crewe on 7 May 1949. It would emerge as 48045. H.C. Casserley, courtesy R.M. Casserley.

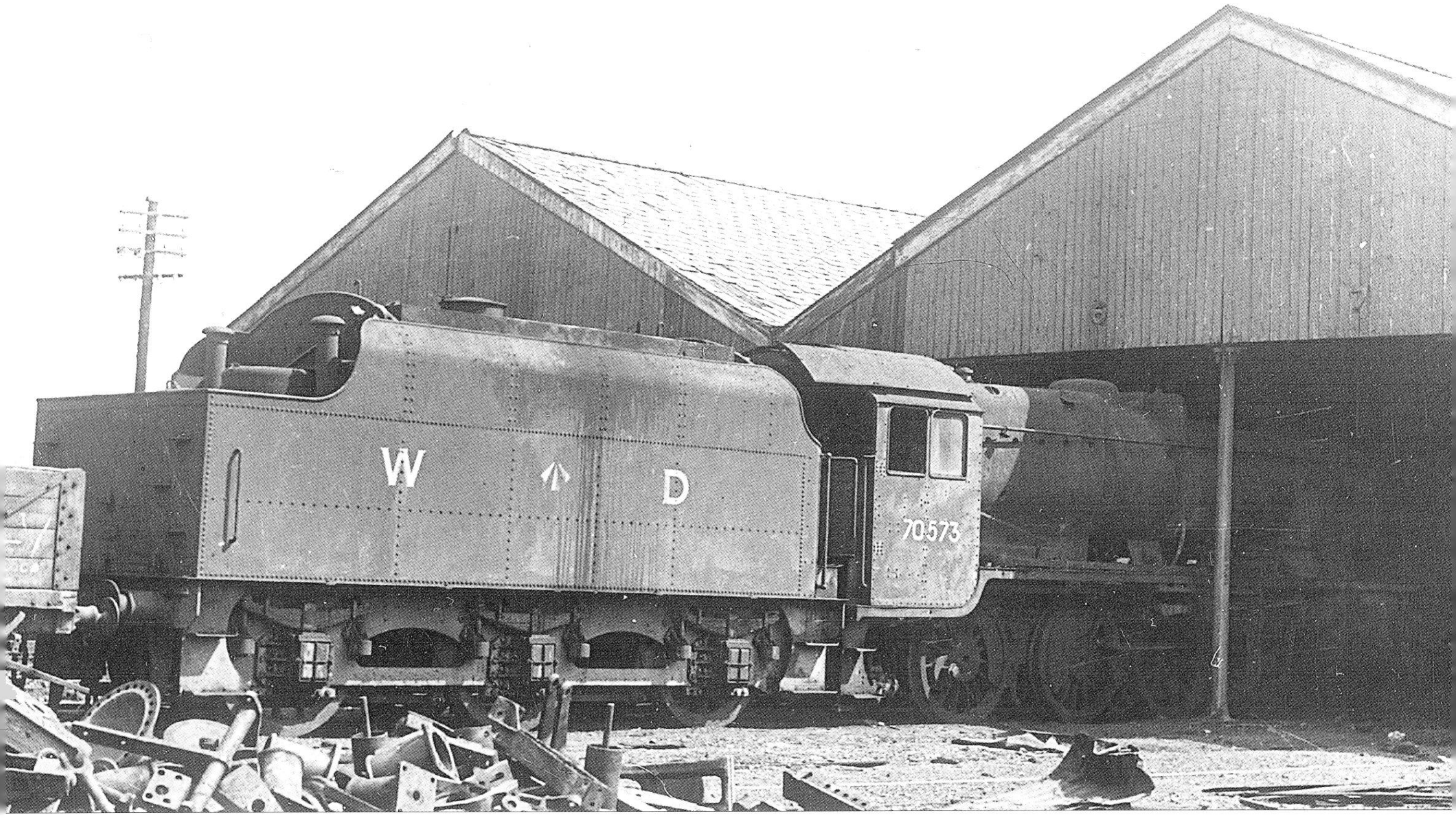

Left. Fowler-type tender with 48045, overhauled and repainted with large 10in numerals, fresh off Darlington in June 1965.

Bottom left. Allan C. Baker writes: Crewe Works and something of a mystery view. The date is 14 June 1964 and the photograph was taken inside what was colloquially known as 'The Melts'. This building, towards the south end of the site, just after Flag Lane Bridge, where the Deviation Works opened out into what was known as the Steel Works, had originally housed the steel furnaces and rolling mills. By the time this photograph was take it was used for cutting up withdrawn locomotives, as well as storage of all sorts of equipment and material. For example, the Crosti pre-heating boiler drums from those 9F locomotives that had been fitted with them, were stored here for a long time. I often wonder what happened to them. Notice all the material lying about in this view. However, I have no idea why these engines have been placed in the shop as they had not been withdrawn and apart from one which was taken out of service a couple of months later, they lived to fight another day. In any event, it was the road farthest to the right, where the breaking up of locomotives took place. I can only assume they might have been placed there while waiting a decision, or perhaps, repaired boilers to be ready for them. Having said all this, they do appear to have had some work undertaken while in this shop – as I say, somewhat of a mystery. The engine are, from right to left: 8F 48010, Standard 9F 2-10-0s 92166 and 92123, Jubilee 45558 WESTERN AUSTRALIA, Standard 2-6-2 tank 84026 and Class 5 45425. It was the Jubilee that was withdrawn in August, so presumably it never left the works. The 8F was withdrawn in January 1968 from Newton Heath. Despite the engines not being where one might have expected them, the intrepid young spotter on the right has found them and is busy recoding the numbers in his note book; it was in the blood you know! B. Webb/B.J. Miller Collection.

Below. 48002 at Crewe on 31 March 1963, standing outside the Number Ten Erecting Shop, Allan C. Baker writes... It would appear to have only had light attention and judging by the new paint, the wheelsets have been attended to along with the brake gear, motion and it looks like some firebox stays; those under the new lagging plates. A few odd jobs still to complete before being reunited with its tender and moved to what was known as the Vacuum Pits, towards the southern end of the works by the Wheel Shop, where engines were steam tested. Having said that, a close inspection shows that the valve chest cover is missing, a temporary one being in its place. This might suggest that the engine had already been steam tested and, with a problem discovered, brought back for remedial attention. Star on the cab side indicating the wheels had increase reciprocating balance, to allow for higher speeds. Notice too, that the engine's number has been stencilled on many parts that have not been removed – the work of overzealous chaps at the Steam Cleaning Pits whose job it was the undertake this task as engines entered the works! The engine behind is 45562 ALBERTA, a Leeds Holbeck engine, which appears to be having some final attention, including a coat of primer. Being a passenger engine it would afterward migrate to the Paint Shop, after steam testing for finish painting. This work is probably being undertaken outside, as the gang has ran out of time on the belt before the next scheduled move of locomotive down the line! Generally speaking the men got round this okay in the fine weather months, less so in deepest winter! R.K. Blencowe Collection.

A 'starred for speed' 48090 recently out of Crewe at Doncaster MPD on 10 September 1959, Chalked on the tender is *2.50PM MON*.

'The star' on 48076 at Wakefield. D. Preston, ColourRail

No	OIL	COAL
8064	10/47	10/48
8079	12/47	8/48
8191	6/47	11/48
8269	10/47	11/48
8273	6/47	12/48
8370	11/47	11/48
8385	6/47	11/48
8386	6/47	12/48
8606	11/47	12/48
8653	10/47	1/49
8696	10/47	1/49

converted 'over there'. The oil burning system was designed so that reversion to coal at some point in the future was straightforward. One spent a week on trials in 1941 between Crewe and Carlisle.
So it was that oil burning was confined to the MoS engines sent abroad – until the great oil burning scheme of 1947 that is. In that Government-inspired episode, eleven 8Fs were converted during that year, to be returned to coal burning a year or so later. Only two of the pre-War engines 8000-8125 were involved, 8064 and 8079. They are tabulated at left.

AWS

Along with so many other classes, the 8Fs were equipped with Automatic Warning System. It was a massive exercise, and was underway from 1960. The receiver was mounted at the front of the truck frames and was protected by a guard attached to the buffer beam. The hook for the swing link coupling was moved from the buffer beam to the bottom edge of the guard. The cylindrical vacuum reservoir and battery box were on the right-hand footplate in front of the cab and the smaller timing reservoir was in the corresponding position on the left-hand side. Around 450 engines were fitted with the equipment before looming withdrawal put an end to the process. Some 8Fs (none of the series in this volume) had earlier got GW-type ATC (Automatic Train Control) when the Western Region acquired them in the 1950s.

Lubrication

There were two Silvertown mechanical lubricators, on the right-hand side, the front one serving the cylinder, slidebars and so on, the other the axleboxes.

Below. **The Erecting Shop at Horwich Works on 8 April 1964. From left to right are 8Fs 48098, 48756 and 48547. These were the last three steam locomotives to be overhauled at Horwich, so this is quite an historic photograph. Presumably the tender on the right belonged to one of them. Unfortunately it was pretty much downhill for Horwich after this as the works never undertook much in the way of repairs to more modern traction. All three engines only appear to be having light repairs, all the boilers staying in position. The first one, 48098, was built at Crewe in January 1939 and withdrawn in March 1967, the next one, 48756 came from Doncaster in November 1945 and was withdrawn in January 1967 while the last one, 48547, was built at Darlington in March 1945 and was withdrawn in March 1966. There is a lot of clutter lying around, including some of the lifting tackle. In the foreground, with the toothed wheels, is the kit for moving the wheels of locomotives when setting the valves. A cylinder cover can be seen on the ground to the right and further down the roadway, a couple of safety valves. A pair of driving wheels from one of the 8Fs protrude on the extreme right. John Marshall.**

THREE AT DARLINGTON Note by Allan C. Baker

48100 at Darlington on 26 June 1965, just out of the Erecting Shop and probably being made ready for steam testing; a few jobs still to be undertaken, followed by painting. The large valve prominent at the bottom of the cylinder is the pressure relief valve; there was another one at the other end. These were designed to release any water that might become trapped in the cylinder when the cylinder cocks were closed; if the boiler was priming for example, before the driver had a chance to open the drain cocks. Enginemen by the way, often referred to the cylinder cocks as the 'taps'. The newly overhauled tender alongside is from an Austerity 2-8-0. N. Skinner.

Livery

The pre-War 8Fs 8000-8125, the subject of this volume, were painted black, and that was about it. The lovely pictures of them, in shimmering black with glistening burnished bare bright metal, varnished teak window frames and red inside frames, portray them in an 'as delivered' never to be attained again condition from Vulcan and all was soon very 'black'. Tenders were lettered (14in) LMS in gold, shaded black serif and the cabside number was similar, but at 12in. The 7F, later 8F, was just below the window.

Block characters appeared from February 1936 and then serif again.

With nationalisation came a flurry of M prefixes, bare tenders and BRITISH RAILWAYS as matters got sorted out. Smokebox numbers were in Gill sans and other forms while tenders lettered LMS rode behind engines with BR numbers for a year or more. There were similar stutterings on all the other new BR Regions.

Cab

It was indistinguishable from that of the Black Five, at 8ft 6in wide. Underneath the curve of the roof at the front were a dozen or more one inch diameter drilled ventilation holes, barely visible in photographs as a curving string of black dots. There was the usual sliding ventilator in the roof. A two inch wide beading ran at the rear edge of the cab roof and then down the rear edge of the cab. Near to the bottom edge of the windows it flared out and ended up as the top fixing point for the cab hand rail, the one used along with that on the tender, to haul yourself into the cab. At the bottom of this cab hand rail, it was curved back into the cab edge and fixed internally. It came loose at the top now and then and from 8096 the beading was flattened back to the cab edge and the cab hand rail fixed by pillars, matching the one on the tender. There was a 'reversion' when the 'Fowler' tenders were fitted. Spectacularly trivial detail it is true, but the essence of 'engine picking'...

48088 at Darlington Works on 1 May 1965; cab numerals 10in as usual, rather than the 8in ones applied at any of the London Midland Region Works. Note small amount of coal placed in the tender for steam testing. I am not sure the reason for the kink in the cylinder lagging and there are some loose parts on the framing above the leading bogie axle; it looks like they may be something to do with one of the axlebox under-keeps. The circular valve just in front of the left-hand front footstep is the drain valve on the vacuum train pipe, which allowed any condensate to drain away whenever the vacuum was completely destroyed. J. Appleton.

48075 undergoing repair, in this case quite a heavy one, at Darlington on 26 September 1964. Having been partly stripped this locomotive, and the one behind, have been moved outside probably to make room in the Erecting Shop, while waiting for repaired parts. Alternatively, in view of the date, they may have been waiting for a decision on whether to continue with the work, or withdrawal. Note the hinged crossbar for the smokebox dart to engage in. D. Hardy.

Top left. The star on 48005 at Mold Junction, 6 October 1964. It also usefully shows how the second hand rail fixing from the front (just above the fifth washout plug) was entirely different from the others – (both sides. Plainly there was some sort of access/fixing here. R.J. Essery.

Above. The earlier boilers 8000-8011, as we've seen, were domeless, a steam collector pipe (internal and not visible) leading to a regulator combined with the superheater header in the smokebox. The reason for the abandonment of these on 8012 onwards was that they were positioned relatively low down and thus more vulnerable to priming when poor water was encountered. The sliding gate regulator positioned as high as possible in a dome was the answer; thus the 8Fs became 'domed', with top feed clacks in front of the said dome. Cox, in *Locomotive Panorama* Vol.1 (Ian Allan, 1965) notes that these clacks ...*at first followed Swindon design exactly, but were soon in trouble and a number of versions were subsequently developed, none of which prevented the occasional rusty line round the boiler where copious leakage of feed water deployed itself inside the clothing*. It's not been possible to identify this from photographs though like anything fashioned from the mind and hand of man they sometimes didn't function perfectly, with a prodigious and unattended period of leaking obvious on 48057 for instance, at Hasland MPD, 30 August 1959. That 'a number of versions' of the clacks were developed surely explains the different top feed outlines to be encountered among the 8Fs, as if designed purely with the engine picker in mind.

Left. A BR 8F emerges, to have an official portrait taken; Gill sans, small number, first emblem, large circular panel and two oblong panels on cylinder casing. The occasion is presumably 48117's Heavy General at Derby 7/4/52-23/5/52. The taper boiler is always regarded as Stanier's hallmark and so it was; LMS boiler practice gained much from Swindon. Cox writes that though the taper boiler 'gave some small advantage in output to weight ratio' over parallel ones this advantage fell away in medium and small boilers. Thus early intentions to reboiler many of the pre-Stanier types came to nought.

Lost at Sea. The SS PENTRIDGE HALL was forced to jettison four 8Fs, as detailed elsewhere, and here's one of them, 8066 at Radcliffe on Soar before the War. The ship left Swansea for Persia and after running into trouble made for Glasgow, though you'd think a return to Swansea would have been more convenient. 8066 presumably lies somewhere to the south west of Wales. It was not a lucky ship working for the government; the website Wrecksite records it scuttled (renamed) with munitions in the North Channel between Scotland and Ulster in 1945, in the service of the Admiralty.

2. On the Record

Health Warning
As pointed out in previous *Books Of*, Engine History Cards, while containing much useful and even fascinating information, should be regarded as a *guide* to what happened to the engines, not a day by day unimpeachable history set in stone. It seems to be stating the obvious that the Cards only show what was written on them at the time, and the temptation to read and interpret too much should be resisted. The Cards are a marvellous, fascinating, invaluable record of what happened, yet they are often infuriatingly silent on events that we enthusiasts half a century or more later consider of vital interest and importance. They were filled in, by hand, by clerks and naturally enough contain errors of omission (quite a few) and commission (a few).

Dates of leaving and entry to works were of course to some extent nominal and a day or two (or weeks often enough) either side should always be assumed. Out and out 'fiddling' of dates was endemic, to massage the monthly figures, either of engines 'in' or engines 'out'. It was thus not entirely unknown for a locomotive to be out on the road with the figures showing it still in works and vice versa – for a few days at least. As with all BR steam locomotives, the record fades from about 1959-60 – what was the point? No-one responsible for the Cards bothered to record the last 'seeing out' mileages on the LMR or other Regions where the 8Fs ended up. The 8Fs, along with the Class 5s, were the great survivors among our steam locomotives of course and this leaves a regrettably lengthy period – often eight years – in which we don't know what happened. As a guide, though, the notional dates of works attention have been taken from the contemporary RCTS *Railway Observer* and added in as *Noted at Works*. It is not possible to ascertain what level of repair was being undertaken, only that particular locos were at particular works at certain periods. From about 1964 many of these were 'foreign' like Darlington, as other Regional works took on LMR steam repairs.

The same fading away was true of allocations and many shed moves at the end did not find their way onto the History Cards. These too have been brought up to date with reference to contemporary published information.

Repairs and Maintenance
The main sheds undertook a vast range of repairs, though it is mainly those conducted at works level that the following pages are concerned with. The highest mileage examination at MPDs would involve removal of all the motion parts, the bearing brasses and crossheads re-metalled, pistons and valves removed for attention, engine and tender split for examination and a host of smaller items. The larger 'Concentration' sheds were well equipped with machine tools, white metalling facilities, coppersmiths and blacksmiths and much else.

The maintenance requirements for the 8Fs involved an X Day examination every 8-10 days as the boiler pressure was 225lb/sq in. At the same time any other examinations, either on a time or mileage basis would be undertaken, along with a boiler washout as appropriate. However, in the case of these locomotives the highest mileage examination was the No.6 at 30-36,000 miles, after which the schedule would start again at a 10-12,000 mile periodicity, the No.6 exam which in their case, involved the full extent of the mileage based work.

Works overhauls were usually designated under one of the 'Classified Repair' codes. These were either 'Heavy' (H) or 'Light' (L), further sub-divided into 'Casual' (C) and 'Intermediate' (I), 'Overhaul' (O), 'Service' (S) or 'General' (G). Occasionally engines were sent to Main Works for other reasons, such as modifications (e.g. fitting of AWS) if this did not coincide with a normally programmed visit and in these cases the code 'NC' (Non-Classified) was used. The other code which appears from time to time on the Engine Repair cards is 'TRO', which stands for 'Tender Repair Only'. Suffixes, usually after 'NC' were '(EO)', which signified 'Engine Only' and 'Rect.', or 'Rect. (EO)' which was used when an engine had to be returned to Works soon after a works visit for 'rectification'; that is, tightening up bits that had come loose and loosening bits that were too tight.
According to the classification prescribed by the Board of Trade, a heavy repair was any one during which an engine was reboilered or had its boiler removed from the frames. Other factors counted, such as fitting new tyres to four or more wheels, new cylinders/axles and so on. 'Light' repairs could seem little different but if only one new axle or cylinder was involved or the boiler was worked on *in situ*, 'Light' it was.

Most Heavy repairs were 'Generals' whilst most Light repairs were 'Intermediates'. General repairs were carried out either at set time intervals or at predetermined mileages beyond which it was deemed that an engine could not safely remain in service. They were designed to return a locomotive virtually to 'as new' condition. Intermediate repairs were normally undertaken when some major component reached the stage where it had to be attended to before the engine was due for general repair, but the aim was to carry out as few intermediate repairs as possible.

Thus HG repairs were usually done at approximately 3 to 4-yearly intervals with typically two Intermediate repairs (either Light or Heavy) between. An HG repair in the LMS period usually took between 25 and 40 weekdays: this was insufficient time to do the necessary work on the boiler, so engines undergoing HG Repairs invariably left Works with a different boiler from that with which they had entered.

Mileages
These were not entirely accurate by any means and nominal figures were issued for certain jobs like ballast work. The point was, the system applied to all locomotives so comparisons and contrasts across classes and individual locomotives can be fairly made.

Improvements and modifications are noted as they appear in the Record though what is there is patchy. Not every 'Imp/Mod' carried out on every loco is there, by any means.

Time for a contemplative fag on 8079. This was one of the eight NOT jettisoned from the SS PENTRIDGE HALL so, while it had gone to sea, it never worked abroad.

48000

Built as 8000 at Crewe Works; 19th June 1935
Renumbered 48000 w/e 3/7/48

Improvement and modifications
17/5/52 New type piston head fastening
25/3/61 Fitting AWS equipment

Repairs

2/3/37-1/4/37**LS**	55,808	
7/6/37-15/7/37**LO**	61,641	
4/11/37-17/12/37**LO**	71,330	
2/8/38-18/8/38**LS**	90,386	
18/11/39-16/3/40**HG**	124,383	
6/11/41-20/12/41**LS**	53,163	
5/12/42-29/12/42**HS**	85,308	
19/7/44-1/9/44**HG**	34,894	
25/1/46-1/3/46**LS**	28,003	
16/2/47-28/3/47**HS**	48,569	Crewe
29/5/48-1/7/48**HS**	26,675	Crewe
28/5/49-31/5/49**TRO**		Shed
3/11/49-25/11/49**LI**	29,318	Crewe
17/2/51-15/3/51**HG**	27,583	Crewe
23/5/52-29/4/52**LC**	24,328	Derby
20/2/53-16/3/53**HI**	39,751	Derby
4/6/55-15/8/55**HG**	47,938	Derby
27/5/57-24/6/57**HI**	41,737	Derby
9/11/59-2/12/59**LI**	57,588	Derby
1/3/61-23/3/61**LC[EO]**	36,444	Derby

Noted at Works: Derby 8/62

Boilers

No.9099	16/3/40	from	8011
No.9098	1/9/44	from	8007
No.9092	1/7/48	from	8009
No.9097	15/3/51	from	8008
No.9096	15/8/55		

Tender
LMS 9134 19/6/35

Sheds

Toton	22/6/35
Wellingborough	10/10/36
Kirkby	12/6/43
Toton	10/5/58
Saltley	14/6/58
Nottingham	20/9/58
Saltley	12/3/60
Nottingham	17/9/60
Saltley	6/4/63
Burton	22/6/63
Derby	28/11/64
Annesley	4/12/65
Stockport	10/9/66

Stored serviceable
28/6/65-21/12/65

Withdrawn w/e 18/3/67

8000, one of the Wellingborough 8Fs more or less from the first, sent to the Midland Division to rescue the London coal traffic from superannuated 0-6-0s, ailing 0-8-0s and Garratts which had operating drawbacks all their own. Here it is at Toton, its original home before early transfer to Wellingborough. Steam brake only so no ejector pipe on left-hand side, or vacuum standpipe on buffer beam.

On 4 July 1963 48000 has found its way to Basingstoke on an up goods, getting back to its new home Burton. From the look of the smokebox, it has had some recent front end attention. H.C. Casserley, courtesy R.M. Casserley.

48000 near the village of Strines with an up freight, close to Manchester in the valley of the Goyt, north of New Mills, 7 August 1948. In the spirit of the times, it has its front number in a sans serif style that was not Gill sans, said to have emanated from Derby, while it carries the proper BR cabside number, in line with the serif LMS of the tender.

48000 at Tramway Crosssing, Gloucester. The period is the early 1960s, after March 1961 when AWS was fitted. The old 8F is in fairly typical condition – 'extreme scruffy' and is bedecked with electrification flashes and the top lamp is still in original high position. 48000 began to be moved around a bit more in the 1960s, like many 8Fs, and is not bearing a shed plate. The loco spent almost its entire working life at Midland Division sheds and was regularly to be found down here in the 'far south west'. It was late 1965 before it moved off its traditional haunts, to Annesley as part of the LM takeover of the GC. Norman Preedy

48000 at Derby on 31 August 1964, carrying its Burton 16F shed plate; AWS conduit clipped to running plate this side. Now with vacuum ejector pipe and still of course, 'domeless' boiler. M. Beckett, ColourRail

48000 languishes stored in one of the Toton roundhouses on 10 October 1965. It was there for much of that year, accompanied by some dead 78000 moguls, prompting suggestions that it would be preserved. It actually went back into service to finish up at Stockport Edgeley.

48001

Built as 8001 at Crewe Works, 28th June 1935
Renumbered 48001 w/e 8/1/49

Improvements and modifications
4/1/49 Stiffening brackets for cab wing plates
19/2/52 Discharge of continuous blowdown into ashpan

Repairs

9/3/37-1/4/37**LS**	57,138	
27/5/39-3/8/39**HG**	119,715	
27/8/40-17/9/40**LO**	37,935	
10/12/40-17/12/40**TRO**		
31/12/40-27/1/41**LS**	45,383	
7/5/41-23/5/41**LO**	50,796	
24/9/41-11/10/41**LO**	60,563	
31/12/41-22/1/42**LO**	66,484	
5/10/42-24/10/42**HS**	95,943	
24/2/43-18/3/43**LO**	11,548	
1/8/44-30/9/44**HG**	54,278	
21/4/46-29/5/46**LS**	46,344	
18/8/47-30/9/47**LO**	37,493	
22/11/48-4/1/49**HG**	64,490	
26/6/50-7/8/50**HI**	40,320	Horwich
22/1/52-19/2/52**LC**	45,287	Derby
8/1/53-2/4/53**HG**	73,649	Derby
4/3/55-31/3/55**LI**	51,817	Derby
31/10/56-26/11/56**LI**	32,328	Derby
25/3/59-1/5/59**HG**	42,807	Derby
26/9/59-15/10/59**LC[EO]**	7,947	Derby
21/8/61-18/10/61**HI**	53,550	Derby
11/3/63-4/4/63**HI**		Crewe

Noted at Works: Crewe 9/65

Boilers

No.9090	13/7/39	from	8002
No.8839	30/9/44	from	8005
No.9094	4/1/49	from	8002
No.9099	2/4/53		
No.9095	1/5/59		

Tender

LMS 9135	28/6/35

Sheds

Wellingborough	29/6/35
Coalville	28/9/35
Toton	9/11/35
Wellingborough	10/10/36
Toton	29/3/41
Leeds	15/5/43
Normanton	7/2/48
Lancaster	31/7/48
Derby[o/l]	12/1/52
Derby	2/2/52
Leeds	8/3/52
Mansfield	16/1/54
Kirkby-in-Ashfield	9/4/60

Withdrawn w/e 9/1/65

8001 near Bedford in 1937, carrying that three link coupling and looking remarkably pristine, doubtless deriving from a recent Light Service repair that year.

8001 in August 1935. The location is unusual; it is Cricklewood but not the MPD. The turntable with hand rails in the background indicate that we are in the 'Brent Ash Pits' actually south of the main roundhouse complex but also parallel to the Edgware Road. Locos off up coal trains could turn and be serviced here without having to visit the MPD.

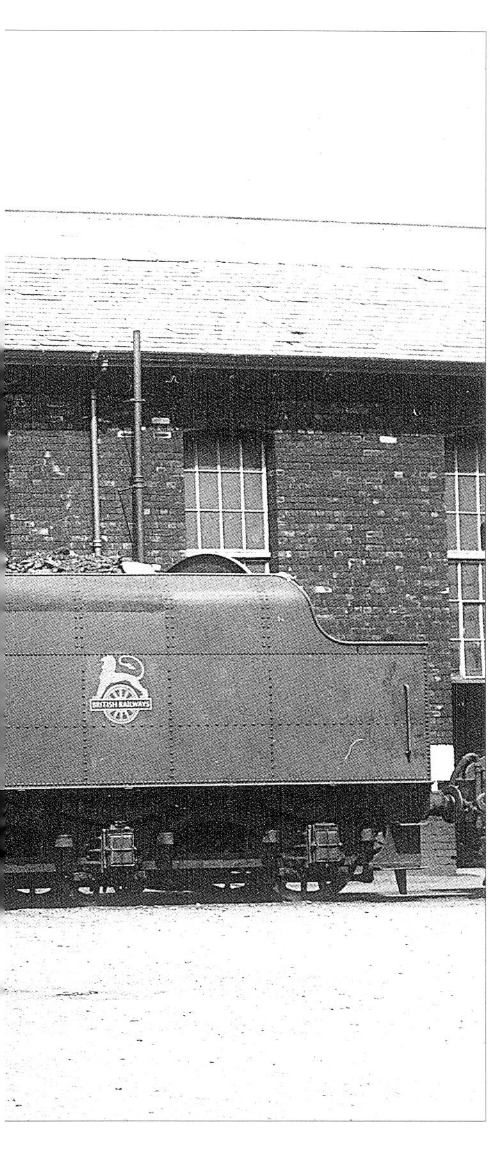

Left. 48001 at Grimesthorpe MPD, Sheffield, a place deep amongst vast steel mills, on 10 July 1955.

Bottom left. 48001 at Mansfield, 4 April 1954 with another 8F alongside.

Below. 48001 at Kirkby in Ashfield MPD, 26 June 1960. Norman Preedy.

48002

Built as 8002 at Crewe Works 9th July 1935
Renumbered 48002 w/e 11/12/48

Improvement and Modifications
7/9/46 Casing and filter for air relief valves
25/12/48 Stiffening brackets for cab wing plates

Repairs

1/6/37-8/7/37**LS**	64,929	
22/8/38-3/9/38**LO**	91,256	
17/5/39-14/7/39**HG**	112,557	
16/10/40-23/10/40**TRO**		
27/2/41-11/3/41**LS**	38,676	
24/8/41-26/9/41**LO**	49,637	
23/12/41-9/1/42**LO**	56,194	
29/5/43-12/7/43**LS**	95,878	
11/9/43-7/10/43**LO**	100,978	
8/7/44-13/10/44**HG**	121,212	
29/6/46-12/8/46**LS**	47,311	
4/11/46-7/12/46**LO**	54,297	
27/9/48-8/12/48**HG**	46,514	
28/2/51-16/3/51**LI**	64,016	Crewe
15/6/52-7/7/52**LC**	36,409	Derby
31/10/53-18/12/53**HG**	68,417	Derby
9/5/56-7/6/56**HI**	61,510	Derby
15/10/56-31/10/56**LC[EO]**	8,034	Derby
21/6/58-28/8/58**HG**	47,420	Derby
10/1/61-16/2/61**LI**	54,633	Derby

Noted at Works: Crewe 8/64

Boilers

No.9094	14/7/39 from	8006
No.9098	8/12/48 from	8002
No.8838	18/12/53 from	8000
No.9098	28/8/58	

Tender
LMS 9219 9/7/35

Sheds

Willesden	13/7/35
Toton	20/12/36
Leicester	27/7/40
Toton	11/3/44
Staveley	15/1/49
Toton	7/10/50
Burton	13/12/52
Hasland	21/9/57
Bourneville	10/1/59
Saltley	7/3/59
Derby	11/4/59
Kettering	4/3/61
Nottingham	16/9/61
Annesley	22/9/62
Woodford Halse	16/2/63
Willesden	19/6/65
Lostock Hall	17/7/65

Withdrawn w/e 24/9/66

Toton's 8002 with piled-up tender (courtesy the Cricklewood coaling plant) hurries north past Radlett over bridge 85 with period wagons on 7 May 1946. A serif number and LMS lurk under the grime.

48002 at Woodford Halse. The engine now has the '50% reciprocating' star on the cabside indicating higher permissible speeds.

48002 at Farington with a short run of minerals on 3 June 1966. RailOnline

48003

Built as 8003 at Crewe Works 28th June 1935
Renumbered 48003 w/e 22/5/48

Improvements and modifications

8/7/38	Manually operated blowdown valves
18/5/46	Providing steel in lieu of copper tube*
12/6/48	Stiffening for brackets over cab wing plates

**presumably main steam pipe*

Repairs

10/7/37-13/8/37**LS**	57,026	
24/3/38-8/7/38**HO**	72,394	
13/6/39-21/6/39**LO**	21,280	
22/6/39-20/7/39**LS**	21,280	
30/7/40-10/9/40**LO**	47,634	
17/12/40-6/1/41**TRO**		
13/3/41-2/4/41**LS**	59,239	
23/6/41-4/7/41**TRO**		
18/9/42-15/10/42**HG**	101,297	
29/7/44-14/9/44**LS**	53,883	
23/7/45-11/8/45**LO**	77,136	
15/4/46-13/5/46**LS**	92,723	
16/4/48-17/5/48**HG**	43,739	
89/5/50-31/5/50**HI**	42,732	Crewe
12/6/51-3/7/51**HI**	26,043	Crewe
27/5/52-11/6/52**LC**	20,650	Derby
30/4/53-25/6/53**HG**	42,069	Derby
24/3/55-19/4/55**LI**	39,175	Derby
16/2/57-21/3/57**HI**	40,596	Derby
6/2/59-6/3/59**HG**	39,445	Derby
24/3/61-10/5/61**LI**	53,487	Derby
11/8/61-15/8/61**LC[TO]**	5,543	Derby

Boilers

No.10086	25/5/38 new	
No.9600	15/10/42 from	8055
No.11799	17/5/48 from	8687
No.11148	25/6/53	
No.11533	6/3/59	

Tenders

LMS 9220	28/6/35
No.10122	15/8/61

Sheds

Willesden	29/6/35
Sheffield	4/4/36
Coalville	11/7/36
Wellingborough	20/9/41
Nottingham	14/10/44
Kirkby	7/10/50

Withdrawn w/e 5/3/66

8003 brand new on 29 June 1935, the day after its official day of completion. It is a sloping throatplate engine, with a regulator dome. No shed plate yet, small single bolted panel on cylinders. This complements the similar view on page 18.

48003 at Bristol Barrow Road on 22 April 1951. It was 'converted' to sloping throatplate with new boiler 10086 of 25/5/38, rendering it into this domed form. Now with larger circular bolted plate on cylinder cover and two rectangular plates on the top edge.

48004

Built as 8004 at Crewe Works 28th June 1935
Renumbered 48004 w/e 24/4/48

Improvements and modifications

14/6/41	Manually operated blowdown valves
7/9/46	Horizontal grid type regulator, casing And filter for air relief valves, additional washout plugs

Repairs

28/7/37-25/8/37**LS**	58,273	
28/6/38-18/8/38**HO**	76,223	
18/9/39-20/10/39**LS**	29,872	
3/6/40-18/7/40**LO**	46,272	
1/5/41-29/5/41**HG**	67,454	
21/3/42-16/4/42**HO**	24,342	
10/12/42-1/1/43**LO**	22,145	
21/8/43-18/9/43**LS**	41,894	
11/10/43-12/11/43**LO**	43,083	
20/4/44-20/5/44**LO**	53,627	
23/10/44-6/12/44**HS**	65,493	
26/7/45-23/8/45**LO**	18,105	
8/8/46-5/9/46**HG**	41,648	
11/3/48-19/4/48**HS**	35,255	Derby
28/12/48-3/2/49**HC**	19,810	Crewe
21/11/49-17/12/49**LI**	44,742	Crewe
21/3/51-21/6/51**HG**	34,095	Crewe
23/8/53-24/9/53**LI**	46,484	Derby
7/3/55-21/4/55**HG**	32,471	Derby
6/3/57-28/3/57**LI**	42,297	Derby
24/3/58-30/4/58**LC**	21,587	Derby
28/9/59-4/11/59**HG**	52,795	Derby
14/7/61-7/9/61**HI**	45,379	Derby

Noted at Works: Crewe 6/63; Crewe 11/63

Boilers

No.9091	18/8/38	from	8003
No.9095	27/5/41	from	8007
No.9096	5/9/46	from	8008
No.8839	21/4/55		
No.9099	4/11/59		

Tenders

LMS 9221	28/6/35
No.10154	1/3/48

Sheds

Willesden	29/6/35
Sheffield	4/4/36
Coalville	11/7/36
Wellingborough	20/9/41
Toton	8/4/44
Stourton	24/7/48
Toton	25/9/48
Kirkby	8/7/50

Withdrawn w/e 6/11/65

Lovely aesthetic balance in form of the Stanier taper boiler locos, shown to perfection in a side-on view at Rugby on 1 December 1935.

48004 bowls along amongst pleasant surrounds at Chinley; the date is not recorded but the loco seems free of electrification flashes and the shed plate is not properly visible. The late 1950s might be a reasonable guess. Norman Preedy.

48004 near Banbury, 3 October 1964. It had been at Kirkby in Ashfield since 1950.

48005

Built as 8005 at Crewe Works 28th June 1935
Renumbered 48005 w/e 4/12/48

Repairs

18/3/37-20/4/37**LS**	53,451	
19/8/37-28/9/37**LO**	61,727	
10/2/39-3/3/39**LO**	99,236	
16/3/39-6/4/39**LO**	100,376	
28/6/39-7/7/39**TRO**		
27/7/39-9/9/39**HG**	101,946	
27/12/40-18/1/41**LS**	43,556	
24/4/42-30/5/42**LS**	84,343	
9/9/42-3/10/42**LO**	98,506	
22/4/43-28/5/43**HS**	118,178	
29/6/44-5/10/44**HG**	33,378	
18/10/45-17/11/45**LO**	27,652	
23/4/46-23/5/46**HS**	39,618	
10/2/48-9/3/48**LS**	46,290	Crewe
28/10/48-3/12/48**LO**	24,068	Crewe
8/12/48-17/12/48**TRO**		Crewe
30/12/49-10/2/50**HG**	56,505	Crewe
28/3/51-21/4/51**LC**	36,651	Horwich
26/4/51-9/5/51**Weighing only**		Horwich
10/12/51-28/1/52**HG**	56,609	Horwich
7/2/52-14/2/52**EO**		Horwich
27/2/53-19/3/53**LC**	37,926	Derby
9/7/54-2/9/54**LI**	73,869	Rugby
8/11/54-9/12/54**LC[EO]**	5,265	Derby
2/7/56-10/8/56**HG**	42,024	Derby
22/10/57-14/11/57**LC[EO]**	27,790	Derby
17/6/59-10/7/59**HI**	62,696	Derby

Noted at Works: Derby 11/61; Crewe 6/64

Boilers

No.8839	9/9/39	from	8001
No.9099	5/10/44	from	8000
No.9091	10/2/50	from	8010
No.9092	28/1/52		
No.9090	10/8/56		

Tender

LMS 9222	28/6/35

Sheds

Willesden	29/6/35
Sheffield	4/4/36
Wellingborough	11/7/36
Leicester	3/10/36
Toton	21/1/59
Hasland	30/9/39
Wellingborough	2/12/39
Hellifield	19/6/43
Skipton	24/1/48
Derby	12/1/52
Leeds	8/3/52
Stourton	27/9/52
Normanton	24/9/55
Nottingham	1/10/55
Derby	20/9/56
Kettering	4/3/61
Annesley	22/9/62
Rowsley	8/12/62
Woodford Halse	13/7/63
Willesden	19/6/65
Fleetwood	17/7/65
Heaton Mersey	26/2/66

Withdrawn w/e 19/3/66

48005 at Woodford Halse MPD, 25 August 1964. 'Improvised' shed plate, star on cab; note now external steam pipe to steam cleaning cock which was high on the loco earlier in 1957 and lower now. Peter Groom.

48005 between Melton Junction and Melton Mowbray (Town) station working very hard with an up freight in April 1957. The driver can now see that he has the road for the main line and will be able to pick up water on Melton troughs if he is going fast enough, but he only has about a mile to do it. Peter Groom.

48006

Built as 8006 at Crewe Works 25th September 1935
Renumbered 48006 w/e 28/5/49

Improvements and modifications
15/7/39 Manually operated blowdown valves
15/7/39 Providing steel in lieu of copper tube*
1/12/51 Discharge of continuous blowdown into ashpan
**presumably main steam pipe*

Repairs

13/12/35-30/12/35**LO**	6,184	
27/7/37-18/8/37**LS**	61,540	
27/7/38-3/8/38**LO**	85,779	
14/3/39-23/6/39**HG**	101,939	
10/7/40-12/7/40**TRO**		
9/7/41-111/8/41**HS**	57,025	
14/4/42-28/4/42**LO**	15,384	
24/3/43-9/4/43**LS**	37,962	
8/3/44-7/4/44**HG**	60,311	
20/1/46-16/2/46**LS**	43,695	
8/8/47-4/10/47**HS**	37,148	Crewe
8/4/49-28/5/49**HG**	35,499	Crewe
13/12/50-6/1/51**LI**	38,138	Crewe
3/11/51-22/11/51**HI**	18,793	Crewe
53-24/4/53**HG**	26,902	Derby
2/10/54-25/10/54**LI**	32,608	Derby
17/10/55-10/11/55**LC[EO]**	21,284	Derby
27/11/56-18/12/56**LI**	43,720	Derby
19/12/58-28/1/59**HG**	42,328	Derby
8/5/61-15/6/61**LI**	60,711	Derby

Noted at Works: Derby 7/63

Boilers

No.9092	23/6/39	from	8004
No.8838	7/4/44	from	8010
No.9093	28/5/49	from	8007
No.9094	24/4/53		
No.9091	28/1/59		

Tenders

LMS 9223	25/9/35
No.9251	27/9/63

Sheds

Crewe	28/9/35
Willesden	5/10/35
Toton	20/12/36
Westhouses	16/3/40
Coalville	20/11/43
Wellingborough	26/8/44
Kirkby	15/11/47

Withdrawn w/e 30/1/65

One of Kirkby's innumerable 8Fs, 48006 after what must have been its final (unrecorded) Heavy General, ex-works at Crewe South on 29 September 1963. Peter Skelton.

48006 at Heaton Mersey, coming north with a freight over the bridges carrying the 1902 Midland Direct line, over (firstly) the CLC and (beyond) the River Mersey on 29 May 1952. The little hipped roof to the left belongs to Heaton Mersey West Box which controlled all movements in and out of Heaton Mersey MPD, which stretched out below to the left. Norman Preedy.

48007

Built as 8007 at Crewe Works 26th September 1935
Renumbered 48007 w/e 5/3/49

Improvements and modifications
19/4/45 New steel in lieu of copper tube
26/3/49 Stiffening brackets for cab wing plates
28/1/61 Fitting of AWS

Repairs

29/5/37-18/6/37**LS**	58,960	
21/5/38-1/6/38**LO**	85,330	
15/1/40-3/4/40**HS**	128,369	
14/2/41-11/3/41**LO**	27,592	
18/11/41-1/12/41**LS**	51,153	
16/10/42-5/11/42**HS**	64,559	
27/5/44-10/7/44**HG**	32,381	
3/3/45-25/4/45**HO**	12,416	
3/6/46-29/6/46**LS**	20,833	Crewe
16/10/47-7/11/47**HS**	29,649	Crewe
29/12/48-28/2/49**HG**	87,435	Crewe
6/12/49-17/12/49**LC**	22,243	Derby
15/5/51-5/6/51**LI**	55,011	Crewe
7/1/52-23/1/52**LC[EO]**	17,406	Derby
8/5/52-22/5/52**LC[EO]**	25,853	Shed
24/9/52-10/11/52**LC**	34,128	Derby
10/12/53-4/2/54**HG**	65,393	Derby
26/8/54-29/9/54**LC[EO]**	16,415	Derby
3/12/55-28/12/55**LI**	43,788	Derby
9/1/56-13/1/56**NC[Rect]**	457	Derby
18/1/58-11/2/58**HG**	48,259	Derby
2/4/59-5/5/59**LC[EO]**	30,042	Derby
14/12/60-9/1/61**NC[EO]**	24,166	Derby

Noted at Works: Derby 9/62

Boilers

No.9098	3/4/40	from	8010
No.9093	10/7/44	from	8009
No.8839	28/2/49	from	8001
No.9098	4/2/54		
No.9092	11/2/58		

Tenders

LMS 9224	26/9/35
No.9183	9/10/62

Sheds

Crewe	28/9/35
Willesden	12/10/35
Toton	20/12/36
Kirkby	31/1/42
Wellingborough	15/5/48
Rose Grove	17/7/48
Sheffield[o/l]	2/4/49
Sheffield	30/4/49
Toton	28/5/49
Leicester	5/3/55
Wellingborough	26/3/60
Kettering	24/9/60
Cricklewood	17/12/60
Toton	16/9/61
Saltley	9/12/61
Annesley	13/10/62
Woodford Halse	16/2/63
Willesden	18/4/64
Bescot	5/9/64

Withdrawn w/e 9/1/65

The southern end of the 347 yard Northchurch tunnels on 19 May 1948; 8007 (serif-style number) slogs its way south, having traversed the later up slow single bore. The original double bore is on the left. H.C. Casserley, courtesy R.M. Casserley.

Willesden's 48007, recently prone to priming, at its London home (vast coaler rearing up beyond) on 10 June 1964. Piping now runs down from the exhaust ejector joint at the smokebox side – this drained water condensing in the system. J.L. Stevenson, courtesy Hamish Stevenson.

48008

Built as 8008 at Crewe Works 3rd October 1935
Renumbered 48008 w/e 3/7/48

Improvements and modifications
8/7/38 Manually operated blowdown valves
10/8/46 Horizontal grid type regulator
26/1/46 Cab wing plates
13/8/49 New design valve casing and filter for air relief valve

Repairs

5/7/37-30/7/37**LS**	59,388	
8/2/39-20/3/39**LO**	98,045	
7/2/40-16/4/40**HS**	119,531	
1/10/41-18/10/41**LS**	42,383	
14/4/42-5/5/42**HO**	56,760	
1/10/42-21/10/42**LO**	12,289	
2/11/43-11/12/43**LS**	44.045	
9/7/44-17/8/44**LO**	56,151	
18/9/45-4/10/45**HG**	80,071	Crewe
2/6/48-3/7/48**LS**	50,012	Crewe
4/2/49-3/3/49**LC**	13,622	Derby
10/6/49-1/8/49**LC**	20,209	Derby
31/7/50-25/8/50**HG**	42,483	Crewe
5/11/52-19/12/52**HG**	61,614	Derby
6/3/54-8/4/54**HI**	37,601	Derby
16/5/56-14/6/56**HI**	53,367	Derby
25/8/58-21/10/58**HG**	44,747	Derby
18/2/60-23/3/60**HI**	49,475	Derby
6/8/60-20/10/60**HI**	46,094	Derby

Noted at Works: Derby 1/62; Crewe 6/64

Boilers

No.9096	16/4/40	from	8003
No.9097	4/10/45	from	8011
No.9099	25/8/50	from	8005
No.9091	19/12/52		
No.8838	21/10/58		

Tenders

LMS 9225	3/10/35
No.9928	29/11/61
No.2616	no date

Sheds

Crewe	5/10/35
Willesden	12/10/35
Toton	20/12/36
Leicester	27/7/40
Derby	11/3/44
Coalville	27/9/47
Wellingborough	11/11/50
Nottingham	5/3/55
Kirkby	25/2/56
Rowsley	23/5/59
Kettering	1/7/61
Rowsley	27/4/63
Westhouses	29/6/63

Withdrawn w/e 2/5/64

Kettering's 48008, with recent attention to the washout 'doors' on the firebox, about 1961. External supply to steam cleaning cock.

At Kettering shed, 6 August 1962. This was more or less what you saw on leaving the station, standing in the station yard and glancing left. RailOnline

48009

Built as 8009 at Crewe Works 7th October 1935
Renumbered 48009 w/e 29/5/48

Improvements and modifications
2/12/39 Manually operated blowdown valves, steel in lieu of copper tube*
**presumably main steam pipe*

Repairs

4/10/37-9/11/37**LS**	66,997	
14/3/38-2/4/38**LO**7	7,290	
6/11/39-27/11/39**HG**	124,032	
24/1/41-1/3/41**LS**	38,410	
12/1/42-4/2/42**HG**	69,8511	
3/2/43-13/3/43**LS**	28,767	
21/10/43-9/11/43**LO**	45,307	
28/3/44-2/6/44**HG**	53,365	
9/3/46-1/4/46**LO**	32,160	
13/6/46-26/7/46**LS**	39,047	
23/4/48-28/5/48**HS**	34,660	Crewe
22/3/49-27/4/49**HC**	19,144	Crewe
12/2/50-1/3/50**LI**	37,899	Crewe
23/11/50-19/12/50**LC**	16,215	Derby
3/5/51-12/6/51**HI**	25,977	Crewe
5/4/53-12/6/53**HG**	41,463	Derby
9/6/55-4/7/55**LI**	43,779	Derby
7/5/57-23/5/57**HI**	39,865	Derby
14/11/59-30/12/59**HG**	50,583	Derby
25/9/61-7/11/61**HI**	44,266	Derby

Noted at Works: Derby 9/62; Derby 1/63 for cutting up

Boilers

No.9093	6/11/39	from
No.9092	2/6/44	from
No.9095	28/5/48	from
No.9093	12/6/53	
No.8839	30/12/59	

Tender
LMS 9226 7/10/35

Sheds

Willesden	no date
Toton	16/11/35
Wellingborough	10/10/36
Toton	29/3/41
Kirkby	12/6/43

Withdrawn w/e 22/12/62
Date actually broken up 14/1/63

8009 at Toton, serif letters, numbers. It was one of the 8Fs to go new to Willesden but very soon it was at Toton. This only lasted a year, 1935-1936 but it was there again during the War. This would be the earlier 1930s period.

At Wellingborough, 24 September 1955. It was in this period that that coal traffic from Toton to London saw exceptionally high volumes with both up loaded trains and the corresponding return empties frequently diverted on to the fast lines between Wellingborough and Brent Sidings. A 'very creditable turn of speed' on the part of the 8Fs enabled such traffic to be sandwiched in between the normal passenger workings 'without undue interference' though the down empties were frequently double headed to avoid unnecessary light engine working. 1954 had also seen the first 9Fs on the Wellingborough coal workings and though their numbers would grow their effect would be blunted because a large proportion were Crosti engines. H.C. Casserley, courtesy R.M. Casserley.

In good nick at Kirkby in Ashfield MPD, 5 July 1953, fresh off a Heavy General. E. Bruton, ColourRail

48010

Built as 8010 at Crewe Works 17th October 1935
Renumbered 48010 w/e 3/9/49

Improvements and modifications
4/11/61 AWS equipment

Repairs

4/1/36-29/1/36**LS**	7,899	
1/6/37-25/6/37**LS**	53,679	
10/2/38-4/3/38**LO**	68,714	
7/12/38-10/1/39**TRO**		
4/1/40-24/2/40**HS**	121,354	
22/7/41-14/8/41**HS**	36,620	
15/12/42-15/1/43**LS**	37,119	
12/2/44-2/3/44**HG**	66,173	
11/10/45-2/11/45**LS**	37,997	
15/3/47-5/5/47**HS**	67,212	
27/4/49-3/9/49**HG**	42,107	Crewe
23/10/50-29/11/50**LC**	30,354	Crewe
5/10/51-9/11/51**HI**	55,267	Crewe
15/7/53-2/9/53**HG**	47,305	Derby
2/1/56-1/3/56**HI**	62,069	Derby
20/2/57-2/5/57**LC[EO]**	26,699	Derby
2/2/59-12/2/59**HG**	66,435	Derby
5/10/61-3/11/61**LI**	73,028	Derby

Noted at Works: Crewe 5/64; Crewe 2/66

Boilers

No.8838	24/2/40	from	8000
No.9091	2/3/44	from	8104
No.8838	3/9/49	from	8006
No.9095	2/9/53		
No.9094	12/3/59		

Tender

LMS 9227	17/10/35

Sheds

Willesden	no date
Toton	16/11/35
Westhouses	16/3/40
Leeds	15/3/41
Canklow	11/10/41
Staveley	13/6/42
Wellingborough	21/7/45
Staveley	28/7/45
Saltley	7/6/47
Wellingborough	16/4/49
Leicester	19/5/56
Wellingborough	26/3/60
Saltley	9/2/63
Woodford Halse	16/2/63
Willesden	19/6/65
Speke Jct	9/10/65
Newton Heath	23/4/66

Withdrawn w/e 20/1/68

48010 at Kettering, by the coal stage, 18 January 1962. The view is from the north end of the station platforms across to the town. The line and more crucially the shed yard (hard against the running lines) is level but the main line dips away south through the station at 1 in 155. K. Fairey, ColourRail

Woodford Halse's 48010 stands on Reading shed, 9 September 1963. Two pipes entering exhaust ejector from cab indicate twin cone ejector; AWS fitted, covers missing from firebox shoulder washout plugs. Electrification flashes, fitted at sheds, could wander around a little; the one 'amidships', usually above the hand rail, is here below it. The rather different second-hand rail fixing seen on, say 48005 at Mold Junction, 6 October 1964 in *Parts and Service*, is there but a similar fixing has appeared for the first hand rail 'knob' too. Peter Groom.

48011

Built as 8011 at Crewe Works 25th October 1935
Renumbered 48011 w/e 28/5/49

Improvements and modifications
31/12/39 Manually operated blowdown valves
14/7/51 Stiffening for brackets over cab wing plates, Additional washout plugs, new type piston head fastening

Repairs

2/8/37-20/8/37**LS**	58,304	
18/1/39-28/1/39**LO**	95,683	
20/11/39-27/12/39**HG**	123,778	
9/7/40-31/7/40**LS**	19,393	
14/12/40-15/1/41**LO**	33,284	
3/2/42-2/3/42**HS**	58,895	
14/7/42-31/7/42**LO**	9,917	
15/3/43-2/4/43**LS**	27,634	
13/12/43-18/1/44**LO**	44,604	
11/6/45-21/7/45**HG**	74,433	
23/7/47-11/9/47**LS**	47,512	Crewe
4/5/49-28/5/49**HI**	38,678	Crewe
17/4/51-26/6/51**HG**	43,041	Crewe
17/10/53-7/12/53**HI**	55,867	Derby
9/10/54-3/11/58**LC[EO]**	16,915	Derby
28/12/55-3/2/56**HG**	39,137	Derby
24/12/57-9/1/58**LC[EO]**	47,360	Rugby
21/1/59-25/2/59**LI**	69,292	Derby
19/6/61-8/8/61**HG**	58,055	Derby

Noted at Works: Darlington 11/64

Boilers

No.9097	21/12/35 from	8009
No.9090	21/7/45 from	8001
No.9097	3/2/56	
No.9093	8/8/61	

Tender
LMS 9228 25/10/35

Sheds

Willesden	no date
Toton	16/11/35
Westhouses	25/2/41
Northampton[o/l]	29/5/48
Northampton	19/6/48
Carlisle Canal[o/l]	28/8/48
Northampton	6/11/48
Willesden	11/2/50
Northwich	4/11/50
Derby[o/l]	12/1/52
Derby	2/2/52
Canklow	11/12/54
Kirkby in Ashfield	9/1/60
Annesley	22/9/62
Woodford Halse	3/8/63
Willesden	19/6/65
Buxton	17/7/65
Bolton	14/8/65
Agecroft	11/9/65
Patricroft	8/10/66

Withdrawn w/e 27/5/67

8011, sadly fallen from grace, at Cricklewood in July 1938. LMS entirely obscured on the tender. Hollow axles, visible even from this distance.

Another Woodford 8F by now, 48011 leaves the Didcot West Curve at Foxhall Junction, and heads towards the Down Main Curve with a westbound freight, in April 1965. The water column for stopped locos, with a bin for sand on this difficult start, stands just beyond the 'off' signal. It is not in the Record, but 48011 underwent what appears to have been a Heavy General at Darlington earlier in the year; completed by the end of January, it accounts for 48011's relatively bright condition, and explains the larger numerals, reminiscent of Scottish works attention. David Anderson.

48011 at Southall MPD, 8 March 1964. K. Fairey, ColourRail

48012

Built as 8012 at Crewe Works 19th December 1936
Renumbered 48012 w/e 3/12/49

Sold to HM Government-withdrawn from LMS Stock w/e 23/12/44
Purchased (WD 577) from Ministry of Supply and returned to ex-LMS stock w/e 3/12/49

Improvement and modifications
11/7/53 Removal of sandguns
10/9/60 AWS

Repairs

19/10/39-16/11/39**LS**	71,420	
12/10/40-18/10/40**LO**	92,787	
4/2/41-6/3/41**HS**	98,902	
20/9/41-21/10/41**LO**	12,312	
29/11/49-15/12/49**HG**		Crewe
[Overseas mileage unknown]		
4/1/52-13/1/52**LC**	53,587	Shed
13/6/52-7/8/52**LI**	65,367	Rugby
26/5/53-25/6/53 **HI**	19,332	Crewe
20/3/54-30/4/54**HC[EO]**	16,788	Crewe
21/4/56-25/5/56**HG**	63,892	Crewe
17/10/56-24/11/56**LC[EO]**	9,988	Crewe
9/4/58-16/4/58**LC[EO]**	43,898	Crewe
22/9/59-31/10/59**HI**	77,562	Crewe
13/8/60-30/8/60**NC[EO]**	21,348	Crewe

Boilers

No.9606	6/3/41 from	8061
No.12023	15/12/49 from	8385
No.10880	25/5/56	

Tenders

LMS 9377	19/12/36
No.10213	29/11/49

Sheds

Normanton	19/12/36
Kirkby	16/3/40
TO WD for overseas	
Into shops	19/9/41
To Dockside	3/11/41
Crewe South	3/12/49
Warwick	14/1/50
Northampton	15/11/58
Rugby	21/2/59
Crewe South	2/1/65
Stoke	30/1/65
Edge Hill	20/5/67

Withdrawn w/e 30/3/68

With 8012 we are now in the realm of the domed, sloping throatplate boiler and this was the first; block style and welded tender at Normanton on 24 May 1938. It was also the first built officially as an 8F rather than 7F. The engine stands on one of the radiating roads of the ancient MR roundhouse, demolished a year or two before to make way for ash and coaling plants.

Battered but unbowed at Suez as 70577 on 3 October 1947; oil fuel tender, 'tropical' roof, lamp and various parts missing. That looks like one of the connecting rods on the running plate. WD number repeated on rear of tender. It had been WD 577 at first, and had arrived at Suez after working in Persia.

48012 back in Blighty, after overhaul at Crewe (not the tender though!) on 28 June 1953. It was a Warwick engine at the time, allocated there from 1950-1958. 48012 is standing just on the station side of Chester Bridge, in the Old Works. The bridge took Edleston Road over the old Chester Line in the Deviation Works. W14 is a works shunting engine target number and an 8F a most unusual engine to be engaged on such duty. Maybe it was covering for a shortage prior to be being released into traffic. The works had its own allocation for shunting, including maintenance spares. They did also occasionally borrow an engine from Crewe South if they were short for any reason. Notice the works shunters have put a three link coupling on the front drawhook to make life easier for them!

48012 at Rugby MPD on 29 September 1962; AWS, with battery box and timing reservoir prominent. Peter Groom.

48012
LOVAT SCOUTS

48016

Built as 8016 at Crewe Works w/e 20th January 1937
Renumbered 48016 w/e 29/10/49

Sold to H M Government-withdrawn from LMS stock w/e 23/12/44
Purchased (WD 591) from Ministry of Supply – returned to ex-LMS Stock w/e 29/10/49

Improvements and modifications
22/3/52 Discharge of continuous blowdown into ashpan
10/9/60 AWS

Repairs

9/2/39-24/2/39**LS**	52,683	
1/8/40-11/8/40**TRO**		
29/11/40-7/12/40**LO**	100,202	
1/5/41-21/5/41**HG**	108,467	
13/9/41 Repaired and prepared for overseas by Southern Rly Co		
28/10/49-12/11/49**HG**		Crewe
[Overseas mileage unknown]		
30/1/52-5/3/52**LI**	57,182	Rugby
30/10/53-13/11/53**LC**	45,459	Shed
19/5/54-12/6/54**HG**	57,673	Crewe
26/2/57-14/3/57**LI**	64,420	Derby
9/6/59-4/7/59**HG**	49,363	Crewe
3/8/60-17/8/60**NC[EO]**	29,218	Crewe

Boilers

No.9827	21/5/41 from	8013
No.10804	12/11/49 from	48257
No.11284	12/6/54	
No.10497	4/7/59	

Tenders

LMS 9381	20/1/37
No.10292	29/10/49

Sheds

Normanton	23/1/37
Kirkby	16/3/40
Into shops	13/9/41
To Dockside	28/12/41
Crewe South	29/10/49
Rugby	10/12/49
Nuneaton	17/6/50
Northampton	14/9/63
Oxley	30/1/65
Saltley	19/6/65

Withdrawn w/e 27/11/65

Nuneaton's 48016 at Willesden, 12 August 1963; AWS and reciprocal masses cleared for speed by application of cabside star. Peter Groom.

Splendidly scruffy 48016, looking like it deserves a rest, in one of the roundhouses at Saltley, 28 November 1965.

48017

Built as 8017 at Crewe Works 25th January 1937
Renumbered 48017 w/e 8/5/48

Improvements and modifications
6/10/51 Discharge of continuous blowdown into ashpan
28/1/56 Provision of new type piston head fastening
8/10/60 AWS
8/10/60 Modification to tube cleaner pipe and fittings

Repairs

30/12/38-10/1/39**LO**	47,679	
18/12/39-5/1/40**LS**	71,570	
2/11/40-25/11/40**TRO**		
29/12/41-4/2/42**HG**	122,565	
25/11/43-11/12/43**HS**	34,822	
20/11/45-29/12/45**LS**	50,692	
20/3/47-3/4/47**LO**	80,788	
48-8/5/48**HG**	79,952	Crewe
2/8/50-19/8/50**HI**	54,306	Crewe
29/8/51-6/10/51**LC[EO]**	27,647	Crewe
11/9/52-29/10/52**HG**	47,944	Horwich
9/12/55-27/1/56**LI**	66,722	Crewe
24/5/58-11/6/58**HG**	46,217	Crewe
19/8/60-5/10/60**HI**	56,602	Horwich
24/4/63-23/5/63**GO**		Horwich

Boilers

No.11140	4/2/42	new	
No.11583	8/5/48	from	8318
No.11152	29/10/52		
No.11503	11/6/58		

Tender

LMS 9382	25/1/37

Sheds

Sheffield	30/1/37
Heaton Mersey	8/11/41
Sheffield	3/7/43
Rose Grove [o/l]	2/4/49
Wakefield [o/l]	9/4/49
Wakefield	30/4/49
Mold Jct [o/l]	9/7/49
Mold Jct	23/7/49
Birkenhead	10/11/51
Widnes	17/10/53
Northwich	15/11/58
Birkenhead	27/2/65
Aintree	24/4/65
Edge Hill	17/6/67

Withdrawn w/e 4/11/67

8017 with ICI hoppers Peak Forest-Northwich at Skelton Junction on the CLC, April 1939. ColourRail

With the curious serif smokebox number plate of the first year or so of BR. The cabside number is in the equally curious 'clipped' block style; the welded tender is anonymous. P. Hughes, ColourRail

AWS equipped 48017 in full BR garb, at Northwich MPD on 14 July 1963. Peter Skelton. Top lamp bracket removed to smokebox door to avoid OHL accidents (and there were a few).

48018

Built as 8018 at Crewe Works 9th February 1937
Renumbered 48018 w/e 3/12/49

Sold to H M Government-withdrawn from LMS stock w/e 23/12/44
Purchased (WD 582) from Ministry of Supply – returned to ex-LMS stock w/e 3/12/49

Improvement and modifications
26/12/53 Removal of sandguns
13/8/60 AWS

Repairs

11/8/38-19/8/38**LO**	33,722	
22/2/39-17/3/39**LS**	48,135	
15/1/40-1/2/40**LO**	75,663	
28/8/40-16/9/40**LO**	92,627	
5/3/41-25/3/41**HS**	102,479	
30/9/41-1/11/41**LS**	8,696	
29/11/49-21/12/49**HG**		Crewe
[Overseas mileage unknown]		
31/7/52-22/8/52**LI**	69,354	Rugby
22/8/53-17/9/53**LC[EO]**	24,907	Shed
11/11/53-22/12/53**HC[EO]**	29,072	Crewe
16/7/55-11/8/55**HG**	64,820	Crewe
2/11/56-15/11/56**LC[EO]**	33,024	Rugby
19/5/58-5/7/58**LI**	70,441	Crewe
27/7/60-12/8/60**NC[EO]**	49,430	Crewe
24/7/61-30/8/61**HG**	75,610	Crewe

Boilers

No.9625	25/3/41 from	8080
No.13250	21/12/49 new	
No.12138	11/8/55	
No.12064	30/8/61	

Tenders

LMS 9383	9/2/37
No.10225	29/11/49

Sheds

Kirkby	13/2/37
Toton	5/3/38
Kirkby	2/3/40
Into shops	27/9/41
To Dockside	11/11/41
Crewe South	3/12/49
Warwick	14/1/50
Northampton	15/11/58
Rugby	7/3/59
Northampton	11/7/64
Stoke	30/1/65
Crewe South	25/3/67
Chester	22/4/67
Crewe South	17/6/67

Withdrawn w/e 21/10/67

Crewe South, and newly complete 8018 is in the shed yard, ready for despatch to Kirkby, where it had been officially allocated the day before!

After service in Persia and transfer to Egypt (it was WD 582) and a ship home, 70582 awaits renovation at Crewe, in the old Carriage Works, on 7 May 1949. H.C. Casserley, courtesy R.M. Casserley.

48018 at work, at Hatton on 7 September 1959. E.R. Morten, courtesy J.R. Morten.

48020

Built as 8020 at Crewe Works 16th February 1937
Renumbered 48020 w/e 17/12/49

Sold to H M Government-withdrawn from LMS stock w/e 23/12/44
Purchased (WD 579) from Ministry of Supply- returned to ex-LMS stock w/e 17/12/49

Improvements and modifications
23/2/52 Discharge of continuous blowdown to ashpan
22/5/54 Removal of sandguns
10/9/60 AWS

Repairs

20/5/38-28/6/38**LS**	41,140	
27/10/39-1/11/39**LO**	86,258	
5/3/40-27/3/40**HS**	96,852	
25/3/41-21/4/41**LO**	35,142	
20/9/41-25/10/41**HS**	52,528	
14/12/49-4/1/50**HG**		Crewe
[Overseas mileage unknown]		
4/1/52-8/2/52**LI**	49,133	Rugby
26/4/54-14/5/54**HG**	57,596	Crewe
11/3/57-8/4/57**LI**	65,930	Crewe
19/9/59-16/10/59**HG**	57,196	Crewe
23/8/60-7/9/60**NC[EO]**	26/858	Crewe
13/6/62-4/7/62**LI**		Crewe
24/7/62-8/8/62**NC[Rect]**		Crewe

Boilers

No.9608	27/3/40	from	8063
No.11849	6/1/50	from	8644
No.11633	14/5/54		
No.9615	16/10/59		

Tenders

LMS 9385	16/2/37
No.10300	14/12/49

Sheds

Wellingborough	20/2/37
Into shops	20/9/41
To Dockside	3/11/41
Crewe South	17/12/49
Nuneaton	14/1/50
Rugby	22/4/50
Nuneaton	17/6/50
Shrewsbury	28/9/63
Croes Newydd	2/11/63
Northampton	5/9/64

Withdrawn w/e 7/8/65

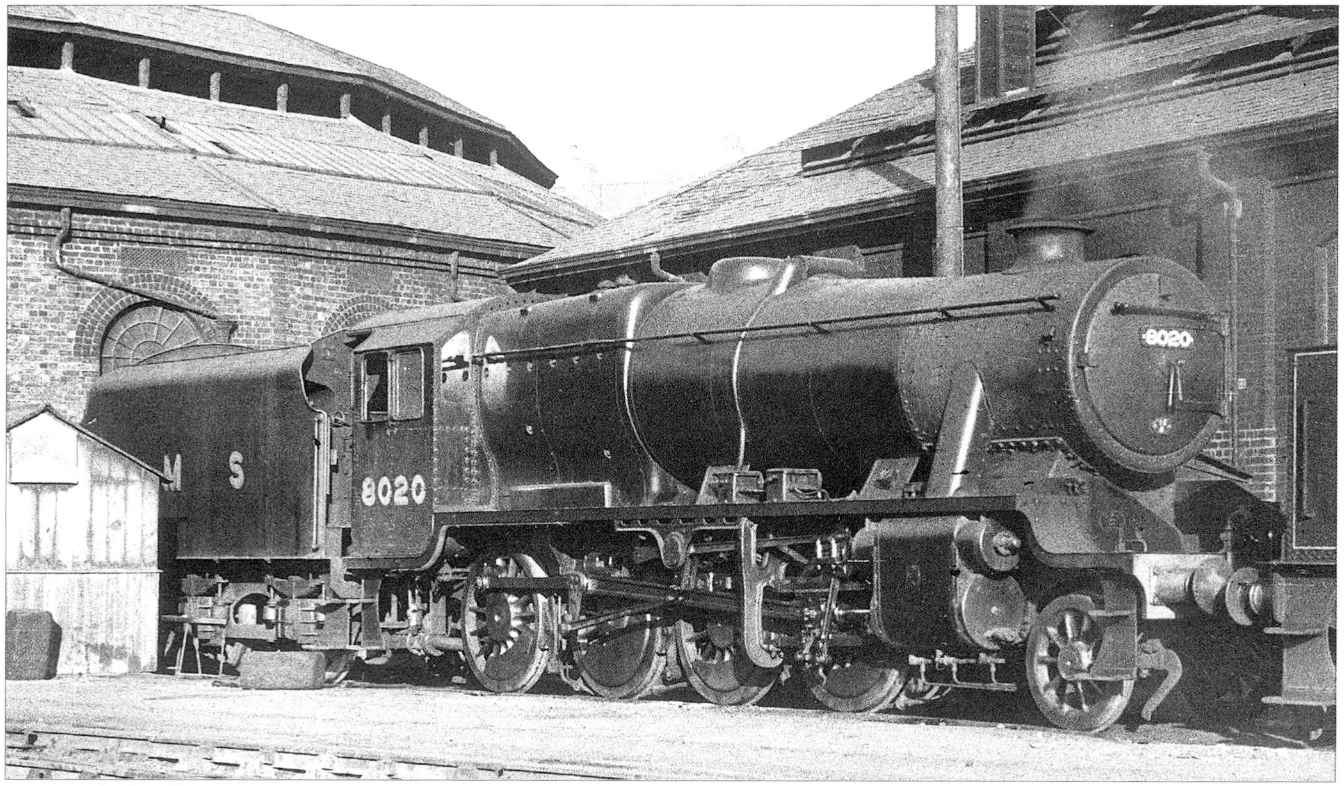

8020 with the shaded lettering showing up as such by some quirk of the light, about 1938. The location is interesting – the seldom photographed pre-War Leicester MPD. To the left is the larger roundhouse, No.2 shed and to the right the three road No.3 shed. 8020 was shipped out as WD 579.

8020 back home, as 70579, at Birkenhead on 25 April 1948; 'tropical' cab roof, modified top feed, bracket for headlamp, buffers stowed at the front. Painted on the front is THE HONOURABLE WB PORT SAID TO NEWCASTLE TWICE DAILY. One suspects drink was involved...

48020 near the end of its days, at Neath on 28 June 1964. It was a Croes Newydd engine by that time. D. Preston, ColourRail

48024

Built as 8024 at Crewe Works 22nd March 1937
Renumbered 48024 w/e 12/2/48

Improvements and modifications
25/3/61 Fitting AWS equipment

Repairs

26/8/38-9/9/38**LO**	34,559	
27/7/39-19/8/39**LS**	65,508	
17/5/40-25/5/40**LO**	88,499	
5/2/41-13/2/41**LO**	102,488	
1/7/41-11/8/41**HG**	108,917	
1/11/42 Repaired also prepared for overseas by GWR		
17/3/44-4/5/44**HG**	65,858	
27/6/45-3/8/45**LS**	41,197	
18/12/46-2/1/47**LO**	74,245	Crewe
31/10/47-16/12/47**HS**	19,387	Crewe
5/12/48-10/2/49**HG**	26,222	Crewe
20/3/51-12/4/51**LI**	56,212	Crewe
27/7/53-9/9/53**HG**	60,716	Derby
8/11/55-1/12/55**HI**	46,431	Derby
29/1/58-20/2/58**HG**	41,350	Derby
30/6/58-18/8/58**LC**	6,342	Derby
15/2/61-16/3/61**LI**	71,671	Derby
11/7/61-18/8/61**LC**	7,160	Derby
9/9/64-6/11/64**HI**	Crewe	

LMS engine histories do not consistently/clearly record requisitions. In summary, 8024 (WD 603) was requisitioned by the WD 11/41 and shipped out of the country, only to return when the vessel got into trouble. So it never did go abroad.

Boilers

No.9579	11/8/41	from	8034
No.11273	4/5/44	from	8196
No.11824	10/2/49	from	8439
No.10441	9/9/53		
No.11509	20/2/58		

Tenders

LMS 9389	22/3/37
No.10122	16/2/61
No.10363	18/8/61

Sheds

Stourton	27/3/37
Toton	1/10/38
Kirkby	2/3/40
To WD for overseas [via Swindon]	
Into shops	1/11/41
To Dockside	30/12/41
Returned temporary to LMS from WD	
Converted from oil to coal burner	
Into shops	25/4/42
Out of shops	30/4/42
Motherwell	2/5/42
Returned to LMS	15/4/43
Motherwell	3/7/43
Kingmoor	23/9/44
Motherwell	3/7/43
Kingmoor	23/9/44
Wellingborough	21/4/45
Kettering	24/2/51
Canklow	8/5/54
Mansfield	19/6/54
Nottingham	20/6/59
Annesley	22/9/62
Nottingham	16/5/64
Leicester	27/3/65
Annesley	22/5/65
Kirkby	17/7/65
Rose Grove	14/8/65

Stored serviceable
14/6/65-5/7/65

Withdrawn w/e 11/11/67

48024, one of the survivors of the SS PENTRIDGE HALL, at Crewe late on – note OHL, and top lamp iron reduced to smokebox door. Requisitioned and shipped out of Swansea as 603 as one of twelve, heavy seas were soon encountered and the Captain ordered four to be jettisoned. It is to be assumed that (fortunately) they were stowed crosswise on rails, so could be slipped over the side rather like a burial at sea. The ship limped into Glasgow where the eight engines were unloaded and sent to St Rollox for storm damage to be repaired and re-converted to coal burning if necessary, using parts from NBL next door. By the time repairs were complete the need for locos in Persia had eased so they were put back to work on the LMS, for a few years in Scotland. Norman Preedy.

'48025'

BECAME 48775
Built as 8025 at Crewe Works 3/37
Sheds: Royston 4/37
Withdrawn from traffic 9/41, to WD 11/41 as 583, shipped to Persia, becomes 41.184. Thence to Egypt/Palestine, becomes 70583; second 1952 WD number 512. One of five sent to UK in 1952 for repair at Derby, then operation from Longmoor/Cairnryan. One of three sold to BR 7/57. Reconditioned at Eastleigh where they were initially renumbered as WDs 90733-90735! Derby was not aware of the 1952 WD renumbering and could not reconcile them with former LMS engines (so confusion is not confined to our own times!) and added the numbers at the end of the 8F series, 48773-48775. '48025' (one number it never actually carried!) became 48775.
The subsequent history is as 48775:

Repairs

7/57'**conv'**		Eastleigh
30/9/59-25/11/59**HI**	43,078	Horwich

Boiler
No.14428

Tenders
No.9390 from new
No.10322

Sheds

Polmadie	7/9/57
Kingmoor	9/11/63
Newton Heath	13/6/64
Agecroft	18/6/66
Patricroft	8/10/66
Lostock Hall	13/7/68

Stored serviceable
11/7/66-17/7/67

Withdrawn w/e 29/12/62 by the Scottish Region
Returned to traffic w/e 9/11/63
Finally withdrawn w/e 3/8/68

8025 with welded tender, a few days old at Crewe South MPD, 3 April 1937.

At Speke Junction, 16 June 1939. For its brief LMS career 8025 was a Royston engine. Plucked from Yorkshire to become WD 583 it was another of the five (see 8021) which came back to Britain from Egypt, arriving at Derby works in August 1952, for overhaul and return. It came back with its new WD 1952 number, 512 and entered Derby Works as that. The engines of course never went back and were eventually put to work on the WD's own lines in Britain. 512 was involved in a very serious fatal accident on the Longmoor Military Railway in October 1956 and was sold to BR as one of the 'final three' in 1957 to become 48775; in fact, the very last one. It seems still to have still been in damaged state from the accident when sold to BR. R.J. Buckley, Initial Photographics.

As 70583, very much derelict at Suez, 15 October 1947. At least the desert climate restricted further corrosion! Daubed on the cabside is TO CARDIFF, while the reversing reach rod is merely stored on the running plate, upside down. The tenders of all five 1952 repatriations stayed behind and duly disappeared.

48026

Built as 8026 at Crewe Works 20th April 1937
Renumbered 48026 w/e 16/4/49

Repairs

1/11/39-22/11/39**LS**	63,203	
21/6/41-30/7/41**LS**	90,220	
27/7/42-25/8/42**HG**	146,077	
27/9/44-14/10/44**LS**	48,710	
27/1/47-1/3/47**HG**	103,746	Crewe
14/3/49-13/4/49**HI**	50,989	Crewe
1/5/51-24/5/51**HI**	47,975	Horwich
25/2/53-25/4/53**HG**	41,574	Horwich
2/8/55-2/9/55**HI**	52,630	Derby
3/11/58-28/11/58**HG**	68,346	Derby
17/4/62-12/5/62**HI**		Crewe
5/5/65-4/6/65**HI**		Darlington

Boilers

No.9599	25/8/42	from	8054
No.11280	1/3/47	from	8203
No.11065	25/4/53		
No.11543	28/11/58		

Tender

LMS 9391	20/4/37

Sheds

Canklow	24/4/37
Sheffield	1/10/38
Heaton Mersey	21/1/39
Canklow	3/7/43
Barrow Hill	29/12/62
Edge Hill	18/4/64
Speke Jct	5/9/64
Agecroft	3/10/64
Newton Heath	18/6/66
Bolton	24/2/68

Stored serviceable
14/11/66-26/11/66
31/1/66-11/9/67

Withdrawn w/e 22/6/68

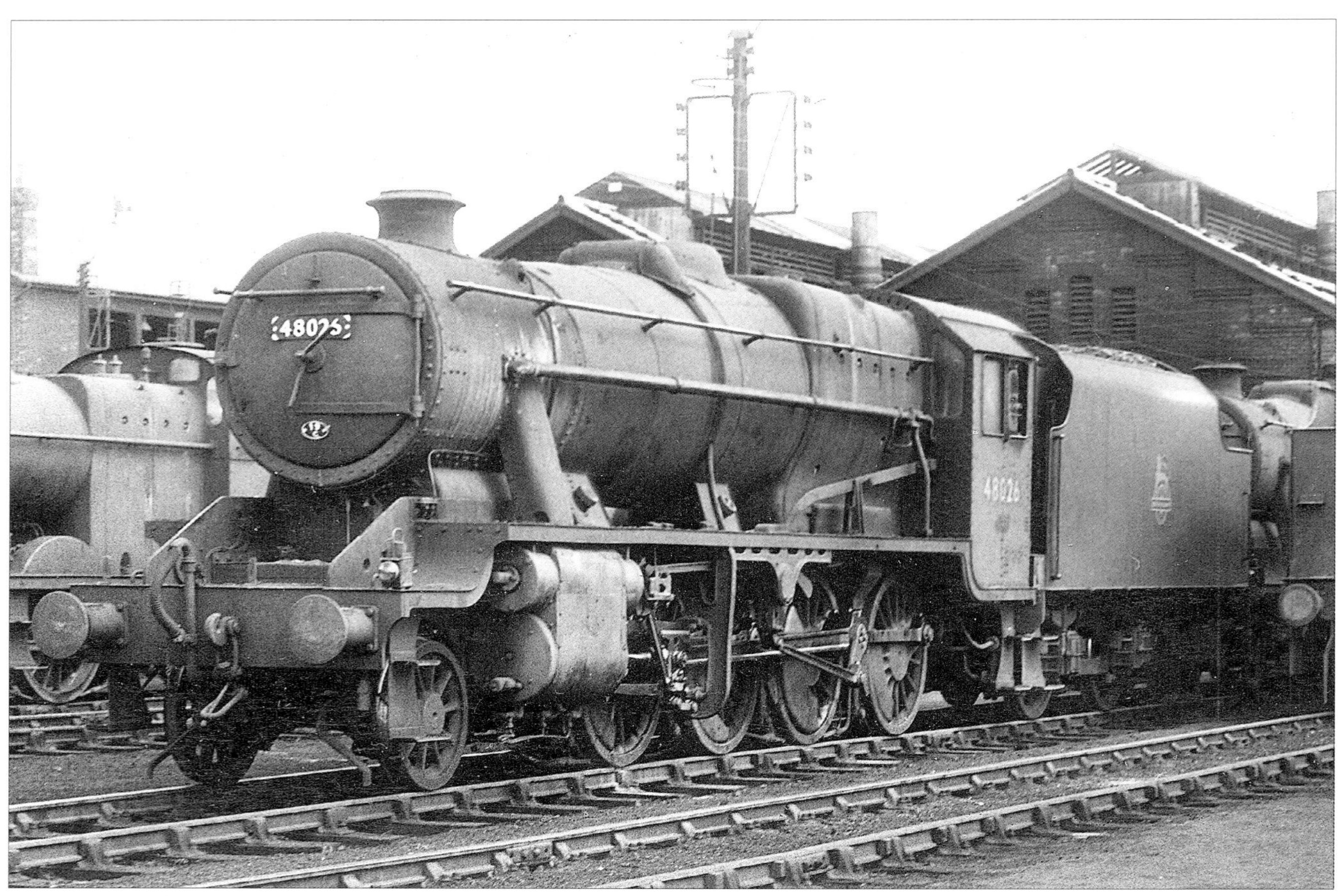

48026 at Westhouses MPD, 13 May 1956. It had been on the Midland since built but spent the last three or four years at various sheds in the North West.

48026, now with much larger 10in cabside numerals acquired at the NER's main works Darlington, with a freight at Armathwaite, 27 July 1965. Repairs to LM engines really appear to have got under way in 1964, as the 'home works', Horwich, Derby in particular, experienced a rundown in steam repairs. There was of course an army of LM engines, of every type on the NE, inherited from the old L&Y/Midland/LNW sheds in Yorkshire in particular. There was a solitary 3F tank under repair at Darlington at the beginning of 1964; this was the only LM type, though clearly Darlington had been repairing BR Standards off the LMR. By the autumn of 1964 there were no less than five 8Fs in for repair, along with Class 5s and Ivatt 2-6-0s. D. Forsyth, ColourRail

48027

Built as 8027 at The Vulcan Foundry Ltd 17th July 1936
Renumbered 48027 w/e 2/7/49

Improvements and modifications
19/2/44 Access to top feed clack on taper boiler
23/3/46 Providing steel in lieu of copper tube*, casing and filter for air relief valve
31/12/60 AWS
**presumably main steam pipe*

Repairs

22/3/38-14/4/38**LS**	52,469	
3/8/39-27/9/39**LS**	96,612	
13/4/40-4/6/40**HO**	115,365	
4/3/41-11/3/41**LO**	16,432	
10/5/41-28/5/41**LO**	19,064	
18/9/41-18/10/41**LO**	26,479	
14/1/42-17/2/42**HG**	33,786	
3/3/42-21/3/42**LO**	765	
4/11/44-20/1/44**HS**	45,317	
4/4/45-2/5/45**LO**	26,177	
8/2/46-14/3/46**LS**	42,267	
13/10/47-3/11/47**HG**	33,616	Crewe
30/5/49-1/7/49**LI**	38,287	Crewe
3/5/49-1/7/49**LI**	38,287	Crewe
5/1/52-12/2/52**HG**	59,504	Crewe
23/3/55-18/4/55**HI**	74,172	Derby
12/2/57-15/3/57**HG**	45,527	Derby
21/3/60-2/5/60**LI**	75,557	Derby
22/11/60-12/12/60**NC[EO]**	18,425	Derby
20/6/62-16/7/62**GO**		Horwich

Boilers

No.9830	4/6/40	from	8015
No.9604	17/2/42	from	8092
No.11195	3/11/47	from	8275
No.11147	12/2/52		
No.10431	15/3/57		

Tender

LMS 9392	17/7/36

Sheds

Toton	18/7/36
Kirkby	16/3/40
Nottingham	29/5/48
Saltley	4/9/48
Leicester	14/1/50
Wellingborough	26/3/60
Woodford Halse	20/7/63

Withdrawn w/e 20/3/65

Willesden used anything that was to hand for the Euston empty stock working, often locos that seemed less than perfectly suited such as elderly Midland or LNW 0-6-0s. Camden bank demanded power after all, and a stall or failure would cause endless trouble. Yet everything seemed to work smoothly enough and at the end BR Class 2 2-6-0s were on the jobs. An 8F would seem a more realistic prospect, given the gradient up past Camden MPD and (rarely) they could be found at various times, such as 48027 on 19 May 1961 forging past the said Camden MPD on empty stock, with every assistance still from the train engine in the rear. It made sense in fact to stay with the train if the engine doing the banking was en-route to Camden (or Willesden for that matter). RailOnline

48027 trundles through Gloucester Central, 27 August 1964. Peter Skelton.

48029

Built as 8029 at the Vulcan Foundry Ltd 7th August 1936
Renumbered 48029 w/e 31/7/48

Improvements and modifications
10/8/46 Providing steel in lieu of copper tube*, casing and filter for air relief valve
1/12/51 Discharge of continuous blowdown into ashpan
**presumably main steam pipe*

Repairs

6/5/38-15/6/38**LS**	51,504	
21/6/39-7/7/39**LO**	86,555	
19/1/40-24/1/40**LO**	106,997	
14/6/40-5/7/40**HS**	123,355	
28/7/41-16/8/41**LS**	35,989	
11/11/41-3/12/41**LO**	48,905	
6/4/42-2/5/42**LO**	60,137	
13/10/42-4/11/42**HG**	72,497	
16/8/43-11/9/43**LO**	25,189	
10/10/44-28/10/44**HS**	46,285	
17/8/45-29/9/45**LO**	16,308	
5/7/46-5/8/46**HS**	34,562	
16/6/48-31/7/48**LS**	41,735	Crewe
20/1/50-22/2/50**HG**	33,886	Crewe
8/10/51-7/11/51**LI**	36,759	Crewe
6/9/53-6/10/53**HI**	39,437	Derby
30/11/55-23/12/55**HG**	49,616	Derby
8/2/58-3/3/58**LI**	47,462	Derby
25/3/61-30/6/61**HG**	67,447	Horwich
31/10/63-5/12/63**LI**		Horwich

Boilers

No.9597	5/7/40	from	8052
No.9837	4/11/42	from	8084
No.9830	5/8/46	from	8180
No.11663	22/2/50	from	8438
No.11529	23/12/55		
No.11797	30/6/61		

Tender

LMS 9394	7/8/36

Sheds

Toton	8/8/36
Kirkby	12/6/43
Canklow	30/1/60
Barrow Hill	26/3/60
Lancaster	7/9/63
Speke Jct	31/10/64
Edge Hill	27/3/65
Speke jct	19/6/65

Withdrawn w/e 25/2/67

8029 on coal work – what else – near Chinley on the Midland Division of the LMS, June 1946.

48029 with the 2.50pm Heysham-Stourton freight passing through Wennington on 12 September 1964. The 10J plate is that of Lancaster Green Ayre. Noel A. Machell.

48033

Built as 8033 at the Vulcan Foundry Ltd 19th August 1936
Renumbered 48033 w/e/ 15/5/48

Improvements and modifications
28/1/61 AWS

Repairs

28/9/38-31/10/38**LS**	57,293	
29/9/39-11/10/39**LO**	87,977	
17/7/40-23/7/40**LO**	112,172	
21/10/40-11/17/40**HG**	118,185	
29/7/41-12/9/41**HO**	13,276	
4/9/42-23/9/42**LS**	24,864	
27/3/43-2/4/43**LO**	34,781	
10/3/44-3/4/44**HS**	50,807	
9/3/45-13/4/45**LO**	12,996	
15/5/46-3/6/46**HG**	47,467	
26/9/46-11/10/46**LO**	10,846	Crewe
15/4/48-14/5/48**LS**	47,979	Crewe
7/3/50-29/3/50**HG**	61,642	Crewe
19/2/51-22/3/51**LC**	26,023	Crewe
9/6/52-10/7/52**HI**	60,858	Derby
24/1/55-25/2/55**HG**	60,456	Horwich
5/2/57-21/2/57**HI**	39,448	Derby
11/4/59-4/5/59**HI**	45,788	Derby
19/10/60-23/11/60**LC[EO]**	41,684	Derby
10/1/61-18/1/61**LC[EO]**	45,054	Horwich

Noted at Works: Derby 11/61; Crewe 10/65

Boilers

No.9589	11/11/40	from	8044
No.9591	12/9/41	from	8046
No.9838	3/6/46	from	8076
No.10882	29/3/50	from	48286
No.12016	25/2/55		

Tender

LMS 9398	19/8/36

Sheds

Toton	22/8/36
Kirkby	16/3/40
Toton	30/9/44
Kirkby	30/9/50
Toton	7/10/50
Burton	3/2/51
Toton	12/5/51
Staveley	13/6/53
Toton	7/12/57
Cricklewood	14/6/58
Toton	23/5/59
Kettering	23/1/60
Birkenhead	21/3/63
Sutton Oak	24/4/65
Springs Branch	17/6/67
Patricroft	30/12/67

Stored serviceable
5/9/66-20/5/67

Withdrawn w/e 29/6/68

48033 at Luton, November 1958. F. Hornby, ColourRail

Tired old 48033 from Birkenhead at Saltley on 12 July 1964, the driver giving it a kick to get it going! The new lower front lamp iron looks like it's only just been welded on. AWS fitted.

48035

Built as 8035 at the Vulcan Foundry Ltd 25th August 1936
Renumbered 48035 w/e 12/6/48

Improvements and modifications
11/7/42 Brake hanger brackets modified to permit working over 6 chain curve
16/6/46 Provision of steel in lieu of copper tube
13/7/46 New design valves casing and filters for air relief valves
3/9/51 New design valve casing and filter for air relief valve
15/11/52 Removal of Sand Guns
27/12/52 Discharge of continuous blowdown into ashpan
13/8/55 Provision and fitting of new type piston head fastenings
5/10/60 AWS

Repairs

7/5/38-17/6/38**LS**	53,346	
28/4/39-6/5/39**LO**	81,361	
8/8/39-15/8/39**LO**	91,013	
13/11/39-16/12/39**HS**	99,206	
18/8/41-3/9/41**LS**	57,360	
24/4/42-23/6/42**LS**	80,116	
8/5/44-3/6/44**HG**	126,218	
29/5/46-15/6/46**HS**	54,774	
7/5/48-8/6/48**LS**	44,206	Crewe
29/3/50-19/4/50**HG**	49,458	Crewe
14/8/51-3/9/51**HO**	17,496	Derby
24/10/52-15/11/52**HI**	63,456	Crewe
30/5/55-29/7/55**HG**	58,631	Derby
16/7/57-25/7/57**LC[EO]**	44,268	Rugby
8/2/58-1/3/58**LI**	55,907	Crewe
21/9/60-29/9/60**NC[EO]**	66,413	Crewe
16/1/61-27/1/61**HG**	73,224	Crewe

Clearly one or other date in error if a Heavy General can take under a fortnight...
Noted at Works: Crewe 8/63

Boilers

No.10088	13/12/39 new	
No.10504	3/6/44 from	8121
No.13223	19/4/50 from	8759
No.12148	29/7/55	
No.12137	27/1/61	

Tenders

LMS 9400	25/8/36
No.9866	13/4/59

Sheds

Wellingborough	29/8/36
Royston	19/6/43
Mansfield	11/10/47
Derby	7/8/48
Wellingborough	8/7/50
Kettering	14/4/51
Wellingborough	21/4/56
Saltley	2/6/56
Rugby	4/1/58
Crewe South	30/1/65
Woodford Halse	24/4/65
Bescot	19/6/65
Oxley	4/12/65
Tyseley	26/2/66
Oxley	5/11/66

Withdrawn w/e 11/3/67

48035 outside Hasland's roofless roundhouse, in company with Garratts, on 3 September 1955. It was not long out of a Heavy General at Derby, hence its marked state of cleanliness. H.C. Casserley, courtesy R.M. Casserley.

48035 now with cabside star, in an excellent state again, not long after its succeeding Heavy General, this time at Crewe. The location is Stockport Edgeley, from the familiar vantage point of the classic 'cinder path' leading down to the shed – off to the right – on 6 February 1961. D. Forsyth, ColourRail

Heavy Generals are a distant memory on 19 February 1966 with 48035 at Over Junction to the north west of Gloucester. The curious darker lower part of the tender is condensation, marking the level of very cold water in the tender. It is February after all. Top lamp iron now lowered, AWS fitted. Norman Preedy.

48036

Built as 8036 at the Vulcan Foundry Ltd 25th August 1936
Renumbered 48036 w/e 4/2/50

Improvements and modifications
30/11/46 Providing steel in lieu of copper tube*, casing and filter for air relief valve
11/9/54 Removal of sand guns
13/8/63 AWS
**presumably main steam pipe*

Repairs

7/4/38-24/5/38**LS**	52,078	
4/12/38-19/12/38**LO**	60,553	
12/12/39-20/1/40**HS**	108,888	
8/4/41-28/4/41**LS**	43,533	
19/2/42-14/3/42**LS**	74,059	
10/9/42-9/10/42**LO**	92,073	
22/3/43-22/4/43**LS**	108,763	
17/3/44-7/4/44**LO**	131,040	
9/11/44-2/12/44**HG**	144,329	
26/2/45-12/3/45**LO**	4,700	
8/3/46-23/3/46**LO**	27,801	
18/10/46-23/11/46**LS**	42,389	Crewe
29/12/47-11/2/48**HO**	19,643	Crewe
21/12/49-4/2/50**HG**	52,669	Horwich
19/4/52-17/5/52**HI**	50,141	Crewe
8/7/54-17/8/54**HG**	56,372	Crewe
17/11/56-8/12/56**LI**	57,352	Crewe
1/9/58-24/9/58**LC[EO]**	50,044	Rugby
3/3/59-1/4/59**HG**	61,602	Crewe
27/6/60-2/8/60**NC[EO]**	41,609	Crewe
2/10/61-27/10/61**LI**	75,0442	

Boilers

No.9580	20/1/40	from	8035
No.10445	2/12/44	from	8110
No.11865	4/2/50	from	8547
No.10090	17/8/54		
No.11269	1/4/59		

Tender

LMS 9401	25/8/36

Sheds

Wellingborough	no date
Heaton Mersey	19/6/43
Cricklewood	24/7/43
Normanton	4/9/43
Kirkby	11/10/47
Bury[o/l]	20/3/48
Bury	5/6/48
Rugby[o/l]	17/12/49
Rugby	7/1/50
Normanton	17/6/50
Newton Heath[o/l]	11/11/50
Willesden[o/l]	9/12/50
Willesden	3/2/51
Crewe South	30/1/65
Willesden	27/2/65
Crewe South	22/5/65
Northwich	25/3/67

Withdrawn w/e 9/3/68

48036 in exalted company at Willesden MPD, 17 April 1962; star on cab, AWS. Peter Groom.

48036 in its last months, at Northwich MPD, its final home, in 1967. Bigger numerals now but the star is a distant memory, buried under grime. M.S. Stokes.

48037

Built as 8037 at the Vulcan foundry Ltd 1st September 1936
Renumbered 48037 w/e 1/5/48

Improvements and modifications
30/11/46 Manually operated blowdown valves
8/9/51 New type piston head fastening
8/9/51 Discharge of continuous blowdown into ashpan

Repairs

29/12/37-15/1/38**LO**	30,809	
30/5/38-20/6/38**LS**	35,896	
9/11/38-10/12/38**LO**	44,264	
15/2/39-3/3/39**LO**	48,594	
25/5/39-27/6/39**LO**	53,459	
30/10/39-17/11/39**LO**	60,512	
4/5/40-20/5/40**LO**	69,405	
29/7/40-21/8/40**HS**	73,395	
3/7/41-12/7/41**LO**	18,742	
21/8/41-26/9/41**HO**	20,341	
8/6/42-10/7/42**LS**	16,508	
2/11/43-2/12/43**HS**	46,721	
12/12/44-22/12/44**LO**	19,215	
3/12/45-5/1/46**LS**	44,586	
31/10/46-15/11/46**LO**	69,142	Crewe
29/3/48-30/4/48**HG**	29,954	Crewe
2/6/49-16/6/49**LI**	36,470	Crewe
10/8/51-8/9/51**HI**	61,043	Crewe
3/6/53-3/8/53**HG**	45,989	Derby
9/3/55-10/3/55**LC**	45,156	Shed
12/11/55-8/12/55**LI**	61,472	Derby
12/12/57-7/1/58**HI**	41,055	Derby
No date-7/10/60**HG**	54,014	Horwich

Boilers

No.9514	21/8/40	from	8029
No.9598	26/9/41	from	8048
No.11543	30/4/48	from	8428
No.9628	3/8/53		
N0.11479	7/10/60		

Tender
LMS 9402 1/9/36

Sheds

Kirkby	19/9/36
Toton	30/9/34
Westhouses	29/3/52
Toton	7/11/53
Wellingborough	4/2/56
Toton	10/3/56
Westhouses	14/4/56
Staveley	16/6/56
Westhouses	22/9/56
Staveley	15/12/56
Grimesthorpe	13/6/59
Staveley	11/7/59
Patricroft	8/12/62
Annesley	25/5/63
Toton	19/6/65

Stored serviceable 14/6/65-25/12/65

Withdrawn w/e 25/12/65

48037 an up train south of Rugby about 1948; GCR girder bridge in the background; view is north-west towards Rugby Midland. The high brick bridge carries the A427 Clifton Road from Rugby to Market Harborough.

A curiosity. We are looking at the mortal remains of 48037, some months after withdrawal, at Crewe on 3 April 1966. It was not the only 8F similarly cannibalised, despite the late date. It is standing on the steam cleaning pits, between the Iron Foundry and Tender Shop to the north and the former 7 and 8 Erecting Shops to the south. All sorts of things happened here including engines being steam cleaned prior to going into Ten Shop. The newly repaired/painted tenders are waiting for their respective engines to emerge, while the tender on the left, with its engine number (it looks like 70023) stamped on, is waiting to go into the Tender Shop. Regarding the 8F, if it had been in the Erecting Shop where the cylinders were removed, it seems strange it still has the tender attached. Engines in theory never went into the Erecting Shop complete with tenders. The crank pins are shiny so it has not been outside for long and the foot framing has been cut off, suggesting that whoever took the cylinders off, knew the engine was for scrap. Latterly, after the Tender Shop went over to electric loco and diesel bogie repairs – the Manchester-Wath locos were done in there – tenders were repaired in the 'Melts'. It is also strange to find a Fowler tender still hanging about!

48039

Built as 8039 at the Vulcan Foundry Ltd 2nd September 1936
Renumbered 48039

Sold to H M Government – withdrawn from ex-LMS stock w/e 23/12/44
Purchased (WD 588) from MoS – returned to LMS stock w/e 15/10/49

Improvements and modifications
23/3/52 Discharge of continuous blowdown to ashpan
26/1/57 Removal of sand guns
20/5/61 Fitting AWS

Repairs

18/1/38-27/1/38**LO**	37,932	
13/6/38-29/6/38**LS**	47,150	
31/1/39-11/2/39**LO**	62,631	
29/2/40-15/3/40**LO**	84,150	
3/6/40-13/6/40**LS**	90,199	
1/8/41-20/8/41**HG**	120,840	
11/9/41 Repaired and prepared for overseas by GWR		
11/10/49-27/10/49**HG**		Crewe
[Overseas mileage unknown]		
24/11/51-30/1/52**HI**	54,262	Rugby
14/4/54-12/5/54**HG**	50,261	Crewe
4/1/57-24/1/57**LI**	61,282	Crewe
24/3/59-5/5/59**HG**	45,231	Crewe
9/6/60-3/9/60**HC**	27,101	Crewe
15/4/61-26/4/61**NC[EO]**	44,438	Horwich

Boilers

No.9631	30/8/41	from	8086
No.11532	27/10/49	from	8415
No.9615	12/5/54		
No.11484	5/5/59		

Tenders

LMS 9404	2/9/36
No.10214	11/10/49

Sheds

Westhouses	19/9/36
Into shops	11/9/41
To Dockside	25/11/41
Crewe South	15/10/49
Rugby	7/1/50
Speke Jct	25/10/52
Widnes	30/1/60
Northwich	28/5/60
Buxton	8/8/64
Lostock Hall	30/1/65

Withdrawn w/e 24/7/65

One that came back; 48039 at Nottingham MPD on 2 June 1957. After work in Persia as 41.187 and then shipping to Egypt (its 1944 number was 70588) it returned to the UK in 1948. Leaving the desert behind, it eventually was to enjoy nearly a decade in the lush pastures of Speke. R.H.G. Simpson.

48039 passing through Farington near Preston under the L&Y on a southbound goods; it carries a Speke Junction 8C plate, so the period is 1952-1960. Norman Preedy.

48045

Built as 8045 at the Vulcan Foundry Ltd 24th September 1936
Renumbered 48045 w/e 23/7/49

Sold to H M Government – withdrawn from ex-LMS stock w/e 23/12/44
Purchased (WD 573) from Ministry of Supply – returned to ex-LMS stock w/e 23/7/49

Improvements and modifications
3/11/51 Discharge of continuous blowdown into ashpan
11/7/53 Removal of sand guns
11/9/60 AWS
4/11/61 Modifications to tube cleaner pipe and fittings
30/12/61 Modifications to tube pipe and fittings

Repairs

13/4/38-28/4/38**LO**	47,882	
21/6/38-15/7/38**LS**	52,818	
20/12/38-24/12/38**LO**	66,854	
22/3/39-5/4/39**LO**	75,830	
2/11/39-7/11/39**LO**	95,926	
20/12/39-8/1/40**LS**	98,798	
26/3/41-15/4/41**HG**	138,919	
13/9/41-15/10/41**HS**	15,927	
18/7/49-5/8/49**HG**		Crewe
[Overseas mileage unknown – Ex Middle East]		
1/5/51-12/5/51**LC**	50,826	Shed
8/9/51-9/10/51**LI**	55,443	Crewe
22/5/53-20/6/53**HG**	43,836	Crewe
31/3/55-20/4/55HI	51,632	Crewe
27/2/57-28/3/57**LI**	52,394	Horwich
10/10/58-23/10/58**NC[EO]**	39,641	Crewe
31/12/58-7/2/59**HG**	43,076	Crewe
8/8/60-25/8/60**NC[EO]**	46,056	Crewe
26/8/61-12/10/61**HI**	68,980	Horwich

Noted at Works: Darlington 4/64; Crewe 6/65

Boilers

No.9634	15/4/41	from	8089
No.11720	5/8/49	from	8662
No.11484	20/6/53		
No.11561	7/2/59		

Tenders

LMS 9410	24/9/36
No.10312	18/7/49
No.3923	23/10/58 (Fowler 3,500)

Sheds

Canklow	26/9/36
Wellingborough	3/10/36
Into shops	14/9/41
To Dockside	3/11/41
Crewe South	23/7/49
Northwich	31/12/49
Toton	11/2/61
Northwich	29/4/61
Widnes	10/6/61
Mold Jct	5/5/62
Speke Jct	7/7/62
Widnes	16/3/63
Warrington	11/1/64
Nottingham	21/3/64
Westhouses	24/4/65
Kirkby	9/10/65
Edge Hill	5/11/66

Stored serviceable
11/10/65-27/10/65

Withdrawn w/e 4/5/68

8045 as oil-fired WD 70573 (it had been WD 573) in Egypt – the date is recorded as 13 October 1947.

Returned in 1948, 70573 emerged from Crewe the following year as 48045 and was allocated to Crewe South (a couple of weeks before the official completion of its Heavy General – a warning there for everyone as to the exactitude of dates in the Record) but before long it was on its way to Northwich where it spent more than a decade. It was back at Crewe for a Light Intermediate in 1951 during which it seems to have had a repaint – at least here it is outside the Paint Shop on 21 October 1951. This would be a somewhat unusual circumstance for an unlined unvarnished loco, even more so as it would have been painted following its refurbishment after repatriation. Amusingly, the bracket for the electric headlamp is still in place on the smokebox top! This had disappeared by 1955 and probably rather earlier than that.

48045 was one of the 8Fs to suffer the indignity of having a 'Fowler' tender attached. Under the wires but yet to get any warning flashes, it is at Crewe in 1960. Large 10in cab numbers added at Darlington in 1964. RailOnline

48046

Built as 8046 at the Vulcan Foundry Ltd 23rd September 1936
Renumbered 48046 w/e 27/8/49

Sold to H M Government- withdrawn from LMS stock w/e 23/12/44
Purchased (WD 599) from Ministry of Supply – returned to ex-LMS stock w/e 27/8/49

Improvements and modifications
21/3/53 Removal of sand guns
11/9/60 AWS

Repairs

21/5/38-15/6/38**LS**	51,998	
6/11/39-16/11/39**LO**	97,758	
20/11/39-5/12/39**LS**	98,010	
12/10/40-19/10/40**TRO**		
4/7/41-25/7/41**HG**	150,209	
18/10/41-20/11/41**LO**	8,848	
22/8/49-9/9/49**HG**		Crewe
[Overseas mileage unknown]		
1/6/51-3/7/51**HI**	51,870	Crewe
8/1/52-6/2/52**LC**	12,390	Crewe
24/2/53-21/3/53**HI**	41,199	Crewe
18/9/54-12/10/54**HG**	44,160	Crewe
14/5/56-15/6/56**HI**	49,070	Horwich
6/6/58-7/6/58**HI**	53,882	Horwich
28/7/58-13/8/58**NC[EO]**	1,624	Rugby
19/11/58-26/11/58**LC**	7,555	Crewe
27/5/59-7/7/59**LC[EO]**	21,409	Crewe
11/8/60-31/8/60**NC[EO]**	47,867	Horwich
10/4/61-20/4/61**NC[EO]**	63,610	Crewe
2/10/61-26/10/61**HG**	74,126	Crewe

Noted at Works: Crewe 10/64

Boilers

No.9639	25/7/41	from	8094
No.11525	9/9/49	from	8410
No.12018	12/10/54		
No.11526	26/10/61		

Tenders

LMS 9411	23/9/36
LMS 9399	20/1/41
No.10301	22/8/49
No.4507	13/8/58 (Fowler 3,500)
No.4504	26/11/58 (Fowler 3,500)
No.4246	26/10/61 (Fowler 3,500)
No.4560	3/3/62 (Fowler 3,500)

Sheds

Canklow	26/9/36
Wellingborough	3/10/36
Into shops	18/10/41
To Dockside	28/12/41
Crewe South	27/8/49
Northwich	31/12/49
Edge Hill[o/l]	28/7/51
Northwich	29/9/51
Birkenhead	20/6/59
Llandudno Jct	7/11/59
Mold Jct	8/7/61
Speke Jct	7/7/62
Nottingham	21/3/64
Westhouses	24/4/65
Newton Heath	26/3/66
Bolton	27/1/68

Stored serviceable 11/10/65-1/2/66

Withdrawn w/e 13/1/68

Crewe South MPD. For 48046 to have an anonymous tender ('awaiting transfers') the period is about 1949, the year of its first Heavy General back on British soil.

48046 at Llandudno Junction MPD in January 1960; passed for fast running now (star on cab) it has acquired one of the Jubilee tenders thus rendering it (a point laboured earlier) 'aesthetically challenged'. ColourRail

As locos like the Jubilees fell increasingly by the wayside, a number of the 8Fs regained 4,000 gallon tenders, as demonstrated by 48046 at Kingmoor (still in traffic, though with the appearance of a blackened hulk) on 7 October 1967. Norman Preedy.

48050

Built as 8050 at the Vulcan Foundry Ltd 6th October 1936
Renumbered 48050 w/e 15/5/48

Improvements and modifications
30/12/61 AWS

Repairs

10/10/38-2/11/38**LS**	65,494	
10/7/39-17/7/39**LO**	85,599	
28/11/39-28/12/39**HS**	105,158	
13/3/41-9/4/41**LS**	43,208	
28/9/42-19/10/42**HG**	87,941	
25/5/44-3/7/44**LS**	47,921	
15/3/46-23/4/46**LS**	95,721	
30/9/46-11/10/46**LO**	99,777	Crewe
5/4/48-11/5/48**HG**	44,060	Crewe
13/1/50-26/1/50**LC**	46,124	Shed
25/5/50-14/6/50**HI**	55,930	Crewe
7/11/51-28/11/51**LC[EO]**	40,887	Shed
27/8/52-6/10/52**HG**	58,622	Derby
10/12/54-13/1/55**LI**	64,827	Derby
27/5/57-25/6/57**HG**	57,273	Derby
25/1/59-3/3/59**HI**	41,704	Derby
30/9/59-3/11/59**NC[Rect]**	14,585	Derby

Noted at Works: Crewe 8/64

Boilers

No.10090	28/12/39	new	
No.9628	9/10/42	from	8083
No.11511	11/5/48	from	8636
No.11143	6/10/52		
No.11263	25/6/57		

Tender

LMS 9415	6/10/36

Sheds

Wellingborough	10/10/36
Kettering	16/7/55
Wellingborough	18/1/64
Warrington Dallam	18/4/64
Aintree	24/4/65

Stored serviceable
20/12/65-31/1/66

Withdrawn w/e19/3/66

A dramatic image of Wellingborough's 8050, with that attractive block front number and still with hints of burnishing; the location might well be Cricklewood. 'MR Co' cast in that impressive water column.

48050 at its home shed Kettering; coal stage at left, shed exit to the north at right; no date. The loco was on the Wellingborough allocation when the 'manual blowdown scheme' (see *Parts and Service*) was introduced involving a total of fifty 8Fs, there and at Toton. Hence the prominent 'X' though with the second emblem up we are well into the 1950s now and no one by now even knew what the letter stood for, probably.

48050 on 29 July 1963; still a Kettering engine, at March on the Eastern Region. AWS by now, with that errant warning flash *below* the hand rail. These things matter to an engine picker... 48050 came to a sticky end in fact; sent to Aintree in April 1965 on 14 July 1966 it was photographed by Colin Stacey (Initial Photographics) at Springs Branch Wigan having suffered severe collision/derailment damage. The cab was distorted and the motion gone, dumped in the tender with the pony truck. Some of its fellow locos in Egypt looked rather better after terrorist bomb attacks. Norman Preedy.

48053

Built as 8053 at the Vulcan Foundry Ltd 14th October 1936
Renumbered 48053 w/e 15/5/48

Improvements and modifications
17/5/52 Removal of sand guns

Repairs

25/7/38-10/8/38**LS**	44,704	
13/12/38-12/1/39**HO**	53,899	
24/5/40-5/6/40**LS**	36,409	
10/6/41-29/6/41**LO**	65,378	
25/11/41-18/12/41**LS**	76,373	
5/2/43-26/2/43**HS**	108,004	
29/3/43-23/4/43**LO**	2,143	
1/6/44-28/6/44**HG**	33,753	
28/1/46-2/3/46**LS**	39,593	
27/2/47-7/3/47**LO**	65,417	Shed
20/4/48-14/5/48**HS**	23,265	Crewe
19/12/49-11/1/50**HI**	34,750	Crewe
3/4/52-8/5/52**LI**	55,290	Horwich
11/6/54-2/7/54**HG**	51,555	Crewe
15/1/57-31/1/57**HI**	61,461	Derby
19/9/58-16/10/58**LC[EO]**	44,333	Rugby
3/7/59-3/9/59**HG**	60,898	Derby
27/9/61-31/10/61**HI**	58,189	Derby

Noted at Works: Crewe 4/64

Boilers

No.10087	12/1/39	new	
No.10444	28/6/44	from	8109
No.11489	14/5/48	from	8602
No.11562	2/7/54		
No.11796	3/9/59		

Tender

LMS 9418	14/10/36

Sheds

Saltley	17/10/36
Staveley	12/12/36
Wellingborough	21/7/45
Staveley	28/7/45
Toton	30/9/50
Burton	3/2/51
Wellingborough	12/5/51
Royston	2/6/51
Wellingborough	16/10/54
Nottingham	5/3/55
Coalville	13/12/58
Leicester	24/4/65
Annesley	22/5/65
Kirkby	17/7/65
Rose Grove	31/7/65

Stored serviceable
14/6/65-5/7/65

Withdrawn w/e 18/3/67

48053 at Werrington, 24 July 1958; there are still plenty of wooden wagons in the train. D. Ovenden, ColourRail

48054

Built as 8054 at the Vulcan Foundry Ltd on 14th October 1936
Renumbered 48054 w/e 2/7/49

Modifications and improvements
12/7/52 Removal of sand guns and equipment
25/2/61 Automatic Train Control

Repairs

22/8/38-27/9/38**LS**	46,924	
1/1/40-16/1/40**LO**	78,739	
16/9/40-28/9/40**LS**	96,528	
24/5/42-23/6/42**HG**	141,451	
14/12/43-3/1/44**HS**	42,076	
30/8/45-27/9/45**LS**	46,361	
13/1/47-8/2/47**HG**	77,931	Crewe
9/6/49-1/7/49**HI**	54,678	Horwich
No boiler change, Crewe confirmed with Horwich		
7/7/49**NC[Rect]**	111	Horwich
21/5/52-4/7/52**HG**	61,954	Crewe
17/3/54-8/4/54**LI**	38,409	Crewe
13/5/57-1/6/57**HG**	69,147	Crewe
10/12/60-14/1/61**HI**	78,292	Crewe
7/2/61-17/2/61**NC[EO]**	1,310	Crewe

Noted at Works: Crewe 6/63

Boilers

No.9640	23/6/42	from	8095
No.11279	8/2/47	from	8202
No.11190	4/7/52		
No.11149	1/6/57		

Tenders

LMS 9419	14/10/36
No.9395	17/1/40
No.9419	11/5/40
No.9093	4/7/52
No.10745	24/11/53
No.10143	14/6/62
No.10754	6/5/63
No.10143	25/6/66

Sheds

Saltley	17/10/36
Staveley	12/12/36
Northampton	19/6/48
Speke Jct	30/9/50
Mold Jct	7/11/59
Nuneaton	8/6/60
Trafford Park	31/7/65

Withdrawn w/e 9/9/67

Nuneaton's 48054 on Newbold troughs, 1963. RailOnline

A lively if inevitably filthy 48054 at Trafford Park MPD its final home, 8 April 1967; AWS, painted smokebox door hinges, daubed 9E shed code.

48055

Built as 8055 at the Vulcan Foundry Ltd 20th October 1936
Renumbered 48055 w/e 13/11/48

Improvements and modifications
11/7/53 Removal of sand guns
11/9/60 AWS

Repairs

27/8/38**TRO**		
28/11/38-21/12/38**LS**	49,444	
23/2/40-23/3/40**LO**	80,159	
5/8/40-5/9/40**LS**	88,199	
1/7/42-3/8/42**HG**	128,589	
9/11/43-10/12/43**HS**	45,724	
17/3/45-14/4/45**LS**	55,595	
2/5/46-31/5/46**LS**	106,224	
2/10/48-8/11/48**HG**	62,566	Crewe
14/6/50-3/7/50**HI**	49,175	Crewe
30/1/52-20/2/52**LC[EO]**	34,177	Shed
20/5/53-17/6/53**HG**	60,411	Crewe
27/3/56-27/4/56**LI**	63,007	Horwich
12/3/58-25/4/58**HG**	44.305	Horwich
26/8/60**NC[EO]**	54,175	Horwich
20/3/61-22/6/61**LI**	65,938	Horwich

Noted at Works: Crewe 6/65

Boiler

No.9627	3/8/42	from	8082
No.11482	8/11/48	from	8527
No.11780	17/6/53		
No.11079	25/4/58		

Tender

LMS 9420	20/10/36

Sheds

Saltley	24/10/36
Westhouses	12/12/36
Lancaster	28/11/42
Canklow	10/12/49
Normanton	24/7/54
Wakefield	15/6/57
Stourton	7/9/57
Mirfield	30/1/60
Wakefield	28/1/67
Royston	17/6/67

Withdrawn 11/67

8055 in stirring form with a freight at Chinley North, 27 June 1937.

48055 'starred for speed', August 1960, location unknown. For once all the tender wheels are visible and they are seen to be spoked, which is as it should be. Except that LNER-built 8Fs had disc wheels and these inevitably seeped into tenders other than those emanating from the LNER, so various combinations could be thrown up.

48055 at home at Royston on 17 September 1967 a month or so before its withdrawal; a useful photograph for the contrast between its own 8in cab number and the 10in version of 48067 alongside. J. Davenport, Norman Preedy Collection.

48056

Built as 8056 at the Vulcan Foundry Ltd 20th October 1936
Renumbered 48056 w/e 8/10/49

Improvements and modifications
11/8/51 Blowdown discharge pipe entered into ashpan
26/12/53 Removal of sand guns
7/10/62 Fitting Automatic Warning System

Repairs

25/8/38-23/9/38**LS**	43,825	
14/3/39-24/3/39**LO**	56,664	
14/9/39-20/9/39**LO**	70,131	
16/2/40-5/3/40**LO**	80,371	
8/8/40-28/8/40**LS**	90,118	
17/6/42-14/7/42**HG**	145,943	
26/2/44-18/3/44**LS**	34,835	
10/7/45-11/8/45**HS**	63,536	
17/12/46-26/12/46**LO**	32,670	Shed
22/8/47-26/9/47**HG**	14,751	Crewe
9/9/49-4/10/49**LI**	49,218	Crewe
29/6/51-4/8/51**LI**	40,395	Horwich
23/10/53-3/12/53**HG**	52,251	Horwich
27/9/55-3/11/55**HI**	35,813	Derby
4/11/57-20/11/57**LC[EO]**	46,795	Rugby
12/6/58-4/7/58**HG**	58,961	Derby
7/2/61-16/3/61**LI**	61,956	Horwich

Noted at Works: Horwich 9/62; Crewe 8/64

Boilers

No.9602	14/7/41	from	8057
No.11192	26/9/47	from	8272
No.12003	3/12/53		
No.11277	4/7/58		

Tenders

LMS 9421	20/10/36
No.10111	8/8/64

Sheds

Saltley	24/10/36
Westhouses	12/12/36
Rowsley	12/1/57
Hasland	23/5/59
Toton	22/9/62
Burton	14/8/65
Edge Hill	10/9/66

Withdrawn w/e 4/5/68

8056 at Westhouses MPD, 7 June 1938, undergoing preparation. It has started out at Saltley but soon moved to Westhouses where it stayed until 1957 – a fixture in fact. At sheds like this the 8Fs represented an enormous leap in power, ease of maintenance (the cylinders were outside for a start) and general usefulness over what had gone before – painfully slow progression from 2F to 3F to 4F 0-6-0. All of a sudden the top freight power was 8F.

A coal engine in its habitat, a vast tip forming the background to Hasland shed yard, on 30 August 1959. The area was riven by coal workings and subsidence in that very year led to the temporary abandonment of the roundhouse while the building was shored up, minus its roof.

48057

Built as 8057 at the Vulcan Foundry Ltd 20th October 1936
Renumbered 48057 w/e 13/8/49

Improvements and Modifications
27/11/43 Fitting Griffiths laminated springs to coupled wheels
1/12/51 New type piston head fastenings
1/12/51 Discharge of continuous blowdown into ashpan
4/11/61 Fitting AWS equipment

Repairs

14/6/38**TRO**		
17/3/39-31/3/39**LO**	57,111	
8/2/40-17/2/40**LO**	79,957	
25/9/40-9/10/40**LS**	93,204	
15/1/42-13/2/42**HG**	123,755	
11/10/43-6/11/43**HS**	39,765	
5/9/45-10/10/45**LS**	45,610	
1/7/47-16/8/47**HG**	40,113	Crewe
18/7/49-13/8/49**LI**	44,946	Crewe
16/10/51-21/11/51**HG**	54,244	Crewe
27/2/54-22/3/54**HI**	55,433	Derby
22/6/56-15/8/56**HG**	55,284	Derby
18/5/59-25/6/59**LI**	49,307	Horwich
14/9/61-3/11/61**HG**	58,389	Derby

Noted at Works: Crewe 8/64

Boilers

No.11141	13/2/42	from	*Stock*
No.11194	16/8/47	from	8274
No.11255	21/11/51		
No.11506	15/8/56		
No.11468	3/11/61		

Tender

LMS 9422	20/10/36

Sheds

Saltley	24/10/36
Westhouses	12/12/36
Rowsley	9/2/57
Westhouses	23/2/57
Toton	30/1/60
Derby	23/6/62
Annesley	22/9/62
Rose Grove	17/7/65
Northwich	11/9/65

Withdrawn w/e 13/5/67

An entirely unexplained procession; presumably engines off PW possessions heading home (at an unknown date) at Dore and Totley, 48057 leading. P. Hughes, ColourRail

48057 banking a mineral train through Westhouses and Blackwell, unusually, tender first. With a shunters pole on the front, this looks like part of a colliery trip job.

48060

Built as 8060 at the Vulcan Foundry Ltd 28th October 1936
Renumbered 48060 w/e 9/4/49

Improvements and modifications
21/3/53 Removal of sand guns
16/7/61 Modifications to tube cleaner pipe and fittings
16/7/61 Fitting AWS

Repairs

12/11/38-5/12/38**LS**	49,699	
6/12/39-15/12/39**LO**	78,150	
29/7/40-13/8/40**LS**	97,730	
16/10/41-4/11/41**HG**	130,334	
12/7/43-16/8/43**LS**	41,560	
14/11/44-2/12/44**HS**	68,563	
4/5/46-13/5/46**LO**	32,846	
14/10/46-31/10/46**HG**	39,299	Crewe
11/3/49-9/4/49**LI**	50,820	Horwich
28/10/50-21/11/50**HG**	35,178	Crewe
9/2/53-10/3/53**LI**	56,544	Horwich
4/1/55-12/2/55**HG**	43,277	Horwich
2/8/55-24/8/55**NC**	9,824	Horwich
27/8/56-2/10/56**LI**	32,589	Derby
27/8/58-26/9/58**HI**	36,568	Derby
15/6/61-13/7/61**HG**	75,551	Horwich

Noted at Works: Crewe 12/64

Boilers

No.9596	4/11/41	from	8091
No.12337	31/10/46	new	
No.13232	21/11/50	from	8768
No.10860	12/2/55		
No.13053	13/7/61		

Tender

LMS 9425	28/10/36

Sheds

Canklow	31/10/36
Westhouses	6/11/37
Toton	3/10/59
Derby	20/1/62
Kettering	9/3/63
Mansfield	5/9/64
Westhouses	14/8/65
Annesley	11/9/65
Speke Jct	31/12/66

Stored serviceable
11/10-65-10/12/65
8/8/66-24/8/66

Withdrawn w/e 20/4/68

Orders are given getting 48060 ready for its next colliery job at Westhouses MPD, about 1958. Is the 12 chalked on the buffer a 'target' number for the next job or a fitter's note?

48060, an Annesley engine by then, makes a move over Horton Road crossing with a Big Prairie, 31 March 1965. AWS and lowered top lamp iron.Norman Preedy.

48061

Built as 8061 at the Vulcan Foundry Ltd 3rd November 1936
Renumbered 48061 w/e 17/9/49

Sold to H M Government – withdrawn from ex-LMS stock w/e 23/12/44
Purchased (WD 614) from Ministry of Supply – returned to ex-LMS stock w/e 17/9/49

Improvements and modifications
6/9/53 Removal of sand guns
27/1/62 AWS

Repairs

2/5/38-26/5/38**LO**	34,717	
29/10/38-4/11/38**LO**	44,408	
25/2/39-14/4/39**LS**	52,176	
16/4/40-2/5/40**LO**	76,445	
28/9/40-3/10/40**LO**	86,386	
30/12/40-25/1/41**HS**	90,497	
27/10/41-31/10/41**LO**	15,085	
1/11/41-29/11/41**LS**	1,545	
16/9/49-3/10/49**HG**		Crewe
[Overseas mileage unknown]		
15/6/51-2/8/51**LI**	42,911	Rugby
3/8/53-28/8/53**LI**	49,275	Crewe
5/9/55-6/10/55**HG**	48,880	Derby
22/7/57-2/8/57**LC[EO]**	46,147	Rugby
18/6/59-29/7/59 **HI**	90,296	Crewe

Noted at Works: Eastleigh 1/65

Boilers

No.9622	25/1/41	from	8077
No.11537	3/10/49	from	8422
No.12337	6/10/55		

Tender

LMS 10293	16/9/49

Sheds

Royston	7/11/36
Hasland	24/4/37
Toton	16/12/39
Hasland	10/2/40
Kirkby	16/3/40
Into shops	1/11/41
To Dockside	22/12/41
Crewe South	17/9/49
Birkenhead[o/l]	19/11/49
Crewe South	24/12/49
Nuneaton	14/1/50
Kettering	17/10/53
Toton	9/1/54
Leicester	8/5/54
Wellingborough	26/3/60
Woodford Halse	20/7/63
Bescot	19/6/65
Oxley	4/12/65
Tyseley	26/2/66
Oxley	5/11/66
Stoke	30/1/65
Rose Grove	12/8/67

Withdrawn w/e 23/9/67

8061 at home on 6 February 1937 with fellow Royston 8F 8088. Royston was a new shed, built to serve new collieries; it was a simple, inexpensive building without luxuries such as doors or complicated ventilation, very much like similar buildings around the Empire, in India for instance.

Top left. 8061 entered WD service as 614 and was shipped to Persia. Its number in that country was 41.200 and it was still bearing that when loading at Port Said for the journey back to Britain on 26 March 1948. Its 1944 WD number, 70614, is also painted on, low down.

Left. Back home at Crewe, with 70395 (later 48257) to the left, on 10 September 1949.

Above. As 48061, taking water at Wellingborough on 5 September 1957.

48062

Built as 8062 at the Vulcan Foundry Ltd 3rd November 1936
Renumbered 48062 w/e 8/1/49

Improvements and modifications

8/9/51	Discharge of continuous blowdown into ashpan
10/8/57	Modified pistons for continuous blowdown valves
25/2/62	Fitting AWS

Repairs

1/12/38-24/12/38**LO**	50,328	
29/3/40-9/5/40**HS**	86,772	
2/6/42-15/6/42**LS**	51,301	
29/1/44-8/2/44**LO**	92,450	
27/6/44-31/7/44**HG**	100,215	
26/12/44-20/1/45**HO**	10,100	
13/3/46-30/3/46**LO**	34,290	
2/1/47-28/2/47**LS**	50,268	Crewe
15/11/48-3/1/49**HG**	45,636	Crewe
6/12/50-5/1/51**HI**	49,184	Horwich
26/6/51-30/7/51**HC**	10,392	Crewe
26/9/52-28/10/52**HI**	46,456	Derby
29/4/55-31/5/55**HG**	49,474	Derby
5/7/57-7/8/57**HI**	47,160	Derby
18/1/60-16/3/60**LI**	47,275	Horwich
24/3/60-13/4/60**LC[EO]**	278	Horwich

Noted at Works: Crewe 1/66

Boilers

No.9592	9/5/40	from	8047
No.9579	31/7/44	from	8024
No.9627	3/1/49	from	8055
No.10883	31/5/55		

Tenders

LMS 9427	3/11/36
No.10130	30/7/51

Sheds

Royston	7/11/36
Cricklewood	10/3/51
Wellingborough	26/11/55
Cricklewood	10/12/55
Toton	23/5/59
Rugby	29/10/60
Buxton	17/12/60
Lostock hall	30/1/65
Birkenhead	27/2/65
Lower Darwen	19/6/65
Rose Grove	6/11/65
Lostock Hall	16/7/66
Rose Grove	7/10/67

Stored serviceable
1/8/66-9/10/67

Withdrawn w/e 3/8/68

48062 gets away with a freight in May 1960; the location is Water Orton East Junction with the line to Derby on the left and the line to Nuneaton (Abbey Street) on the right. David Woods.

48062, a Rose Grove engine for its last few months, where it survived till that fateful August, at Bolton shed on 7 March 1968. AWS and lowered top lamp iron. J. Corkill.

48063

Built as 8063 at the Vulcan Foundry Ltd 10th November 1936
Renumbered 48063 w/e 25/12/48

Improvements and modifications

30/10/43	Fitting Griffith laminated springs
8/7/44	Fitting Griffith laminated springs
8/8/53	Removal of sand guns

Repairs

8/10/38-28/10/38**LS**	44,460	
18/12/39-6/1/40**HS**	76,359	
2/7/40-24/7/40**LS**	14,924	
7/2/42-11/3/42**LS**	55,575	
28/9/42-8/10/42**HS**	71,108	
4/10/43-22/10/43**LS**	25,100	
3/7/45-24/7/45**HG**	65,281	
17/1/47-24/2/47**LS**	33,676	Crewe
22/11/48-21/12/48**HS**	44,492	Crewe
9/5/50-28/5/50**LC**	31,001	Shed
15/5/51-9/6/51**HG**	54,775	Horwich
15/6/53-7/8/53**LI**	50,121	Horwich
3/6/55-22/6/55**HI**	40,635	Derby
5/10/56-9/11/56**HG**	30,382	Derby
1/12/58-30/12/58**HI**	44,351	Derby
1/3/61-10/4/61**LI**	53,013	Derby

Noted at Works: Crewe 1/66

Boilers

No.10089	6/1/40	new
No.10506	24/7/45	from 8123
No.11721	9/6/51	from 48453
No.11255	9/11/56	

Tender

LMS 9428	10/11/36

Sheds

Canklow	14/11/36
Westhouses	6/11/37
Rowsley	23/2/57
Kirkby	23/5/59
Coalville	26/12/64
Kirkby	22/5/65
Northwich	25/2/67
Heaton Mersey	24/2/68

Stored serviceable
2/9/67-11/12/67

Withdrawn w/e 9/3/68

48063 gets its down empties underway at Trent, north end, on 14 May 1963. The line to the right is the North Curve, for Derby. RailOnline

With 'reciprocating masses star' 48063 stands at Willesden MPD on 8 July 1964. It will have to turn before making its way back north. J.L. Stevenson, courtesy Hamish Stevenson.

48064

Built as 8064 at the Vulcan Foundry Ltd 11th November 1936
Renumbered 48064 w/e 23/10/48

Improvements and modifications
27/12/47 New type piston head fastening
31/12/60 AWS

Repairs

28/3/39-1/4/39**Tender only**		
27/9/39-11/10/39**LO**	69,994	
26/1/40-16/2/40**LS**	77,089	
5/5/42-30/5/42**HG**	142,686	
24/4/44-6/5/44**LS**	51,438	
24/7/45-29/8/45**LS**	83,793	
20/11/46-30/11/46**LO**	117,530	Shed
2/10/47-29/10/47**HG**	17,297	Crewe
Converted to oil burning		
4/10/48-20/10/48**NC**	19,784	Crewe
Re-converted to coal burning		
4/7/49-6/7/49**TRO**		Shed
6/2/50-1/3/50**HI**	50,632	Crewe
3/1/51-3/2/51**LC**	20,255	Crewe
3/4/52-26/5/52**HG**	50,751	Derby
15/10/54-5/11/54**LI**	56,951	Derby
10/10/56-26/10/56**LC[EO]**	46,022	Rugby
27/3/57-24/5/57**HG**	57,651	Derby
21/3/60-27/4/60**LI**	77,050	Derby
22/11/60-9/12/60**NC[EO]**	16,688	Derby

Boilers

No.9514	30/5/42 from 8037
No.11568	29/10/47 from 8307
No.11257	26/5/52
No.11707	24/5/57

Tender

LMS 9429	11/11/36

Sheds

Canklow	14/11/36
Leeds	15/3/41
Canklow	11/10/41
Staveley	13/6/42
Nottingham	15/11/47
Annesley	22/9/62
Mansfield	18/4/64
Burton	9/10/65

Withdrawn w/e 21/5/66

48064, one of the shed's finest for some fifteen years, at Nottingham MPD on 22 June 1952; the vast 16A coaling plant stands in the distance. 48064 owes its good looks to a recent Heavy General at Derby. B.K.B. Green, courtesy Norman Preedy.

48064 with a Uttoxeter-Colwick freight at West Hallam, 3 November 1962. Tony Cooke, ColourRail

48065

Built as 8065 at the Vulcan Foundry Ltd 11th November 1936
Renumbered 48065 w/e 10/12/49

Improvements and modifications
8/9/51 Discharge of continuous blowdown into ashpan

Repairs

13/1/39-24/2/39**LS**	51,313	
16/10/39-26/10/39**LO**	65,516	
15/3/40-19/4/40**TRO**		
10/2/41-28/2/41**HS**	97,700	
13/12/41-22/12/41**TRO**		
21/4/42-11/5/42**LS**	33,111	
30/6/43-17/7/43**TRO**		
25/2/44-10/3/44**HS**	76,124	
30/5/46-29/6/46**HG**	50,262	
12/8/47-20/9/47**LS**	29,237	Crewe
14/11/49-5/12/49**LI**	52,827	Crewe
20/6/51-3/8/51**HG**	34,937	Crewe
16/2/54-10/3/54**LI**	57,715	Horwich
9/12/55-6/1/56**HG**	44,265	Derby
14/10/57-31/10/57**HI**	40,271	Derby
29/3/60-3/6/60**LI**	60,686	Horwich

Noted at Works: Derby 1/63

Boilers

No.9611	28/2/41	from 8066
No.11290	29/6/46	from 8213
No.13234	8/8/51	from 48770
No.11537	6/1/56	

Tenders

LMS 9430	1/11/35
LMS 9432	1/12/41
LMS 9430	22/12/41

Sheds

Canklow	14/11/36
Hasland	6/11/54
Burton	18/8/62
Leicester	27/3/65

Withdrawn w/e 12/2/66

Canklow's 8065 at Derby on a rainy 23 October 1937. In thirty years the 8F worked from only four sheds. A hint of burnishing lingers on the valve covers.

48065 (it never got AWS) has found its way to Oxford on 14 September 1965. It was withdrawn in February the following year. External pipework to tube cleaning cock. B. Miller Collection.

48067

Built as 8067 at the Vulcan Foundry Ltd 18th November 1936
Renumbered 48067 w/e 5/11/49

Improvements and modifications
24/1/48 Additional washout plugs, new type piston head fastening
6/10/51 Blowdown discharge pipe entered into ashpan
11/7/53 Removal of sand guns
14/8/60 AWS

Repairs

29/1/38-4/2/38**LO**	35,241	
25/12/38-5/1/39**LO**	59,108	
30/6/39-20/7/39**LS**	74,581	
27/1/40-4/4/40**LO**	92,674	
30/5/40-13/6/40**LO**	96,262	
17/2/41-8/3/41**LO**	121,990	
22/11/41-5/1/42**HG**	145,237	
25/5/43-19/6/43**LS**	36,878	
6/1/44-7/2/44**LO**	49,463	
9/6/45-11/7/45**HS**	82,792	
30/10/46-21/11/46**LO**	35,138	
9/12/47-19/1/48**HG**	23,118	Crewe
22/2/48**NC**	2,158	Leeds
5/10/49-4/11/49**LI**	68,654	Horwich
15/8/51-13/9/51**LI**	64,111	Horwich
27/4/53-22/6/53 **HG**	60,781	Horwich
16/5/55-24/6/55**LI**	67,554	Horwich
17/5/57-11/6/57**LI**	65,984	Horwich
24/8/59-9/10/59**HG**	67,058	Horwich
8/8/60**NC[EO]**	26,569	Horwich

Noted at Works: Darlington 4/65

Boilers

No.9621	5/1/42	from 8076
No.9574	19/1/48	from 8064
No.11182	22/6/53	
No.10437	9/10/59	

Tenders

LMS 9432	18/11/36
LMS 9393	17/2/41
LMS 9432	1/5/41
LMS 9430	1/12/41
LMS 9432	22/12/41
No.10254	12/6/57

Sheds

Toton	21/11/36
Bath	4/1/41
Leeds	13/9/41
Canklow	11/10/41
Kettering	25/5/46
Leeds	7/2/48
Royston	9/9/61

Withdrawn 10/67

8067 with the 'ghost train', the special block train of bogie coal wagons dedicated to Stonebridge Park power station, built for the Euston-Watford electrification. It is running north past Headstone Lane (one of the sub-stations for the third rail scheme in the right background) in 1937.

48067 with a more conventional working, mineral wagons passing Eastfield MPD in Glasgow, 26 October 1957. It's a thing worthy of note just to see an 8F in Scotland, apart from the 'final three', which went to Polmadie. 48067 was at Holbeck at the time, so is almost certainly 'out of course' in its working; you'd imagine Holbeck freight diagrams didn't go beyond Carlisle... J.L. Stevenson, courtesy Hamish Stevenson.

48069

Built as 8069 at the Vulcan Foundry Ltd 26th November 1936
Renumbered 48069 w/e 13/11/48

Improvements and modifications
8/9/51 Discharge of continuous blowdown into ashpan
2/11/57 Provision of Metaflex joints
2/11/57 Modified piston for continuous blowdown gear
25/1/61 Fitting ATC equipment

Repairs

14/5/38**TRO**		
10/8/38-31/8/38**LS**	53,128	
26/6/39-1/7/39**LO**	78,686	
24/1/40-13/2/40**LS**	94,880	
3/6/41-3/7/41**HG**	136,128	
3/11/41-5/12/41**HS**	13,6,128	
[Mileage from 5/12/41 to 10/5/42 not available]		
4/7/44-29/7/44**LS**	82,801	
28/6/45-11/8/45**LS**	118,322	
24/10/46-29/11/46**HG**	163,014	
8/10/48-10/11/48**LS**	47,011	Crewe
31/8/50-20/9/50**LI**	47,762	Crewe
17/6/51-20/7/51**LC**	19,179	Crewe
2/11/51-10/12/51**LC[EO**]	27,271	Crewe
2/3/53-16/4/53**HG**	61,370	Derby
29/4/55-19/5/55**HI**	51,437	Derby
16/9/57-17/10/57**HG**	52,375	Derby
22/2/60-28/3/60**HI**	57,795	Derby
14/1/61-8/2/61**LC[EO]**	24,720	Derby

Noted at Works: Derby 6/62; Crewe 8/64 for scrap
LMS engine histories do not consistently/clearly record requisitions. In summary, 8069 (WD 615) was requisitioned by the WD 11/41 and shipped out of the country, only to return when the vessel got into trouble. So it never did go abroad.

Boilers

No.9828	3/7/41
No.12316	29/11/46 new
No.11155	16/4/53
No.11354	17/10/57

Tenders

LMS 9434	26/11/36
No.9183	10/12/51
No.9876	22/6/63

Sheds

Wellingborough	28/11/36
Canklow	8/7/39
Wellingborough	18/11/39
Into shops	1/11/41
To Dockside	26/12/41
Returned temp. to LMS from WD	
Converted from oil to coal	
Into shops	6/5/42
Out of shops	9/5/42
Motherwell	16/5/42
Returned to LMS	15/5/43
Motherwell	3/7/43
Kingmoor	11/5/46
Royston[o/l]	29/3/47
Coalville	5/4/47
Wellingborough	26/4/47
Kettering	22/11/47
Wellingborough	15/2/64
Kirkby	18/4/64

Withdrawn w/e 7/11/64

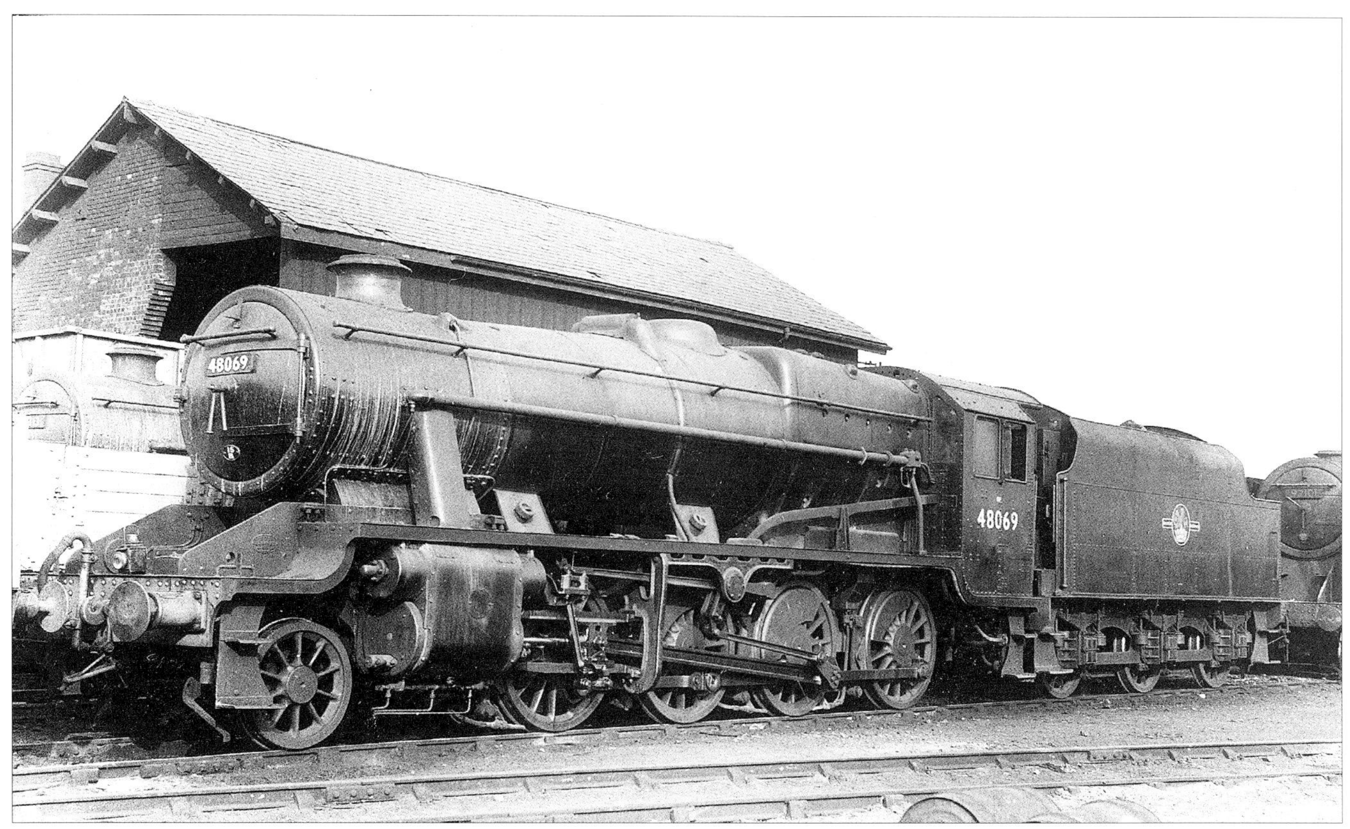

48069, another to have taken the short voyage of the SS PENTRIDGE HALL (see 8024 page 95 for instance) at Kettering MPD in the 1950s – after 1957 at any rate, from the second emblem. A very respectable looking 8F, its appearance due in no small part, no doubt, to its late 1957 Heavy General. J. Davenport, courtesy Norman Preedy.

A lovely show from 48069 in the cold air at Great Glen (near Oadby, Leicester) with up coal, 2 February 1963. Like the others off the SS PENTRIDGE HALL this 8F had the distinction of being equipped for oil burning without actually working as such. Also, because they were restored to working order at St Rollox (the ship berthing in Glasgow after its calamitous voyage) they worked from Scottish sheds like Motherwell before drifting back to the English Midlands. Tony Cooke, ColourRail

48070

Built as 8070 at the Vulcan Foundry Ltd 26th November 1936
Renumbered 48070 w/e 17/12/49

Improvements and modifications
24/1/48 Casing and filter for air relief valves
30/12/51 Discharge of continuous blowdown into ashpan
29/12/51 Removal of sand guns
11/9/60 AWS

Repairs

5/2/38-26/2/38**LO**	27,758	
14/7/38-16/8/38**LO**	35,471	
15/2/39-27/2/39**LO**	42,955	
1/8/39-11/8/39**LO**	51,983	
28/8/39-4/9/39**LO**	53,333	
1/12/39-13/1/40**LS**	59,590	
2/11/40-23/11/40**HO**	78,057	
14/11/41-8/12/41**LS**	28,859	
13/4/42-29/4/42**LO**	38,686	
5/10/42-21/10/42**LO**	52,208	
2/7/43-6/7/43**LO**	72,412	
3/8/43-6/9/43**LS**	75,046	
18/11/46-27/11/46**LO**	22,131	Shed
17/12/47-17/1/48**HG**	20,142	Crewe
24/2/48**NC**	2,281	Leeds
20/11/49-17/12/49**LI**	71,418	Horwich
13/10/50-10/11/50**LC**	29,182	Horwich
31/10/51-5/12/51**HG**	60,740	Horwich
21/8/53-25/9/53**HI**	59,258	Horwich
29/8/55-1/10/55**LI**	62,653	Horwich
17/9/56-16/10/56**HG**	24,063	Derby
28/11/58-2/1/59**LI**	47,884	Horwich
21/3/60-28/4/60**LC[EO]**	28,554	Horwich
17/8/60**NC[EO]**	34,988	Horwich

Boilers

No.9623	23/11/40	from	8078
No.11257	6/9/43	from	8180
No.9604	17/1/48	from	8027
No.13186	5/12/51		
No.12139	16/10/56		

Tenders

LMS 9435	26/11/36
No.10185	17/12/49

Sheds

Kirkby	28/11/36
Nottingham	18/2/39
Toton	30/11/46
Leeds	7/2/48
Royston	17/7/54

Withdrawn 11/67

8070 in an unusual view; this is the old Leicester MPD (see also 8020) with the curious 'birdcage' above, which led north-east off Swain Street/ Sparkenhoe bridge at the southeast end. E.R. Morten, courtesy J.R. Morten.

48070 at Mirfield MPD in the 1960s; the scribble on the cab reads BAD LOCO which is a new category!

48070 at Royston, its home for most of its time as a BR engine. Middle warning flash in another eccentric position. AWS and BR modified pipework to steam heating cock.

48073

Built as 8073 at the Vulcan Foundry Ltd 9th December 1936
Renumbered 48073 w/e 25/9/48

Improvements and modifications
22/2/53 Provision of new type pistons head and rods

Repairs

15/8/38-26/8/38**LO**	40,527	
1/3/39-22/3/39**LO**	53,497	
15/6/39-20/7/39**LS**	58,664	
15/3/40-23/3/40**LO**	74,777	
17/7/40-30/7/40**HO**	83,478	
1/3/41-12/3/41**TRO**		
18/8/41-11/9/41**LS**	34,428	
24/4/42-11/5/42**TRO**		
23/2/43-27/3/43**LS**	92,267	
9/6/43-9/7/43**LO**	100,010	
13/11/44-25/11/44**HG**	148,021	
14/5/46-22/6/46**HS**	52,682	
10/11/47-22/12/47**LS**	45,458	Crewe
19/8/48-22/9/48**LO**	14,986	Derby
1/7/49-6/8/49**HG**	33,488	Crewe
30/3/51-23/4/51**HI**	38,683	Horwich
6/5/52-9/6/52**HI**	21,970	Derby
26/6/54-27/8/54**HG**	43,988	Crewe
9/3/56-27/3/56**HI**	35,159	Derby
10/3/58-27/3/58**LI**	43,798	Derby
22/9/60-9/1/61**HG**	58,695	Derby

Noted at Works: Crewe 6/63; Crewe 4/64

Boilers

No.9588	30/7/40	from	8043
No.9592	25/11/44	from	8062
No.11518	6/8/40	from	8403
No.11524	27/8/54		
No.11353	9/1/61		

Tenders

LMS 9438	9/12/36
No.10264	27/8/54

Sheds

Nottingham	12/2/36
Leeds	3/9/41
Kirkby	24/1/48
Mansfield	26/12/64
Westhouses	14/8/65
Annesley	8/10/66
Saltley	31/12/66
Chester	25/3/67

Stored serviceable
10/10/66-1/12/66

Withdrawn w/e 8/4/67

Another new 8F, 8073 at Nottingham shed, 20 November 1937. The question arises as to why only 126 of them were built before the War and the answer seems to lie in the contemporaneous rebuilding of so many ex-LNW 0-8-0s to better suit them to modern needs.

At Nottingham shed, the castle in the background, as with 48064. Plenty of coal!

A neglected 48073 at Westhouses MPD, 19 June 1966. Its running valence and tender has attracted the attentions of a Nottingham Forest supporter...

48074

Built as 8074 at the Vulcan Foundry Ltd 8th December 1936
Renumbered 48074 w/e 4/2/50

Improvements and modifications
22/3/52 Discharge of continuous blowdown into ashpan
3/12/60 AWS

Repairs

26/8/38-5/9/38**LO**	42,506	
27/12/38-5/1/39**LO**	50,110	
15/4/39-4/5/39**LO**	55,948	
20/6/39-21//39**LS**	59,257	
2/5/40-22/6/40**HO**	76,080	
12/6/41-29/7/41**LO**	26,357	
2/2/42-21/2/42**LO**	40,813	
7/12/42-13/1/43**HG**	59,303	
18/10/44-3/11/44**LS**	50,489	
12/2/46-9/3/46**HS**	82,611	
24/10/47-5/12/47**HG**	48,102	Crewe
14/1/50-1/2/50**LI**	55,874	Crewe
12/2/52-19/3/52**HG**	56,391	Crewe
24/4/53-28/4/53**LC[EO]**	33,645	Shed
20/9/54-22/10/54**HI**	69,595	Rugby
22/8/56-5/10/56**HG**	45,753	Horwich
14/6/58-25/6/58**LC[EO]**	47,548	Rugby
4/4/59-5/5/59**HI**	66,181	Horwich
3/11/60-17/11/60**NC[EO]**	36,286	Horwich
25/9/61-30/10/61**HG**	54,261	Crewe

Noted at Works: Derby 2/64; Crewe 2/64

Boilers

No.9629	22/6/40	from	8084
No.9840	13/1/43	from	8026
No.11510	5/12/46	from	8606
No.11074	19/3/52		
No.12318	5/10/56		
No.13610	30/10/61		

Tenders

LMS 9439	8/12/36
No.9448	24/3/59

Sheds

Nottingham	12/12/36
Heaton Mersey	21/1/39
Derby	30/1/43
Stourton	17/8/46
Kirkby	11/10/47
Wellingborough	15/5/48
Peterborough	2/10/48
Carlisle Canal	16/9/50
Willesden	2/6/51
Bletchley	20/6/59
Speke Jct	22/8/59
Mold Jct	7/11/59
Nuneaton	18/6/60
Rugby	7/7/62
Nuneaton	16/3/63
Trafford Park	21/5/66
Heaton Mersey	12/8/67

Stored serviceable
30/1/67-14/8/67

Withdrawn w/e 25/11/61

8074 sails through Baguley station on the CLC, with hoppers, in 1939. It had moved to Heaton Mersey at the beginning of the year and stayed there well into the war years.

Trundling through a station now, this time Hawkesbury Lane on the Coventry-Nuneaton line, 21 July 1962. Tony Cooke, ColourRail

48075

Built as 8075 at the Vulcan Foundry Ltd 8th December 1936
Renumbered 48075 w/e 26/3/49

Improvements and modifications
8/10/60 AWS
8/10/60 Modifications to tube cleaner pipe and fittings

Repairs

30/11/38-7/12/38**LO**	54,763	
8/9/38-7/10/38**RTO**		
31/3/39-20/4/39**LS**	66,516	
20/1/40-31/1/40**LO**	94,028	
20/3/41-17/4/41**HG**	131,816	
11/5/42-5/6/42**LO**	27,820	
28/10/43-24/12/43**LS**	58,388	
19/5/45-9/6/45**HS**	91,431	
22/12/46-16/1/47**LO**	43,679	Crewe
10/7/47-29/8/47**LS**	10,800	Crewe
21/2/49-23/3/49**HG**	44,058	Crewe
7/12/50-13/1/51**HI**	46,602	Crewe
7/9/53-6/11/53**HG**	80,100	Derby
3/3/56-26/3/56**LI**	56,840	Derby
21/6/58-6/8/58**HG**	47,990	Derby
16/9/60**LI**	38,854	Horwich

Noted at Works: Darlington 10/64

Boilers

No.9610	17/4/41	from	8065
No.10508	9/6/45	from	8125
No.11789	23/3/49	from	8649
No.11543	6/11/53		
No.11823	6/8/58		

Tender

LMS 9440	8/12/36

Sheds

Nottingham	12/12/36
Toton	3/4/37
Leeds	6/9/41
Canklow	11/10/41
Royston	10/10/42
Toton	9/9/44
Canklow	9/4/55
Ardsley	6/9/59
Stourton	30/1/60
Royston	13/7/63

Withdrawn 5/67

48075 after front end work at Horwich, 1 September 1962. D. Forsyth, ColourRail

48075 at Mirfield MPD late on, in 1966-67; the large 10in cabside numerals were applied during a Heavy General at Darlington in 1965.

48076

Built as 8076 at the Vulcan Foundry Ltd 22nd December 1936
Renumbered 48076 w/e 14/8/48

Improvements and modifications
20/4/46 Providing steel in lieu of copper tube*, casing and filter for air relief valve
8/10/60 AWS
**presumably main steam pipe*

Repairs

9/12/38-9/1/39**RTO**		
14/2/39-1/3/39**LO**	62,802	
22/7/39-4/8/39**LS**	77,361	
4/7/40-22/7/40**LS**	101,152	
1/9/41-18/10/41**HG**	135,479	
16/1/43-28/1/43**LO**	45,108	
29/3/43-30/4/43**LS**	52,102	
24/1/44-5/2/44**HS**	71,189	
5/3/46-1/4/46**HG**	43,007	
18/9/47-3/10/47**LO**	13,834	Shed
18/6/48-13/8/48**HS**	16,856	Crewe
27/9/50-23/10/50**HI**	50,414	Crewe
12/1/53-4/4/53**HG**	55,661	Horwich
27/2/56-24/3/56**HI**	62,318	Horwich
10/7/57-14/8/57**LC[EO]**	27,429	Horwich
10/2/59-20/3/59**HG**	64,594	Horwich
14/9/60**NC**	32,235	Horwich

Noted at Works: Horwich 6/62; Crewe 7/66

Boilers

No.9838	18/10/41 from	8024
No.9839	1/4/46 from	8080
No.11499	13/8/48 from	8614
No.11493	4/4/53	
No.11809	20/3/59	

Tender
LMS 9441 22/12/36

Sheds

Toton	26/12/36
Kettering	12/6/43
Westhouses	7/8/43
Normanton	24/2/51
Wakefield	18/5/57
Stourton	7/9/57
Mirfield	30/1/60
Royston	11/8/62
Farnley Jct	25/1/64
Royston	5/11/66

Withdrawn 11/67

48076 in for AWS fitting at Horwich, 3 September 1960. D. Forsyth, ColourRail

48076 (MALCOLM has offered his imprimatur on the cylinder) at Royston in 1962. Since the fitting of AWS at Horwich it has swapped smokeboxes, with that lower steam cleaning cock and the external pipe to it. The ending of the repairs record about 1960 sadly means that details of these late works visits are lost to us. J. Davenport, courtesy Norman Preedy.

48077

Built as 8077 at the Vulcan Foundry Ltd 22nd December 1936
Renumbered 48077 w/e 24/12/49

Sold to H M Government, withdrawn from ex-LMS stock 12/6/41
Purchased (WD 611) from Ministry of Supply – returned to ex-LMS stock w/e 24/12/49

Improvements and modifications
22/3/52 Discharge of continuous blowdown into ashpan
19/5/56 Removal of sand guns
13/8/60 AWS

Repairs

19/12/38-5/1/39**LS**	63,182	
30/3/40-6/4/40**LO**	96,306	
23/11/40-13/12/40**HG**	118,867	
25/10/41-22/11/41**LS**	29,160	
22/12/49-13/1/50**HG**		Crewe
[Overseas mileage unknown]		
12/2/52-21/3/52**LI**	49,755	Rugby
7/9/53-7/10/53**LI**	39,737	Rugby
3/4/56-3/5/56**HG**	59,878	Crewe
7/3/58-17/3/58**LC[EO]**	42,876	Rugby
2/9/59-7/10/59**LI**	76,047	Crewe
19/7/60-3/8/60**NC[EO]**	23,955	Crewe

Noted at Works: Crewe 5/62; Crewe 4/65

Boilers

No.9638	13/12/40 from 8093
No.11792	13/1/50 from 48077
No.9620	3/5/56

Tenders

LMS 9442	22/12/36
No.10315	22/12/49

Sheds

Toton	26/12/36
Into shops	25/10/41
To Dockside	22/12/41
Crewe South	24/12/49
Nuneaton	14/1/50
Willesden	4/8/62
Bletchley	19/1/63
Lancaster	17/7/65
Carnforth	23/4/66

Withdrawn w/e 9/3/68

8077 at Kettering shed, where the yard adjoined the north end of the station, in 1938. A comparison with a similar view of 48010 shows that the shear legs disappeared, and that by 1962 the gradient south through the station had sharpened somewhat.

8077 became WD 611 and after work in Persia ended up at Jaffa in what would become Israel, as 70611 (1944 WD number). Here it is in near-perfect nick it would seem at, apparently, Jaffa, near Tel Aviv, in October 1947. It arrived back in Britain the following year.

48078

Built as 8078 at the Vulcan Foundry Ltd 23rd December 1936
Renumbered 48078 w/e 7/8/48

Improvements and modifications
17/5/52 Removal of sand guns
8/10/60 AWS

Repairs

9/3/38-19/3/38**LO**	36,087	
2/3/39-5/4/39**LS**	65,959	
18/3/40-22/3/40**LO**	100,528	
8/10/40-25/10/40**HG**	117,098	
27/10/41-28/11/41**LS**	40,357	
22/4/43-7/7/43**HS**	82,034	
31/8/43-14/9/43**LO**	6,836	
16/10/44-2/11/44**LS**	46,040	
16/3/45-5/4/45**LO**	61,086	
17/9/45-25/10/45**HG**	76,080	
4/10/46-1/11/46**LS**	38,846	
21/1/48-12/2/48**LO**	31,720	Shed
5/7/48-7/8/48**LS**	89,559	Crewe
30/5/50-29/6/50**HG**	44,799	Horwich
26/3/52-29/4/52**HI**	43,838	Horwich
4/11/54-26/11/54**HG**	57,208	Crewe
3/12/56-18/12/56**LC[EO]**	50,927	Rugby
29/4/57-5/6/57**LI**	60,392	Horwich
30/3/59-26/5/59**HG**		Horwich*
20/9/60**NC**	26,965	Horwich

* No mileage figure recorded

LMS engine histories do not consistently/clearly record requisitions. In summary, 8078 (WD 616) was requisitioned by the WD 10/41 and shipped out of the country, only to return when the vessel got into trouble. So it never did go abroad.

Boilers

No. 9582	25/10/40 from 8037
No.10443	25/10/45 from 8108
No.10445	29/6/50 from 8036
No.11525	26/11/54
No.11586	26/5/59

Tenders

LMS 9443	23/12/36
No.9432	28/5/57

Sheds

Toton	26/12/36
Into shops	30/10/41
To Dockside	26/12/41
Returned temp. to LMS from WD	
Converted from oil to coal burner	
Into shops	7/5/42
Out of shops	9/5/42
Motherwell	16/5/42
Returned to LMS	15/4/43
Motherwell	3/7/43
Kingmoor	11/5/46
Royston	28/12/46
Toton[o/l]	16/10/48
Royston	11/12/48
Edge Hill	11/8/62

Withdrawn w/e 28/8/65

48078 at Horwich for a Light Intermediate repair, 4 May 1957. R.A. Panting.

48078 at Royston, its home for most of the BR period, on 19 February 1961. In the 1950s over a third of Royston's sixty or so locos were 8Fs, with the rest made up largely of 0-6-0s. By the mid-1960s there were still twenty or more there, though the shed's steam allocation had fallen to little more than thirty. D. Preston, ColourRail

48078 at Kingmoor, which must have been the far limit for Royston's 2-8-0s.

48079

Built as 8079 at the Vulcan Foundry Ltd 23rd December 1936
Renumbered 48079 w/e 21/8/48

Improvements and modifications
22/3/52 Blowdown discharge pipe entered in ashpan
10/8/57 Provision and fitting new type piston rod fastening

Repairs

10/1/39-23/1/39**Tender only**		
13/2/39-10/3/39**LS**	63,850	
5/2/40-20/2/40**LO**	99,080	
2/5/41-23/5/41**HG**	139,342	
8/11/41 Prepared for overseas by GWR		
27/5/44-14/6/44**LS**	71,254	
4/12/44-27/12/44**LO**	88,888	
12/11/45-7/12/45**HG**	124,646	
3/4/46-21/5/46**LO**	15,482	
13/10/47-4/12/47**LS**	63,539	Crewe
Converted to oil burning		
29/12/47-9/1/48**NC**	349	Crewe
20/1/48-29/1/48**NC**	911	Crewe
2/8/48-19/8/48**NC**	7,240	Crewe
Re-converted to coal burning		
10/10/49-1/11/49**LC**	36,389	Crewe
7/3/51-11/4/51**LC**	35,552	Derby
26/1/52-6/3/52**HG**	55,428	Crewe
22/11/54-16/12/54**LI**	69,653	Derby
30/10/56-13/11/56**LC[EO]**	45,830	Rugby
28/6/57-2/8/57**HG**	60,627	Derby
30/12/59-15/2/60**LI**	57,486	Derby

LMS engine histories do not consistently/clearly record requisitions. In summary, 8079 (WD 602) was requisitioned by the WD 11/41 and shipped out of the country, only to return when the vessel got into trouble. So it never did go abroad.

Boilers

No.9831	23/5/41	from	8018
No.9617	7/12/45	from	8088
No.3216	6/3/52		
no.11773	2/8/57		

Tenders

LMS 9444	23/12/36
LMS 9910	15/11/44
LMS 9444	5/12/44
LMS 9458	27/12/44
LMS 10028	23/5/46

Sheds

Toton	26/12/36
Into Shops	8/11/41
To Dockside	30/12/41
Returned temp. to LMS from WD	
Converted from oil to coal burner	
Into shops	25/4/42
Out of shops	6/5/42
Motherwell	9/5/42
Returned to LMS	15/5/43
Motherwell	3/7/43
Kingmoor	11/5/46
Royston[o/l]	7/12/46
Royston	28/12/46
Derby	3/4/48
Kettering	25/2/61
Annesley	22/9/62
Toton	19/6/65
Carnforth	17/7/65
Lancaster	6/11/65
Lostock Hall	23/4/66
Rose Grove	16/7/66

Stored serviceable
14/6/65-5/7/65

Withdrawn w/e 31/12/66

8079 at home at Toton in July 1938. Requisitioned as 602, it set sail with the others on the SS PENTRIDGE HALL and after restoration at St Rollox worked in Scotland for the rest of the War.

The southern approaches at Carlisle, 27 August 1965. 48079 is on the North Eastern link from London Road Junction to Canal Yard and the Goods Committee tracks. Over on the right are the North Eastern passenger lines between London Road and Citadel which were used by Midland Settle & Carlisle trains as well as those from Newcastle. The bridge in the foreground carried the goods tracks (recently lifted) from Upperby Junction to the North Western's Crown Street goods depot near Citadel station. The next bridge was used by trains on the West Coast main line from Lancaster. D. Forsyth, ColourRail

48080

Built as 8080 at the Vulcan Foundry Ltd 23rd December 1936
Renumbered 48080 w/e 19/2/49

Improvements and modifications
6/9/52 Removal of sand guns
8/10/60 AWS

Repairs

20/4/38-28/4/38**LO**	35,218	
14/9/39-5/0/39**LS**	74,614	
12/2/40-14/3/40**LO**	85,356	
5/9/40-20/9/40**LO**	99,173	
8/1/41-19/2/41**HG**	107,255	
3/11/41 Prepared for overseas by GWR		
1/9/43-25/9/43**LS**	51,398	
2/5/44-30/5/44**LS**	75,551	
6/12/44-13/1/45**LO**	98,748	
4/12/45-14/1/46**HG**	135,332	
4/8/47-1/10/47**HS**	56,364	
21/1/49-18/2/49**LI**	32,805	Crewe
22/5/50-3/6/50**LC**	37,102	Leeds
3/7/50-5/8/50**HG**	38,229	Crewe
1/8/52-27/8/52**LI**	42,568	Horwich
7/2/55-15/3/55**HG**	60,887	Derby
1/1/57-11/1/57**LC[EO]**	47,078	Rugby
3/2/58-19/2/58**LI**	73,245	Derby
14/9/59-22/10/59**HG**	36,310	Horwich
6/10/60**NC**	23,691	Horwich

LMS engine histories do not consistently/clearly record requisitions. In summary, 8080 (WD 604) was requisitioned by the WD 11/41 and shipped out of the country, only to return when the vessel got into trouble. So it never did go abroad.

Boilers

No.9839	19/2/41	from	8025
No.11066	14/1/46	from	8128
No.11699	5/8/50	from	8464
No.12006	5/3/55		
No.11525	22/10/59		

Tender

LMS 9445	23/12/36

Sheds

Normanton	26/12/36
Into shops	3/11/41
To Dockside	30/12/41
Returned temp. to LMS from WD	
Converted from oil to coal burning	
Into shops	8/5/41
Out of shops	15/5/41
Polmadie	16/5/41
Returned to LMS	15/5/43
Polmadie	26/6/43
Perth	24/6/44
Kingmoor	11/5/46
Royston[o/l]	7/12/46
Royston	15/5/48
Stourton	16/5/48
Royston	18/11/50
Low Moor	17/5/58
Stourton	30/1/60
Royston	13/7/63
Farnley Jct	7/9/63

Withdrawn 11/66

Retaining the looks of a new engine, Normanton's 8080 stands in the yard at Stourton shed in 1937. 8080 (as 604) also took the brief voyage on the SS PENTRIDGE HALL and worked in Scotland for the rest of the War after attention at St Rollox.

48080 rattles a coal train along at Hellifield in 1962; AWS protector plate prominent. M. Chapman, ColourRail

48081

Built as 8081 at the Vulcan Foundry Ltd 2nd January 1937
Renumbered 48081 w/e 21/5/49

Improvements and modifications
27/12/52 Removal of sand guns and equipment

Repairs

5/4/39-24/4/39**LS**	58,113	
2/5/40-12/5/40**LO**	86,839	
24/6/40-5/7/40**LS**	90,251	
10/1/41-7/2/41**HO**	104,692	
18/2/42-28/3/42**LS**	37,052	
17/6/43-10/7/43**HS**	87,305	
27/11/44-16/12/44**HG**	59,807	
24/1/46-20/2/46**LS**	45,983	
1/8/47-20/9/47**LS**	49,653	Crewe
21/4/49-16/5/49**HG**	36,482	Crewe
23/4/51-15/6/51**LI**	44,383	Crewe
24/3/52-2/4/52**LC[EO]**	19,228	Shed
25/10/52-15/11/52**LI**	32,115	Crewe
17/12/54-14/1/55**HG**	44,726	Derby
4/2/57-5/3/57**HI**	44,839	Derby
7/4/59-22/4/59**LI**	43,546	Derby
19/2/61-28/3/61**HG**	48,762	Derby

Noted at Works: Derby 2/62; Crewe 8/64

Boilers

No.10439	16/12/44 from	8104
No.11477	16/5/49 from	8522
No.10443	14/1/55	
No.13232	28/3/61	

Tender
LMS 9446 2/1/37

Sheds

Staveley	2/1/37
Leeds	15/3/41
Skipton	13/11/43
Kirkby	24/1/48
Rowsley	23/5/59
Woodford Halse	13/67/63
Willesden	19/6/64
Rose Grove	17/7/65

Withdrawn w/e 23/3/68

Staveley (Barrow Hill) 8F 8081 (its block style front number had given way to a serif version by 1947) in the shed yard at Peterborough (Spital Bridge) about 1938. What looks like a novel addition to the boiler top behind the dome is in fact a distant detail of the sand house chimney.

As 48081 with cabside star at Stockport Edgeley MPD, 4 July 1959. The huge sign at the left announces the imminent electrification Manchester-Crewe. D. Forsyth, ColourRail

Shunting in the yard at Todmorden station goods yard when a Rose Grove engine, 20 February 1967. It never got AWS. Norman Preedy.

48081

48082

Built as 8082 at the Vulcan Foundry Ltd 11th January 1937
Renumbered 48082 w/e 19/6/48

Improvements and modifications
27/1/63 Fitting Automatic Warning System
27/1/63 Modifications to tube cleaner pipe and fittings

Repairs

16/11/38-5/12/38**LS**	49,048	
28/10/39-11/11/39**LO**	73,970	
18/5/40-30/5/40**LS**	87,285	
3/1/41-15/1/41**LO**	104,271	
10/2/41-28/2/41**LO**	105,640	
27/10/41-14/11/41**HG**	125,303	
27/3/43-6/5/43**LS**	34,437	
30/6/44-14/7/44**HS**	63,419	
12/11/45-20/12/45**LS**	37,721	
12/11/46-22/11/46**LO**	62,855	Crewe
17/5/48-19/6/48**HG**	30,038	Crewe
27/11/50-28/12/50**LI**	67,560	Crewe
1/9/52-16/9/52**LC[EO]**	51,357	Shed
13/3/53-28/4/53**HG**	65,991	Derby
8/6/55-30/6/55**LI**	63,052	Derby
30/4/58-13/6/58**HG**	66,857	Derby
27/11/60-23/12/60**LI**	70,323	Horwich

Noted at Works: Horwich 12/62

Boilers

No.9589	14/11/41 from	8033
No.9628	19/6/48 from	8050
No.11205	28/4/53	
No.11824	13/6/58	

Tender
LMS 9447 11/1/37

Sheds

Staveley	16/1/37
Wellingborough	28/7/45
Toton	6/7/55
Westhouses	13/8/55
Toton	22/9/62
Kettering	11/1/64
Wellingborough	15/2/64

Withdrawn w/e 15/4/67

48082 at Leicester MPD on 7 October 1962; once again (see opposite) it has had attention to the smokebox. RailOnline

48083

Built as 8083 at the Vulcan Foundry Ltd 2nd January 1937
Renumbered 48083 w/e 3/7/48

Improvements and modifications
1/11/52 Removal of sand guns and equipment
13/7/57 Modified pistons for continuous blowdown valves

Repairs

18/1/39-17/2/39**LS**	54,135	
31/1/40-13/2/40**LO**	77,473	
10/8/40-22/8/40**LO**	89,455	
21/11/40-5/12/40**LS**	98,011	
20/5/42-9/6/42**HG**	161,077	
28/9/43-4/10/43**LO**	36,721	
23/3/44-12/4/44**HS**	49,118	
11/10/44-26/10/44**LO**	13,249	
25/3/46-25/4/46**HS**	44,101	
3/6/48-3/7/48**HS**	52,039	Crewe
9/6/50-27/6/50**HG**	49,241	Crewe
17/9/52-17/10/52**LI**	47,998	Horwich
30/7/54-3/9/54**HG**	40,691	Crewe
2/10/56-18/10/56**LC[EO]**	48,004	Rugby
8/6/57-2/7/57**HI**	62,397	Derby
16/7/60-23/9/60**HG**	71,581	Derby

Boilers

No.9605	9/6/42	from	8060
No.12317	25/4/46	new	
No.13208	27/6/50	from	8744
No.11804	3/9/54		
No.12001	23/9/60		

Tenders

LMS 9448	2/1/37
LMS 9934	4/4/44

Sheds

Westhouses	2/1/37
Canklow	26/5/51
Derby	9/1/54
Westhouses	10/9/66
Annesley	8/10/66

Stored serviceable
28/6/65-11/10/65
8/8/66-12/9/66

Withdrawn w/e 12/11/66

48082, filthy except for the smokebox (clearly there has been some work at the front end – there was a Light Intermediate around this time) works a train at Mill Hill around 1950-51.

48083 at Derby shed, 26 June 1955.

Still at Derby a decade on, 2 January 1966. J.B. Hall, ColourRail

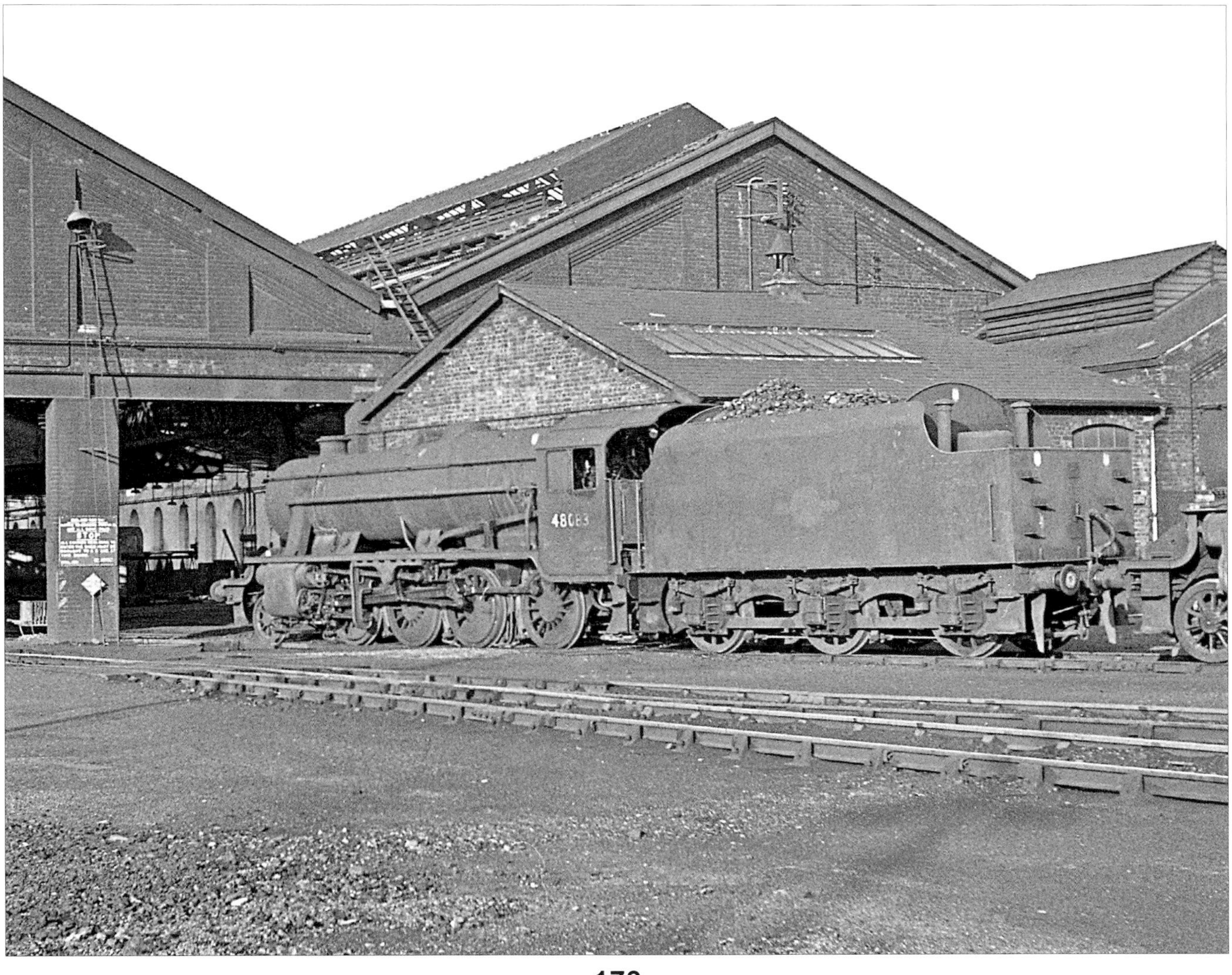

48084

Built as 8084 at the Vulcan Foundry Ltd 13th January 1937
Renumbered 48084 w/e 2/7/49

Improvements and modifications
8/9/51 Blowdown discharge pipe entered into ashpan
26/12/53 Removal of sand guns
31/12/60 AWS

Repairs

20/4/39-1/6/39**LS**	58,197	
23/4/40-15/6/40**HO**	86,411	
8/9/41-1/10/41**LS**	31,881	
6/7/42-15/8/42**HG**	48,690	
14/12/44-4/1/45**HS**	51,141	
17/10/45-17/11/45**HO**	19,739	
14/3/47-8/5/47**LS**	33,079	Crewe
7/6/49-2/7/49**LI**	47,633	Horwich
30/6/51-25/8/51**HG**	45,569	Horwich
30/8/51-6/9/51**NC**	11,210	Horwich
20/11/53-16/12/53**HI**	55,593	Horwich
20/1/55-10/2/55**LC**	22,762	Horwich
28/2/56-5/4/56**HG**	47,027	Derby
9/7/58-25/8/58**HI**	54,680	Derby
29/11/60-14/12/60**LC[EO]**	42,358	Horwich
22/6/61-1/9/61**HG**	62,813	Horwich

Noted at Works: Darlington 12/64

Boilers

No.9837	15/6/40	from	8022
No.9609	15/8/42	from	8064
No.9584	17/11/45	from	8090
No.10506	25/8/51	from	48063
No.13234	5/4/56		
No.12011	1/9/61		

Tender

LMS 949	13/1/37

Sheds

Normanton	16/1/37
Wakefield	15/6/57
Stourton	7/9/57
Royston	28/1/67

Withdrawn 11/67

48084 at Saltley MPD, 13 February 1966. Darlington-applied 10in numbers, AWS.

48084 at Royston shed on 5 February 1967. It had been transferred there a few days before; it was only its fourth shed, and all were in a particular part of Yorkshire. Norman Preedy.

48085

Built as 8085 at the Vulcan Foundry Ltd 12th January 1937
Renumbered 48085 w/e 17/4/48

Improvements and modifications
2/1/54 Removal of sand guns
10/9/60 AWS

Repairs

23/3/39-31/3/39**LO**	55,544	
31/10/39-17/11/39**LS**	71,532	
17/1/41-21/2/41**HG**	105,047	
8/11/41-13/12/41**LS**	15,960	
Mileage from 13/12/41 to 27/4/42 not available		
3/7/44-15/8/44**HS**	88,377	
27/12/45-26/1/46**HG**	57,685	
10/3/48-17/4/48**LS**	64,768	Crewe
31/10/49-23/11/49**LI**	40,253	Crewe
16/9/51-5/10/51**HG**	49,756	Crewe
7/12/53-31/12/53**HI**	57,924	Crewe
15/5/56-14/6/56**HG**	61,704	Crewe
21/3/58-27/3/58**LC[EO]**	43,232	Rugby
10/4/59-14/5/59**LI**	68,237	Crewe
23/8/60-7/9/60**NC[EO]**	35,198	Crewe
18/9/61-23/10/61**HG**	59,558	Crewe

Noted at Works: Crewe 6/65

LMS engine histories do not consistently/clearly record requisitions. In summary, 8085 (WD 618) was requisitioned by the WD 11/41 and shipped out of the country, only to return when the vessel got into trouble. So it never did go abroad.

Boilers

No.9633	21/2/41	from	8088
No.10089	26/1/46	from	8063
No.11744	5/10/51		
No.12012	14/6/56		
No.10919	23/10/61		

Tender

LMS 9450	12/1/37

Sheds

Normanton	16/1/37
Into shops	9/11/41
To Dockside	26/12/41
Returned temp. to LMS from WD	
Converted from oil to coal burner	
Into shops	7/4/42
Out of shops	27/4/42
Motherwell	2/5/42
Returned to LMS	15/5/43
Motherwell	3/7/43
Kingmoor	11/5/46
Royston[o/l]	7/12/46
Royston	28/12/46
Crewe South	19/6/48
Rugby	26/11/49
Crewe South	17/9/60
Willesden	23/6/62
Bletchley	15/12/62
Birkenhead	15/10/63
Saltley	2/11/63
Stoke	31/12/66
Northwich	29/5/67

Withdrawn w/e 12/8/67

48085 working hard at St Andrews, Birmingham, about 1964. As 8085, it had been requisitioned and put aboard the SS **PENTRIDGE HALL** as WD 618 for the abortive voyage from Swansea. Like all eight it was put into good order at St Rollox and worked in Scotland for the rest of the War. Norman Preedy.

48085 at Northwich MPD, June 1967. Note Ivatt pattern top feed cover; introduced in 1948, it had a protective fairing over new-type clackboxes, the screws of which projected above the centre portion. An obvious contrast to the earlier variety on the 8F behind.

48088

Built as 8088 at the Vulcan Foundry Ltd 20th January 1937
Renumbered 48088 w/e 13/8/49

Repairs

15/6/39-21/8/39**LS**	55,550	
25/11/40-3/1/41**HS**	92,691	
8/11/41-6/12/41**LS**	24,104	
1/7/43-7/8/43**LS**	51,096	
1/6/44-24/6/44**HS**	87,076	
25/6/45-24/8/45**HG**	42,892	
25/10/46-22/11/46**LS**	54,806	St Rollox
23/6/48-3/9/48**LS**	34,651	Rugby
1/3/49-10/3/49**LC**	8,275	Shed
20/6/49-13/8/49**HG**	13,250	Crewe
16/10/50-26/10/50**LC**	23,475	Shed
14/3/51-11/4/51**LI**	30,703	Crewe
28/6/52-15/8/52**HG**	22,538	Derby
17/11/54-9/12/54**HI**	43,500	Derby
13/12/56-30/1/57**HG**	38,572	Derby
3/4/59-22/5/59**HI**	41,202	Derby
6/9/61-9/10/61**HG**	55,205	Crewe

Noted at Works: Darlington 2/65

LMS engine histories do not consistently/clearly record requisitions. In summary, 8088 (WD 620) was requisitioned by the WD 11/41 and shipped out of the country, only to return when the vessel got into trouble. So it never did go abroad.

Boilers

No.9617	3/1/41	from	8072
No.10437	24/8/45	from	8102
No.11522	13/8/49	from	8407
No.9640	5/8/52		
No.11777	30/1/57		
No.13250	30/9/61		

Tender

LMS 9453 20/1/37

Sheds

Royston	23/1/37
Normanton	3/8/40
Into shops	9/11/41
To Dockside	26/12/41
Returned temp. to LMS from WD	
Converted from oil to coal burner	
Into shops	20/4/42
Out of shops	7/5/42
Polmadie	9/5/42
Returned to LMS	15/5/43
Polmadie	26/6/43
Perth	24/6/44
Kingmoor	11/5/46
Royston	28/12/46
Mansfield	11/10/47
Kirkby	9/4/60
Rowsley	20/4/63
Woodford Halse	20/7/63
Willesden	19/6/65
Bolton	17/7/65
Buxton	14/8/65

Withdrawn w/e 17/12/66

8088, another 'survivor' which remained on board the SS PENTRIDGE HALL and made it safely to Glasgow. After working from some Scottish sheds it finally got back 'home' to Royston at the end of 1946.

48088 (48319 at rear) at Toton on 27 September 1959; an Ivatt-style form of top feed cover, steam cleaning cock low down. W.A.C. Smith, transporttreasury

48088 at Southall shed on the WR, 8 November 1964; top feed cover has reverted to the norm, steam cock now has external feed. Norman Preedy.

48089

Built as 8089 at the Vulcan Foundry Ltd 26th January 1937
Renumbered 48089 w/e 6/8/49

Improvements and modifications
29/11/52 Removal of sand guns
29/11/52 Blowdown discharge pipe entered in ashpan
23/2/63 Fitting Automatic Warning System

Repairs

12/12/38-29/12/38**LO**	50,775	
20/3/39-30/3/39**LO**	56,441	
15/6/39-26/6/39**LO**	60,795	
6/10/39-3/11/39**LS**	69,669	
15/7/40-26/7/40**LO**	88,874	
28/8/40-5/10/40**LO**	91,069	
27/12/40-22/2/41**HS**	97,591	
17/8/42-12/9/42**LS**	38,892	
27/8/43-25/9/43**LO**	62,539	
6/12/43-4/1/44**HS**	67,125	
1/11/45-24/11/45**HG**	38,819	
31/5/47-1/7/47**LO**	35,861	Shed
5/1/47-20/12/47**LS**	9,371	Crewe
9/6/49-6/8/49**HI**	30,042	Horwich
31/10/50-1/12/50**HG**	26,846	Horwich
4/10/51-26/10/51**HC**	21,244	Horwich
21/10/52-22/11/52**HI**	41,286	Horwich
27/9/54-3/11/54**HI**	42,619	Horwich
13/3/57-17/4/57**HG**	49,355	Horwich
1/2/58-21/2/58**LC[EO]**	17,431	Horwich
30/6/59-11/8/59**LI**	7,579	Horwich
31/10/60-12/12/60**HI**	39,064	Horwich

Noted at Works: Horwich 1/63

Boilers

No.9637	22/2/41	from	8092
No.9610	24/11/45	from	8075
No.13187	1/12/50	from	48723
No.11196	17/4/57		

Tender

LMS 9454	26/1/37

Sheds

Peterborough	30/1/37
Nottingham	6/9/38
Heaton Mersey	21/1/39
Hasland	1/2/58
Wellingborough	7/7/62
Heaton Mersey	18/8/62

Withdrawn w/e 19/2/66

Heaton Mersey's 8089 passing Cheadle station with hoppers in June 1939; block style front number. W. Potter.

Now with serif style number, at home at Heaton Mersey in August 1948. 19D was the original LMS code for Heaton Mersey.

Now with standard BR Gill sans numbering and AWS, again at Heaton Mersey MPD, 12 January 1964. The loco spent the great part of its time allocated to the Stockport shed, in two separate spells. Noel A. Machell.

48090

Built as 8090 at the Vulcan Foundry Ltd 28th January 1937
Renumbered 48090 w/e 29/4/50

Improvements and modifications
17/5/52 Discharge continuous blowdown into ashpan
27/2/54 Removal of sand guns
10/9/60 AWS

Repairs

9/12/39-22/12/39**LS**	71,365	
2/9/41-27/10/41**HG**	120,754	
12/9/42-14/10/42**TRO**		
31/5/43-10/7/43**LS**	64,287	
8/8/44-4/9/44**LO**	103,130	
14/5/45-13/6/45**HG**	127,389	
17/9/47-4/11/47**LS**	68,585	Crewe
21/1/49-2/3/49**L C**	25,096	Rugby
31/3/50-26/4/50**HG**	49,843	Crewe
1/4/52-16/5/52**LI**	46,665	Rugby
8/2/54-26/2/54**HI**	42,925	Crewe
24/1/56-6/2/56**LC[EO]**	47,279	Rugby
5/7/56-11/8/56**HG**	58,115	Crewe
13/4/58-21/4/58**LC[EO]**	47,495	Rugby
23/3/59-21/4/59**LI**	70,851	Crewe
7/8/60-22/8/60**NC[EO]**	34,352	Crewe
16/1/61-23/2/61**HC**	44,235	Crewe

Noted at Works: Crewe 9/65

Boilers

No.9584	27/10/41	from	8039
No.11061	13/6/45	from	8093
No.12142	26/4/50	From	8398
No.10089	11/8/56		

Tender

LMS 9455	28/1/37

Sheds

Canklow	30/1/37
Sheffield	11/1/41
Leeds	13/9/41
Staveley	24/1/48
Northampton	19/6/48
Mold Jct	12/1/63
Chester	23/4/66
Newton Heath	25/3/67
Bolton	24/2/68

Withdrawn w/e 6/4/68

Two sides to Mold Junction's 48090 a long way from home at Bristol Barrow Road MPD, in the spring of 1965. Ivatt top feed cover.

48092

Built as 8092 at the Vulcan foundry Ltd 9th February 1937
Renumbered 48092 w/e 4/12/48

Improvements and modifications
17/5/52 New type piston head fastening
30/12/62 Fitting Automatic Warning System

Repairs

18/10/38-8/11/38**LO**	34,608	
11/7/39-29/8/39**LS**	44,819	
27/4/40-14/5/40**LO**	59,968	
3/6/40-26/6/40**LO**	62,933	
26/10/40-27/11/40**HS**	68,94	
4/9/41-29/10/41**HG**	15,650	
24/2/42-31/3/42**HS**	6,970	
12/4/43-8/5/43**LS**	24,803	
3/4/44-14/4/44**TRO**		
30/12/44-15/1/45**LO**	57,302	
23/6/45-27/7/45**HG**	72,368	
20/2/47-28/3/47**LS**	33,970	Crewe
19/5/48-4/6/48**LO**	25,642	Shed
1/11/48-1/12/48**LS**	17,087	Crewe
14/6/49-2/7/49**LC**	11,783	Crewe
11/4/50-17/4/50**TRO**		shed
25/6/50-7/8/50**HG**	32,728	Crewe
27/2/52-1/4/52**LI**	36,609	Derby
2/9/53-21/9/53**LC[EO]**	32,427	Shed
14/12/53-20/1/54**HI**	37,767	Derby
9/8/55-7/9/55**HG**	34,420	Derby
2/10/57-24/10/57**HI**	45,575	Derby
18/4/60-26/5/60**HG**	55,811	Derby
20/9/60-6/10/60**LC[EO]**	8,241	Derby

Noted at Works: Horwich 11/62; Crewe 5/66

Boilers

No.9604	27/11/40	from	8059
No.9616	29/10/41	from	8022
No.9615	31/3/42	from	8066
No.10433	27/7/45	from	8098
No.11481	7/8/50	from	8526
No.11851	7/9/55		
No.12067	26/5/60		

Tender
LMS 9457 9/2/37

Shed
Kirkby 13/2/37

Withdrawn w/e 30/4/66

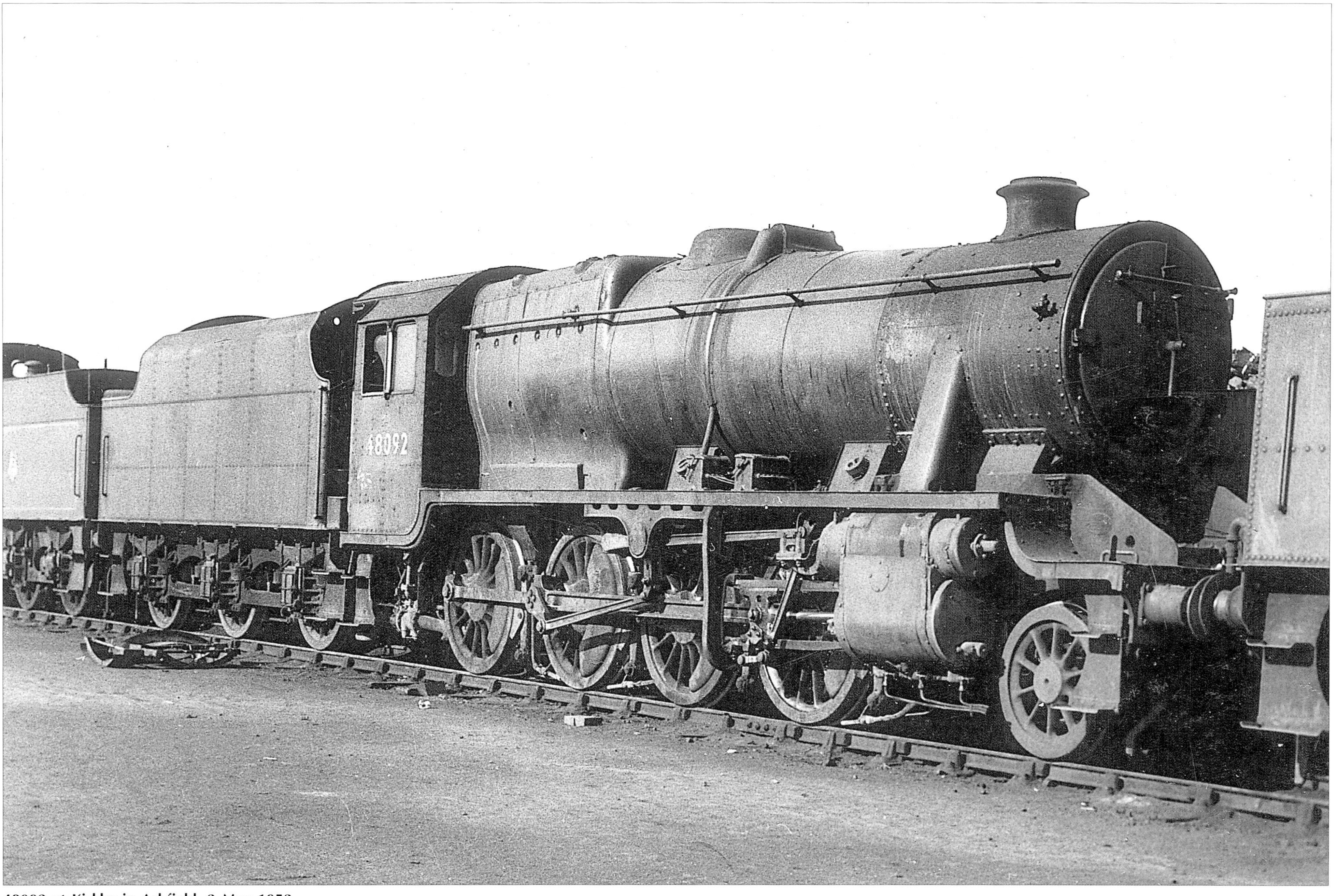

48092 at Kirkby in Ashfield, 2 May 1953.

48093

Built as 8093 at the Vulcan Foundry Ltd 9th Feb 1937
Renumbered 48093 w/e 12/2/49

Improvements and modifications
12/7/52 Removal of sand guns
3/12/60 AWS

Repairs

8/12/38-21/12/38**LO**	41,274	
20/6/39-8/9/39**LS**	51,816	
9/11/39-13/12/39**LO**	55,740	
11/10/40-5/11/40**HO**	72,968	
9/10/41-18/10/41**LO**	16,351	
10/11/41-20/12/41**LS**	22,232	
11/8/43-10/9/43**LS**	70,107	
1/10/43-8/12/43**LO**	72,706	
6/11/44-22/12/44**HS**	123,273	
12/3/45-28/3/45**LO**	11,055	
5/6/46-3/8/46**LS**	67,422	
16/12/48-12/2/49**HG**	55,731	Crewe
30/8/50-23/9/50**LI**	39,414	Horwich
5/6/52-4/7/52**HI**	40,083	Horwich
5/1/53-2/2/53**LC[EO]**	12,308	Horwich
6/11/54-9/12/54**HG**	54,646	Horwich
4/12/56-5/1/57**LI**	47,320	Horwich
18/7/58-3/9/58**HG**	37,665	Horwich
11/11/60**NC[EO]**	45,502	Horwich

Noted at Works: Darlington 9/65

LMS engine histories do not consistently/clearly record requisitions. In summary, 8093 (WD 621) was requisitioned by the WD 11/41 and shipped out of the country, only to return when the vessel got into trouble. So it never did go abroad.

Boilers

No.11061	5/11/40 new
No.10496	22/12/44 ex Crewe
No.13053	12/2/49 new
No.11722	9/12/54
No.11780	3/9/58

Tenders

LMS 9458	9/2/37
LMS 9444	27/12/44
LMS 9889	20/3/45
LMS 9877	6/9/46

Sheds

Kirkby	13/2/37
Into shops	7/11/41
To Dockside	26/12/41
Returned temp. to LMS from WD	
Converted from oil to coal burner	
Into shops	9/5/42
Out of shops	13/7/42
Polmadie	18/7/42
Returned to LMS	15/5/43
Polmadie	26/6/43
Perth	24/6/44
Kingmoor	11/5/46
Saltley	21/6/47
Royston	12/11/49
Mirfield	13/6/59
Royston	28/11/59
Stourton	27/3/65
Royston	28/1/67

Withdrawn 11/67

8093 at Derby shed, 14 March 1937, before the ill-fated voyage of the SS PENTRIDGE HALL. Its subsequent wartime work in Scotland saw it one the few – maybe the only – 8F to work from Perth. Compare numbering/lettering style and configuration to page 23 for example.

Royston's 48093, carrying that shed's pre-1956 LMR code of 20C; on passing to the NER it became 55D. The date is not given but with nothing on the tender we could be as far back as 1949 (there was a Heavy General early in that year). The location is not known either, but it certainly has the look of Royston.

48093, now a Stourton loco, at Derby shed on 10 October 1965. The rumples in the tender match the state of the cylinder casing; AWS conduit. The large numerals have been acquired at the NER's main works Darlington. Washout plugs prominent on boiler barrel top front and aft; the atomiser cock cover 'dart' is high up in conventional place but earlier on it was – perhaps uniquely – positioned lower down without a protective cover. This former position is marked by the little bracelet of bolts a foot or so below the atomiser cock. This earlier state of affairs is apparent in the view of 8093 at the end of the War in the Introductory Notes.

48094

Built as 8094 at the Vulcan Foundry Ltd 17th February 1937
Renumbered 48094 w/e 24/12/49

Sold to H M Government – withdrawn from ex-LMS stock w/e 23/12/44
Purchased (WD 606) from Ministry of Supply – returned to ex-LMS stock w/e 24/12/49

Improvements and modifications
8/10/60 AWS

Repairs
8/3/38-19/3/38**LO** 25,157
14/1/39-4/2/39**LS** 44,749
16/10/39-16/11/39**LO** 60,613
31/12/40-1/1/41**TRO**
29/4/41-4/6/41**HS** 96,842
4/10/41 repaired & prepared for overseas by Southern Rly Co
20/12/49-10/1/50**HG** Crewe
[Overseas mileage unknown]
9/2/53-18/3/53**LI** 80,073 Horwich
22/6/55-6/8/55**HG** 52,410 Crewe
1/9/57-21/9/57**LI** 48,984 Crewe
5/3/60-3/6/60**HG** 46,272 Horwich
1/9/60-16/9/60**NC** 6,578 Horwich
Noted at Works: Derby 4/62

Boilers
No.9620 4/6/41 from 8075
No.10795 10/1/50 from 48249
No.11580 6/8/55
No.11519 3/6/60

Tenders
LMS 9459 9/2/37
No.10314 20/12/49
No.10238 23/6/55

Sheds
Royston 30/2/37
Westhouses 16/10/37
Into shops 4/10/41
To Dockside 28/12/41
Crewe South 24/12/49
Mold Jct 18/2/50
Birkenhead 20/10/51
Speke Jct 17/10/53
Warrington 11/2/56
Birkenhead 29/9/62
Mold Jct 20/7/63

Withdrawn w/e 25/9/65

8094 before shipment abroad as 606, at Crewe South. It worked in Persia on the 'back door' to the Soviet Union and then (a reading of the runes in Rowledge's *Heavy Goods Engines of the War Department* Volume 2 indicates) came back on the ingeniously fashioned narrow gauge wagons, first to Baghdad, then Palestine/Egypt.

Back in Crewe in the old Carriage Shed as a near-wreck and numbered WD 70606 (it also still carried its old Persian number 41-230) on 19 June 1949. For the 8Fs it was a long way home, as might be expected. Apart from those drowned deep, some were withdrawn and cannibalised for spare parts while others stayed.

Finally as 48094, a Warrington Dallam engine since 1956, in for the fitting of AWS at Horwich, on 3 September 1960. Star on cabside. D. Forsyth, ColourRail

48095

Built as 8095 at the Vulcan Foundry Ltd 25th February 1937
Renumbered 48095 w/e 11/6/49

Improvements and modifications
28/11/53 Removal of sand guns
5/10/57 Provide Metaflex joints to boiler top feed
27/1/63 Fitting Automatic warning System

Repairs

8/5/39-8/6/39**LS**	57,481	
25/5/40-4/6/40**LO**	86,640	
7/10/40-18/10/40**LS**	96,257	
28/4/42-15/5/42**HG**	130,127	
23/2/44-4/3/44**LO**	45,582	
7/7/44-4/8/44**HS**	50,077	
28/9/45-19/10/45**LS**	32,675	
9/12/46-14/1/47**LO**	61,534	Crewe
27/6/47-4/8/47**HG**	72,934	Crewe
24/5/49-11/6/49**HI**	46,888	Horwich
15/5/51-6/6/51**LI**	48,978	Horwich
27/10/53-20/11/53**HG**	57,432	Crewe
13/3/54-7/4/54**LC[EO]**	8,454	Derby
6/4/56-25/4/56**HI**	55,800	Derby
31/8/57-2/10/57**HG**	31,297	Derby
11/5/60-10/6/60**LI**	71,064	Horwich

Noted at Works: Horwich 12/62

Boilers

No.9832	15/5/42	from	8017
No.11302	4/8/47	from	8225

Tender

LMS 9460	25/2/37

Sheds

Staveley	27/2/37
Bath	4/1/41
Royston	5/7/41
Hasland	6/11/54
Toton	22/9/62
Saltley	6/4/63

Withdrawn w/e 20/2/65

48095 with tanks at Churchdown, near Gloucester, 21 November 1964. Norman Preedy.

48095 at Saltley MPD, 23 August 1964. It's been in works for attention to the front end from the glossy look of the smokebox, while that top feed cover's been off as well. AWS battery box open and empty. L.W. Perkins.

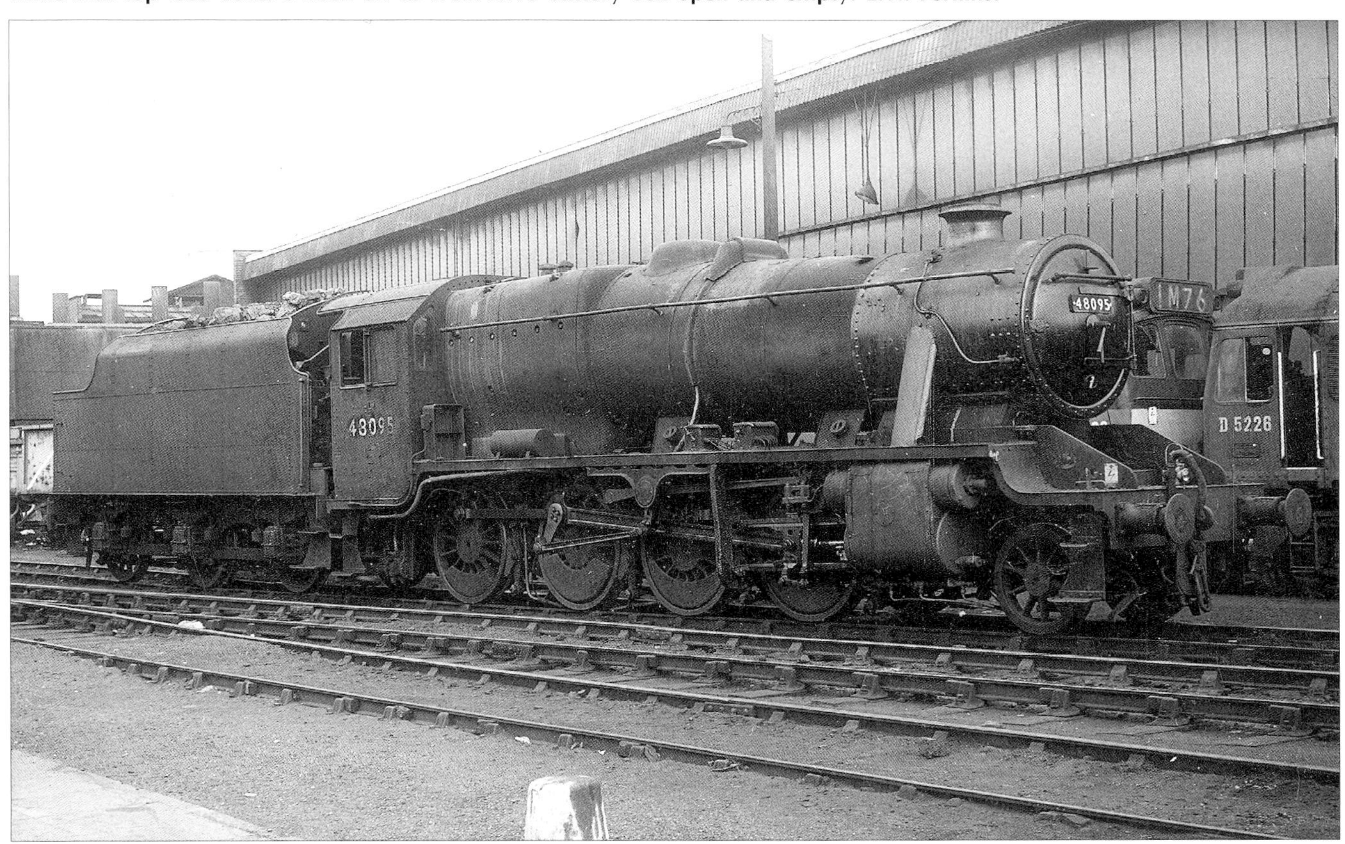

48096

Built as 8096 at Crewe Works 20th December 1938
Renumbered 48096 w/e 19/2/49

Improvements and modifications
27/2/43 Fitting Griffiths laminated springs to coupled wheels
8/7/44 Fitting Griffiths laminated springs to coupled wheels

Repairs

29/5/39-31/5/39**TRO**		
3/6/41-19/6/41**LS**	74,506	
5/5/42-13/5/42**LO**	99,799	
23/10/43-12/11/43**HG**	131,859	
18/9/45-18/10/45**HS**	36,026	
24/4/46-1/5/46**LO**	12,097	
9/10/46-26/10/46**LO**	22,005	Derby
2/6/47-5/7/47**LS**	39,465	Derby
19/7/47-22/8/47**LO**	389	Derby
25/12/48-16/2/49**HG**	30,869	Crewe
21/11/50-9/12/50**LI**	39,730	Crewe
7/7/52-14/8/52**HI**	34,579	Derby
25/3/54-5/5/54**HG**	36,906	Derby
25/2/56-14/3/56**LI**	39,950	Derby
13/3/58-2/5/58**HG**	43,816	Derby
12/7/60-20/9/60**HI**	48,432	Derby
25/1/63-20/2/63**HI**		Crewe

Boilers

No.10438	12/11/43 from	8103
No.11850	16/2/49 from	8703
No.11570	5/5/54	
No.9611	2/5/58	

Tender
LMS 9728 20/12/38

Sheds

Willesden	7/1/39
Kirkby	11/10/41

Withdrawn w/e 30/10/65

Willesden's 8096 a long way from home at the tumble-down ancient shed at Carlisle Upperby on 31 August 1939. Intriguingly it carries one of those paper 'special' codes on the front, W523. W was the designation for Western Division trains as opposed to C Central, M Midland etc. The higher numbers were generally those allocated to specials and might be used over and over again. Most of the main line trains had a W code, but they were not always carried on the engines as in most cases everybody that needed to know knew what the trains were. However, in the case of specials it was usual to carry them to avoid confusion, like sending them the wrong way at junctions! So somewhere that day, 8096 had had charge of a passenger train.

48096 at Chinley, on 17 May 1952. Norman Preedy.

48096 at Shrewsbury about 1964. It was one of the least-travelled 8Fs, in terms of sheds as it were; after two years at Willesden from new it went to Kirkby in 1941 and stayed there till withdrawal in 1965. F. Rowley.

48097

Built as 8097at Crewe Works 29th December 1938
Renumbered 48097 w/e 26/2/49

Improvements and modifications
14/7/62 AWS

Repairs

3/9/41-26/9/41**LS**	86,414	
31/7/43-31/8/43**HG**	130,811	
28/9/44-3/10/44**LO**	21,524	
13/4/45-26/5/45**LS**	31,552	
30/5/46-11/6/46**LO**	52,887	
28/1/47-6/3/47**HS**	68,435	Crewe
25/12/48-26/2/49**HG**	38,693	Crewe
20/9/50-9/10/50**LI**	33,873	Crewe
10/10/51-22/10/51**LC[EO]**	24,840	Shed
2/4/52-28/4/52**HI**	35,260	Derby
6/4/54-17/5/54**HG**	41,231	Derby
26/5/56-12/6/56**LI**	44,682	Derby
3/9/57-26/9/57**HI**	25,569	Derby
3/12/59-15/1/60**HG**	47,236	Derby
28/7/61-6/9/61**LC[EO]**	38,396	Crewe
29/5/62-21/6/62**HI**		Derby

Boilers

No.9616	31/8/43	from	8092
No.11794	26/2/49	from	8659
No.11999	17/5/54		
No.11192	15/1/60		

Tender

LMS 9729	29/12/38

Sheds

Willesden	7/1/39
Wellingborough	1/11/41
Kirkby	31/1/42

Withdrawn w/e 24/7/65

8097 with serif number, taking water about 1939.

48097 late on at Kirkby MPD in 1964; it was another 8F that came to the little coalfield shed early on and stayed for twenty or more years. Still with 'block' style front number. J.C. Haydon.

48098

Built as 8098 at Crewe Works 2nd January 1939
Renumbered as 48098 w/e 22/1/49

Improvements and modifications
30/11/57 Modified pistons for continuous blowdown
16/6/62 AWS

Repairs

24/6/41-22/7/41**LS**	80,689	
24/6/42-1/7/42**LO**	103,527	
29/12/42-4/1/43**LO**	114,770	
22/2/43-18/3/43**LS**	117,429	
15/1/45-20/2/45**HG**	150,665	
16/12/46-14/1/47**HS**	38,035	Crewe
19/1/48-26/1/48**LO**	21,681	Shed
1/1/49-21/1/49**LI**	41,236	Crewe
5/8/50-1/9/50**HG**	35,828	Crewe
27/3/52-28/4/52**LI**	33,084	Derby
18/10/53-11/11/53**HI**	31,913	Derby
23/11/53-2/12/53**NC[Rect][EO]**	206	Derby
22/8/55-16/9/55**HG**	38,674	Derby
22/10/57-7/11/57**LI**	44,896	Derby
26/1/60-14/3/60**HI**	47,938	Derby

Noted at Works: Derby 5/62; Horwich 2/64

Boilers

No.10498	20/2/45	from	8115
No.11066	14/9/50	from	8080
No.9633	16/9/55		

Tender
LMS 9730 2/1/39

Sheds

Willesden	7/1/39
Kirkby	11/10/41
Speke Jct	25/2/67

Withdrawn w/e 11/3/67

Immaculate 48098 at Derby shed at an unrecorded date; clearly the loco is ex-works after a Heavy General and will literally shine amongst the other 8Fs when it returns to Kirkby in a day or two. It got AWS in 1962, by which time it would have been overdue for a Heavy repair, so this may indeed be 1962. D98 is not much help in dating the picture; it was built in 1961. Norman Preedy.

48098 working powerfully at Buxworth Junction, 28 June 1952. Norman Preedy.

48099

Built as 8099 at Crewe Works 11th January 1939
Renumbered 48099 w/e 17/4/48

Improvements and modifications
3/12/60 AWS

Repairs

3/9/41-1/10/41**LS**	85,984	
7/9/42-6/10/42**HS**	113,224	
16/9/43-26/9/43**LO**	23,358	
8/5/44-30/5/44**HG**	30,558	
11/7/45-18/8/45**LS**	26,630	
1/8/47-10/10/47**LS**	39,985	Rugby
12/3/48-15/4/48**LO**	8,027	Derby
26/5/49-2/7/49**HG**	30,734	Horwich
10/7/51-16/8/51**HI**	39,387	Crewe
5/5/54-8/6/54**HG**	60,289	Crewe
31/3/57-1/5/57**LI**	64,527	Horwich
19/1/60-10/3/60**HG**	62,979	Derby
10/11/60-29/11/60**NC[EO]**	20,365	Horwich

Noted at Works: Derby 3/62

Boilers

No.11284	30/5/44	from	8207
No.11540	2/7/49	from	8425
No.9840	8/6/54		
No.12022	10/3/60		

Tender

LMS 9731	11/1/39

Sheds

Willesden	21/1/39
Sheffield	11/10/41
Heaton Mersey	18/10/41
Toton	19/7/58
Nottingham	7/1/61
Annesley	22/9/62
Fleetwood	7/12/63

Withdrawn w/e 24/7/65

48099 at Nuneaton; the background suggests something of the look of the MPD, from the Coventry line, but that's just a feeling... The loco carries a Toton plate which marks the period as July 1958-January 1961. Norman Preedy.

8099 on a prodigious freight, near Bourne End on the LNW main line, days before War, on 19 August 1939. H.C. Casserley, courtesy R.M. Casserley.

48100

Built as 8100 at Crewe Works 16th January 1939
Renumbered 48100 w/e 6/11/48

Improvements and modifications
27/11/43 Fitting Griffiths laminated springs to coupled wheels
8/7/44 Fitting Griffiths laminated springs to coupled wheels

Repairs

8/4/41-26/4/41**LS**	73,478	
25/4/42-2/5/42**LO**	100,646	
28/10/43-13/11/43**HG**	132,133	
1/11/45-27/11/45**LS**	37,501	
18/3/47-6/5/47**LS**	62,723	Crewe
6/10/48-2/11/48**HS**	30,506	Crewe
31/5/50-19/6/50**LI**	35,080	Crewe
8/5/51-30/5/51**LC**	20,745	Crewe
28/5/52-19/6/52**HI**	42,370	Derby
3/2/54-4/3/54**HG**	28,122	Derby
2/12/55-19/12/55**LI**	40,982	Derby
19/2/58-18/4/58**HG**	45,931	Derby
28/3/60-11/5/60**LI**	44,834	Derby
11/9/62-29/9/62**HI**		Derby
2/10/63-18/10/63**LC**		Horwich
2/5/65-29/6/65**HI**		Darlington

Boilers

No.9623	13/11/43 from	8070
No.11517	2/11/48 from	8402
No.11823	4/3/54	
No.11630	18/4/58	

Tenders

LMS 9732	16/1/39
LMS 9942	no date
No.9910	11/6/52

Sheds

Willesden	21/1/39
Kirkby	11/10/41
Northwich	23/4/66

Withdrawn w/e 30/9/67

48100, another long-term Kirkby resident, got a Heavy repair and repaint at Darlington in May-June 1965, which left it looking smart and with large cab numbers when photographed at Heaton Mersey soon after. The coal stage is unmistakable in its profound dereliction.

48100 and 48528 hurry along the Mansfield Colliery branch on 28 January 1959, either to collect trains or to return home to Kirkby MPD.

48101

Built as 8101 at Crewe Works 18th January 1939
Renumbered 48101 w/e 5/6/48

Repairs

29/5/39-12/6/39**TRO**		
8/8/40-1/9/40**LS**	66,391	
7/9/42-25/9/42**LS**	115,684	
12/5/43-5/6/43**LO**	129,593	
12/10/44-2/11/44**HG**	157,982	
9/10/46-8/11/46**HS**	40,479	Crewe
23/4/48-31/5/48**LS**	37,553	Crewe
6/8/49-8/9/49**HG**	27,491	Crewe
22/3/51-21/4/51**LI**	33,906	Horwich
24/3/52-31/3/52**LC[EO]**	20,995	Shed
27/11/52-31/12/52**HG**	34,364	Derby
17/1/55-9/2/55**LI**	43,279	Derby
11/10/56-7/11/56**LI**	35,033	Derby
1/1/58-1/2/58**HG**	25,468	Crewe
23/1/61-8/3/61**LI**	71,501	Crewe
20/12/62-11/1/63**GO**		Crewe

Boilers

No.10503	2/11/44	from	8120
No.10432	8/9/49	from	8217
No.11353	31/12/52		
No.13205	1/2/58		

Tender

LMS 9733	18/1/39

Sheds

Willesden	21/1/39
Toton	23/3/40
Willesden	26/10/40
Normanton	1/11/41
Kirkby	11/10/47
Saltley	24/2/59
Woodford Halse	21/3/64
Saltley	1/1/66

Withdrawn w/e 20/8/66

48101 light engine at Woodford Halse (where it would later be allocated) on 25 June 1961. The station is in the background which would mean the view is north, with the shed lying in the far distance, beyond fields and a couple of roads, a fifteen minute walk on cinder paths. It might be that 48101 has arrived on a freight from the north and is now reversing to the shed. RailOnline

48101 winds through Chester with a Warrington-Birkenhead freight in 1960. RailOnline

48102

Built as 8102 at Crewe Works 24th January 1939
Renumbered 48102 w/e 14/1/50

Improvements and modifications
30/12/51 Discharge of continuous blowdown into ashpan
30/12/51 Removal of sand guns
23/2/63 Fitting Automatic Warning System

Repairs

14/3/41-3/4/41**LS**	71,568	
26/3/42-16/4/42**LO**	102,365	
9/3/43-25/3/43**LS**	127,328	
7/3/45-24/3/45**HG**	171,483	
20/12/46-18/1/47**LS**	40,019	Crewe
30/11/48-13/1/49**LI**	44,591	Rugby
11/11/49-13/1/50**HG**	18,794	Crewe
6/11/51-13/12/51**HI**	45,762	Horwich
2/1/52-26/1/52**NC[EO]**	533	Horwich
18/9/53-21/10/53**LI**	43,365	Derby
13/10/55-16/11/55**HG**	47,207	Derby
31/12/57-28/1/58**HI**	48,147	Derby
2/5/60-2/8/60**HG**	51,277	Derby
8/1/63-31/1/63**LI**		Horwich

Boilers

No.10499	24/3/45	from	8116
No.11659	13/1/50	from	8434
No.11465	16/11/55		
No.9340	2/8/60		

Tender
LMS 9734 24/1/39

Sheds

Willesden	28/1/39
Westhouses	1/11/41
Nottingham	1/10/49
Kirkby	7/7/56

Withdrawn w/e 21/8/65

48102 with a long line of iron ore tipplers, a line so long they can only be empties, at Ashton on 6 July 1961. RailOnline

48103

Built as 8103 at Crewe Works 31st January 1939
Renumbered 48103 w/e 4/6/49

Improvements and modifications
13/6/53 Removal of sand guns

Repairs

8/4/41-25/4/41**LS**	65,003	
19/5/42-2/6/42**LO**	96,157	
30/7/43-3/9/43**HG**	125,401	
21/5/45-22/6/45**LS**	50,781	
15/7/46-25/7/46**LO**	81,257	
17/1/47-5/3/47**HS**	92,526	Crewe
9/5/49-4/6/49**LI**	54,217	Horwich
3/4/51-30/4/51**LI**	46,302	Horwich
9/5/51-10/5/51**Rect**	Nil	Horwich
23/3/53-27/5/53**HG**	46,20	Horwich
21/3/55-22/4/55**HI**	46,160	Horwich
3/7/57-15/8/57**LI**	43,633	Horwich
20/2/60-22/4/60**HG**	47,714	Horwich
21/11/62-14/12/62**HI**		Horwich
11/12/64-12/1/65**HC**		Crewe

Boilers

No.10086	3/9/43	from	8003
No.11291	5/3/47	from	8214
No.11184	27/5/53		
No.11273	22/4/60		

Tender

LMS 9735	31/1/39

Sheds

Willesden	4/2/39
Royston	1/11/41
Staveley	10/12/55
Patricroft	8/12/62
Derby	25/5/63
Kirkby	22/6/63
Derby	16/11/63

Stored serviceable
28/6/65-11/10/65
1/8/66

Withdrawn w/e 8/10/66

48103 in the all-over grime sooner or later attained by an 8F between Heavy repairs, alongside the roundhouses at Toton about 1956. RailOnline

48103 fresh out from a Heavy General at Horwich, 23 April 1960. It had been at Barrow Hill (Staveley) since 1955 but the old Midland shed had been transferred to the Eastern Region in 1958 and thus 48103 carries the ER plate 41E. It returned to the LMR fold at Patricroft at the end of 1962. D. Forsyth, ColourRail

48104

Built as 8104 at Crewe Works 31st January 1939
Renumbered 48104 w/e 28/1/50

Improvements and modifications
24/1/48 New type piston head fastening
23/2/52 Discharge of continuous blowdown into ashpan
24/2/52 Removal of sand guns
8/10/60 AWS
4/11/61 Modification to tube cleaner pipe and fittings

Repairs

23/7/40-25/7/40**TRO**		
7/8/40-7/9/40**LS**	60,363	
16/3/42-21/3/42**LO**	101,345	
17/6/42-15/7/42**LS**	105,351	
23/2/43-12/3/43**TRO**		
12/9/44-14/10/44**HG**	144,860	
20/10/45-1/1/46**TRO**		
1/6/46-13/6/46**LO**	28,365	
11/11/46-14/12/46**HS**	36,594	Crewe
2/12/47-17/1/48**LS**	21,664	Crewe
12/2/48**NC**	1,720	Leeds
19/2/49-28/1/50**HG**	69,063	Horwich
9/10/50-30/11/50**LC**	24,518	Horwich
2/1/52-5/2/52**LI**	62,013	Horwich
13/2/52-18/2/52**Rect[EO]**	Nil	Horwich
12/5/52-13/6/52**HC[EO]**	9,780	Horwich
27/2/53-25/3/53 **LC[EO]**	37,924	Horwich
24/4/54-9/6/54**HG**	78,507	Horwich
22/4/56-24/5/56**LI**	63,739	Horwich
24/4/57-16/5/57**LC**	35,201	Horwich
8/1/59-6/2/59**HG**	79,309	Crewe
10/9/60-23/9/60**NC**	51,030	Horwich
11/9/61-13/10/61**HI**		Horwich
1/4/63-26/4/63**HI**		Horwich
2/7/64-29/8/64**LC**		Crewe

Boilers

No.10442	14/10/44 from	8108
No.11722	28/1/50 from	8455
No.13213	9/6/54	
No.11486	6/2/59	

Tender
LMS 9736 31/1/39

Sheds

Willesden	4/2/39
Toton	23/3/40
Willesden	26/10/40
Kirkby	1/11/41
Leeds Holbeck	24/1/48

Withdrawn 7/67

Engine Shed Junction box lies beyond and in the yard at Holbeck MPD stands 48104, one of the shed's own 8Fs. R.K. Blencowe.

48104 passing Durran Hill Junction box at Carlisle on 1 June 1963. It had been at Holbeck in Leeds almost from the very first day of British Railways, Holbeck having about a dozen 8Fs in the 1950s.

48105

Built as 8105 at Crewe Works 31st January 1939
Renumbered 48105 w/e 21/1/50

Improvements and modifications
12/7/52 Removal of sand guns

Repairs

17/11/41-9/12/41**LS**	88,669	
8/11/43-6/12/43**HG**	154,060	
18/12/45-18/1/46**LS**	51,434	
21/6/47-9/7/47**LO**	88,217	Shed
12/11/47-3/1/48**LS**	18,341	Crewe
12/2/48**NC**	3,359	Leeds
6/12/49-16/1/50**HG**	54,948	Crewe
29/5/52-25/6/52**LI**	56,484	Horwich
26/11/53-23/12/53**HI**	38,686	Horwich
31/12/53-12/1/54**NC[Rect]EO**	Nil	Horwich
26/5/56-29/6/56**HG**	69,071	Horwich
18/6/58-11/7/58**HI**	60,257	Horwich
6/1/61-22/2/61**HI**	61,181	Derby
5/2/62-2/3/62**LC**		Derby
23/8/63-25/9/63**HG**		Crewe

Boilers

No.10507	6/12/43	from	8124
No.10922	16/1/50	from	48295
No.11706	29/6/56		

Tenders

LMS 9737	31/1/39
No.9568	25/9/63

Sheds

Willesden	4/2/39
Toton	1/11/41
Belle Vue	1/7/44
Sheffield	2/9/44
Hellifield	17/1/48
Toton	13/9/58
Saltley	7/2/59
Kirkby	7/1/61
Coalville	28/11/64
Kirkby	22/5/65
Oxley	25/2/67

Withdrawn w/e 11/3/67

48105 at Leicester, north of the station, 12 December 1963. It is starred for the balanced running and a stencilled 8105 survives on the front drop plate, a reminder of the last overhaul. It will be running back to Leicester MPD, by the look of it.

Now a Coalville engine, 48105 stands in the shed yard there on 9 August 1964. Norman Preedy.

Snowplough fitted 48106 near the end of it days, at Mirfield MPD about 1966. It had been a Bolton engine since April 1965, and has a crude 9K painted on the smokebox door. The little plough will presumably come off soon.

48106

Built as 8106 at Crewe Works 2nd February 1939
Renumbered 48106 w/e 18/3/50

Improvements and modifications
8/4/53 Removal of sand guns
/12/60 Modifications to tube cleaner pipe and fittings
AWS, date not known

Repairs

/10/41-3/12/41**LS**	90,433	
/12/43-14/1/44**HG**	152,400	
/6/46-31/7/46**LS**	44,530	
1/1/48-10/2/48**HS**	30,162	Crewe
0/2/50-17/3/50**LI**	43,239	Crewe
6/1/53-10/4/53**HG**	59,604	Horwich
8/7/55-1/9/55**LI**	57,697	Horwich
8/12/57-25/1/58**HG**	48,469	Crewe
4/10/60-17/11/60**LI**	66,946	Horwich

Noted at Works: Horwich 9/63

Boilers

No.11283	14/1/44	from	8206
No.11492	10/2/48	from	8626
No.11271	10/4/54		
No.13184	25/1/58		

Tender

LMS 9738	2/2/39

Sheds

Willesden	4/2/39
Wellingborough	1/11/41
Coalville	8/4/44
Huddersfield	27/3/48
Birkenhead	10/12/49
Mold Jct	17/10/53
Birkenhead	4/12/54
Buxton	11/2/56
Birkenhead	28/4/5
Warrington	17/5/58
Willesden	18/2/61
Warrington	6/5/61
Newton Heath	6/5/61
Patricroft	31/10/64
Bolton	24/4/65

Withdrawn w/e 24/6/67

48107

Built as 8107 at Crewe Works 8th February 1939
Renumbered 48107 w/e 5/11/49

Improvements and modifications
30/1/54 Removal of sand guns
25/3/61 AWS
7/9/63 Modifications to tube cleaner pipe and fittings
7/9/63 Repositioning of head lamp irons

Repairs

10/6/41-27/6/41**LS**	77,352	
17/2/43-20/3/43**LS**	141,970	
21/8/44-16/9/44**HG**	176,250	
16/4/45-26/5/45**LO**	11,823	
21/1/46-26/2/46**HS**	26,356	
26/7/47-20/8/47**HS**	31,842	Crewe
22/9/49-31/10/49**HI**	44,492	Crewe
12/6/51-29/6/51**HG**	42,414	Crewe
21/12/53-19/1/54**HI**	72,410	Crewe
15/6/56-11/7/56**HG**	57,417	Derby
23/5/58-7/7/58**HI**	46,144	Bow
10/9/59-29/9/59**LC[TO]***	33,676	Derby
24/1/61-2/3/61**LI**	66,171	Crewe
8/7/63-30/8/63**HG**		Horwich

*collision

Boilers

No.10087	16/9/44	from	8053;
No.11201	20/8/47	from	8281
No.11183	29/6/51	from	48280
No.10506	11/7/56		
No.10092	5/67		

Tender
LMS 9739 8/2/39

Sheds

Willesden	11/2/39
Wellingborough	1/11/41
Coalville	8/4/44
Wellingborough	11/11/50
Cricklewood	16/9/60
Kettering	28/10/61
Coalville	30/1/65
Leicester	22/5/65
Annesley	1/1/66
Edgeley	10/9/66
Heaton Mersey	27/1/68

Stored serviceable
31/5/65-9/12/65

Withdrawn w/e 6/4/68

8107 in lovely condition at Crewe, in its first days as a Willesden engine, in February 1939.

In fine fettle once again, at Cricklewood MPD in March 1961, after overhaul and fitting of AWS at Crewe. RailOnline

48107, by now a Kettering engine, has found its way to Gloucester Horton Road on 27 August 1964. AWS and front lamp now low down; with a steep decline in native WR types LM and Standard engines often gave the place more the look of an LMR outpost. Peter Skelton.

48108

Built as 8108 at Crewe Works 8th February 1939
Renumbered 48108 w/e/18/9/48

Improvements and modifications
23/2/52 Discharge of continuous blowdown into ashpan
9/10/54 Removal of sand guns
24/3/62 Fitting of AWS

Repairs

28/9/40-25/10/40**LS**	61,357	
25/3/42-2/4/42**LO**	98,755	
25/1/43-6/2/43**LS**	119,245	
12/3/45-11/4/45**HG**	157,663	
20/11/46-20/12/46**HS**	35,936	Crewe
19/8/48-13/9/48**HS**	13,025	Crewe
2/5/50-22/5/50**HG**	37,830	Crewe
9/1/52-5/2/52**HI**	37,868	Crewe
21/1/54-5/3/54**LC[EO]**	43,289	Shed
12/8/54-18/9/54**HG**	53,257	Crewe
9/11/56-30/11/56**LI**	51,844	Derby
15/9/58-1/10/58**LC[EO]**	45,404	Rugby
8/8/59-2/10/59**HG**	67,226	Derby

Noted at Works: Derby 2/62; Darlington 11/64

Boilers

No.9835	11/4/45	from	8081
No.12018	22/5/50	from	8381
No.11491	18/9/54		
No.11531	2/10/59		

Tender

LMS 9740	8/2/39

Sheds

Willesden	11/2/39
Kirkby	1/11/41
Mansfield	2/8/52
Nottingham	25/7/53
Warrington	21/3/64
Aintree	24/4/65
Buxton	21/5/66

Withdrawn w/e 2/9/67

48108 at Scarborough MPD on 20 August 1960. The 8F is standing on the half of the eight road that had to be demolished because of subsidence.

48108 hurries along light in the 1960s. AWS now, and larger Darlington-style numbers. RailOnline

48109

Built as 8109 at Crewe Works 14th February 1939
Renumbered 48109 w/e 4/6/49

Improvement and modifications
5/10/57 Modified piston for continuous blowdown valve
10/9/61 Fitting AWS

Repairs

20/6/41-9/8/41**LS**	76,314	
1/11/43-26/11/43**HG**	126,018	
13/4/46-8/5/46**LS**	35,440	
8/11/47-20/12/47**HS**	31,877	Crewe
6/5/49-1/6/49**HG**	9,903	Crewe
6/1/51-2/2/51**LC**	44,935	Shed
31/5/51-16/6/51**LI**	53,820	Crewe
27/7/52-8/8/52**LC[EO]**	36,993	Shed
4/5/53-23/6/53**HG**	59,665	Derby
14/2/55-14/3/55**HI**	46,334	Derby
29/7/57-13/9/57**LI**	52,782	Bow
16/5/60-8/7/60**HG**	49,951	Horwich
28/7/61-23/8/61**NC[EO]**	32,033	Horwich
13/9/62-10/10/62**HI**		Derby

Boilers

No.10502	26/11/43	from	8119
No.11639	1/6/49	from	8350
No.11821	23/6/53		
No.10870	8/7/60		

Tender

LMS 9741	14/2/39

Sheds

Willesden	18/2/39
Kirkby	11/10/41
Cricklewood	14/2/48
Toton	23/5/59
Saltley	9/12/61

Withdrawn w/e 22/1/66

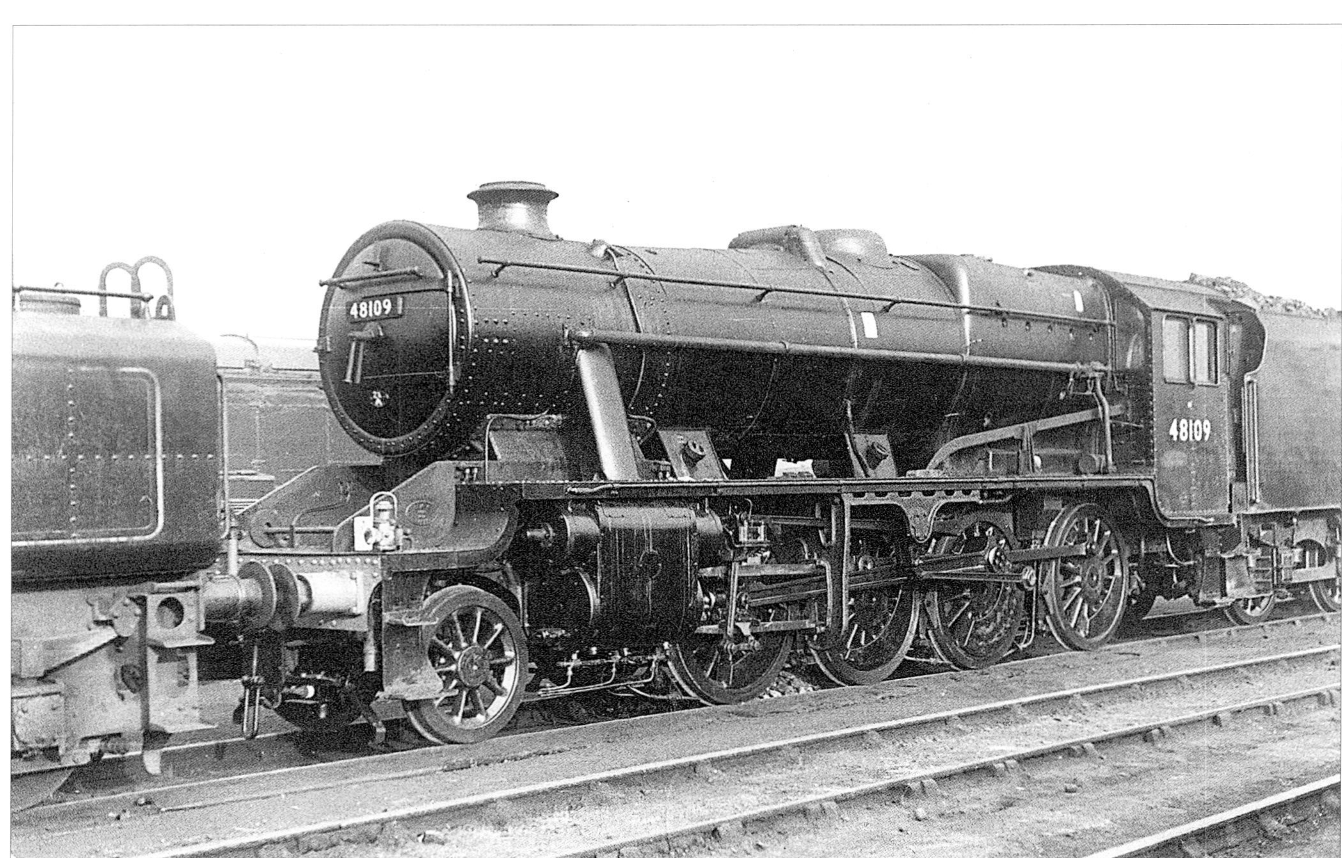

Fresh from a Heavy Intermediate at the adjacent works, 48109 stands in line at Derby shed, October 1962.

A blackened 48109 comes south with coal for Brent, through St Albans on the Slow Lines in 1956. The station is in the distance while the tank and smoke vents of the two road St Albans engine shed are visible above the middle of the train.

48110

Built as 8110 at Crewe Works 14th February 1939
Renumbered 48110 w/e 28/8/48

Modifications and Improvements
17/5/52 Discharge of continuous blowdown into ashpan
24/4/54 Removal of sand guns

Repairs

9/6/41-6/7/41**LS**	74,102	
3/11/42-2/12/42**LS**	116,529	
13/4/43-4/5/43**LO**	128,785	
2/7/44-11/8/44**HG**	168,907	
12/1/46-23/2/46**LS**	49,778	
15/7/47-11/9/47**HS**	42,445	Crewe
10/8/48-24/8/48**LS**	29,677	Crewe
5/1/50-4/3/50**HG**	30,960	Horwich
5/4/52-9/5/52**LI**	60,090	Crewe
4/3/54-2/4/54**HI**	66,058	Crewe
7/2/56-9/3/56**HG**	61,035	Crewe
24/2/58-29/3/58**LI**	69,633	Crewe
9/2/60-2/4/60**LI**	59,443	Crewe

Noted at Works: Crewe 5/65

Boilers

No.11202	11/8/44	from	8282
No.12012	4/3/50	from	8376
No.12021	9/3/56		

Tender
LMS 9742 14/2/39

Sheds

Willesden	18/2/39
Kirkby	4/10/41
Toton	1/11/41
Leeds	12/6/43
Toton	7/2/48
Belle Vue	29/5/48
Willesden	21/10/50
Newton Heath	11/11/50
Shrewsbury	9/12/50
Tyseley	22/6/63
Stoke	8/2/64

Withdrawn w/e 1/7/67

Out of Crewe after a Light Intermediate, a shiny black 48110, with cabside star, stands in the shed yard at Stockport Edgeley on 7 April 1960. The OHL (overhead line) is marching forward remorselessly on the main line beyond – compare to its earliest days on page 167. D. Forsyth, ColourRail

With coal on the Tuffley Junction 'loop' on 25 October 1963. This is the Midland line south of Gloucester, where the LMS and GWR ran parallel. Peter Skelton.

Typical end state for an 8F! Poor old 48110, latterly of Stoke and covered in priming deposits, has found its way to Shrewsbury 23 March 1966. The wonder, one supposes, is that it worked for another year after this. J.L. Stevenson, courtesy Hamish Stevenson.

48111

Built as 8111 at Crewe Works 27th February 1939
Renumbered 48111 w/e 19/6/48

Improvements and modifications
8/10/60 AWS

Repairs

18/11/41-15/12/41**LS**	71,019	
7/12/42-12/12/42**LO**	98,207	
10/1/44-5/2/44**HG**	126,745	
5/12/45-14/1/46**LS**	41,660	
17/4/47-1/5/47**LO**	73,223	Shed
26/1/48-18/2/48**HG**	19,662	Crewe
26/5/48-17/6/48**NC**	6,099	Derby
25/1/50-13/2/50**HI**	38,812	Crewe
12/11/51-23/11/51**LC[EO]**	47,671	Shed
9/7/52-1/9/52**HG**	65,655	Derby
14/12/54-13/1/55**HI**	61,175	Derby
5/3/55-24/3/55**LC[EO]**	3,192	Derby
10/12/56-1/1/57**LI**	38,795	Derby
20/4/59-9/6/59**HG**	60,360	Derby
14/9/60-30/9/60**NC[EO]**	34,082	Crewe
18/12/61-19/1/62**HI**		Crewe
21/4/65-3/8/65**LI**		Crewe

Noted at works: Eastleigh 12/64

Boilers

No.11294	5/2/44	from	8217
No.11196	18/2/48	from	8276
No.10438	1/9/52		
No.11786	9/6/59		

Tender

LMS 9783	27/2/39

Sheds

Northampton	4/3/39
Warwick	20/5/39
Northampton	24/5/41
Westhouses	11/10/41
Staveley	18/10/41
Wellingborough	11/11/50
Nottingham	12/12/53
Crewe South	4/1/58
Nuneaton	15/8/59
Agecroft	18/6/66
Bolton	8/10/66

Stored serviceable
20/2/66-12/3/66

Withdrawn w/e 16/3/68

48111 ex-works at Derby in June 1959. It was still a Crewe South engine, as the 5B plate denotes, but it would very soon go to Nuneaton.

48111 comes south on the LNW main line south of Oxenholme – Windermere branch to the left – with a long train of vans. One wonders how many were fitted and piped up – more than the minimum of four with that lamp code it is to be hoped. Coming down Shap with that lot you'd want some brake power. Norman Preedy.

48111 in semi-dismantled state at Eastleigh works on 6 March 1965. Like Darlington and Swindon, Eastleigh was taking on repairs to LMR locomotives; it seems to have all been rather leisurely (presumably spares and material were a problem) and 48111 had turned up back on 28 November 1964, hauling 48510 and on the same day 45699 GALATEA had also appeared, towing a third 8F, 48471. All four engines were intended for overhaul at Eastleigh. The puzzle is that though 48111 did indeed undergo repairs (only completed at last in August 1965) in the Record this is noted as taking place at Crewe, yet from the state of it here it is pretty much inconceivable that it was sent back to Crewe for the work.

48112

Built as 8112 at Crewe Works 28th February1939
Renumbered 48112 w/e 23/4/49

Improvements and modifications
27/11/43 Fitting Griffiths laminated springs to coupled wheels
8/7/44 Fitting Griffiths laminated springs to coupled wheels
16/6/57 Provision and fitting new type piston head fastening
16/6/57 Modified pistons for continuous blowdown valve

Repairs

17/9/41-15/10/41**LS**	60,176	
20/10/43-19/11/43**HG**	98,078	
23/5/45-23/6/45**LS**	37,487	
18/12/46-11/1/47**LO**	77,360	Crewe
27/1/47-14/3/47**HS**	78,413	Crewe
9/3/49-22/4/49**HG**	59,583	Crewe
28/4/49-13/5/49**NC**	121	Crewe
31/8/50-14/9/50**LC**	41,684	Shed
23/4/51-15/5/51**LI**	55,235	Horwich
20/3/53-8/5/53**HG**	53,687	Derby
30/4/55-26/5/55**LI**	57,430	Derby
21/5/57-10/6/57**LI**	48,252	Derby
11/4/60-20/5/60**HG**	71,933	Derby
26/7/61-15/9/61**HC**	34,897	Derby

Boilers

No.9597	19/11/43 from	8029
No.11871	22/4/49 from	8555
No.11495	8/5/53	
No.10496	20/5/60	

Tender

LMS 9784	28/2/39

Sheds

Northampton	4/3/39
Warwick	20/5/39
Northampton	24/5/47
Leeds	1/11/41
Normanton	8/11/41
Toton	9/9/44
Wellingborough	4/2/56
Toton	10/3/56
Westhouses	28/4/56

Withdrawn w/e 13/11/65

Westhouses with 48112 in June 1963, when the shed was coded 18B.

48112 at Westhouses MPD, where it had been allocated since 1956, a while later, on 8 September 1963. Now the shed plate is 16G. RailOnline

48113

Built as 8113 at Crewe Works 7th March 1939
Renumbered 48113 w/e/3/9/49

Improvements and modifications
19/4/52 Removal of sand guns
25/3/61 Fitting Automatic Warning System

Repairs

20/2/42-6/3/42**LS** 77,199		
5/9/44-30/9/44**HG**	140,532	
22/3/47-7/5/47**HS**	5,393	Crewe
24/6/49-3/9/49**HG**	55,690	Horwich
10/9/49-22/9/49**Rect**	Nil	Horwich
7/5/51-25/5/51**LI**	41,814	Horwich
4/3/52-28/3/52**LC[EO]**	19,738	Horwich
29/6/53-7/8/53**LI**	50,130	Horwich
29/8/55-30/9/55**HG**	41,660	Horwich
5/7/57-29/8/57**HG**	44,996	Horwich
31/1/61-17/3/61**HI**	68,120	Horwich

Boilers

No.10501	30/9/44	from	8118
No.11685	3/9/49	from	8452

Tender
LMS 9785 7/8/39

Sheds

Warwick	11/3/39
Shrewsbury	24/5/41
Royston	1/11/41

Withdrawn w/e 2/10/67

48113 at Bolton on 9 August 1953. It has had attention at Horwich works and like all engines off the works there has been consigned to Bolton shed for running in. Such ex-works locos were a welcome addition so far as the Running Foreman was concerned and he was not averse to extending their use way beyond the strict requirements of 'running in'.

48113, like a number of 8Fs, spent virtually its entire career at Royston, where by spring 1965 they still made up two thirds of the allocation of thirty-odd locos (as well as several diesel shunters). In the shed's last weeks its 8Fs looked just like 48113 at the front of the building on 17 September 1967; shabby but serviceable; lowered front lamp iron. J. Davenport, courtesy Norman Preedy.

48114

Built as 8114 at Crewe Works 14th March 1939
Renumbered 48114 w/e 24/4/48

Improvements and modifications
27/11/43 Fitting Griffiths laminated springs to coupled wheels
8/7/44 Fitting Griffiths laminated springs to coupled wheels
23/2/52 New type piston head fastening
23/2/52 Discharge of continuous blowdown into ashpan

Repairs

19/7/40-24/7/40**TRO**		
28/5/41-17/6/41**LS**	62,488	
16/4/42-2/4/42**LO**	84,495	
5/4/43-12/4/43**LO**	106,887	
15/10/43-4/11/43**HG**	118,207	
29/4/46-27/5/46**LS**	47,184	
18/3/48-25/4/48**HS**	43,016	Crewe
18/1/49-10/2/49**HC**	16,647	Crewe
24/5/50-13/6/50**LI**	45,718	Crewe
17/1/52-22/2/52**HG**	38,577	Crewe
2/6/54-1/7/54**HI**	51,093	Derby
17/8/56-14/9/56**HG**	43,765	Derby
27/10/58-24/11/58**HI**	43,353	Derby
20/3/61-21/4/61**HG**	58,069	Derby

Noted at Works: Horwich 2/64

Boilers

No.9629	4/11/43	from	8074
No.11257	23/4/48	from	8070
No.12005	22/2/52		
No.10498	14/9/56		
No.9589	21/4/61		

Tender
LMS 9786 14/3/39

Sheds

Northampton	18/3/39
Toton	23/3/40
Northampton	26/10/40
Kirkby	11/10/41
Heaton Mersey	5/7/47
Kirkby	19/7/47
Springs Branch	26/12/64

Withdrawn w/e 1/4/67

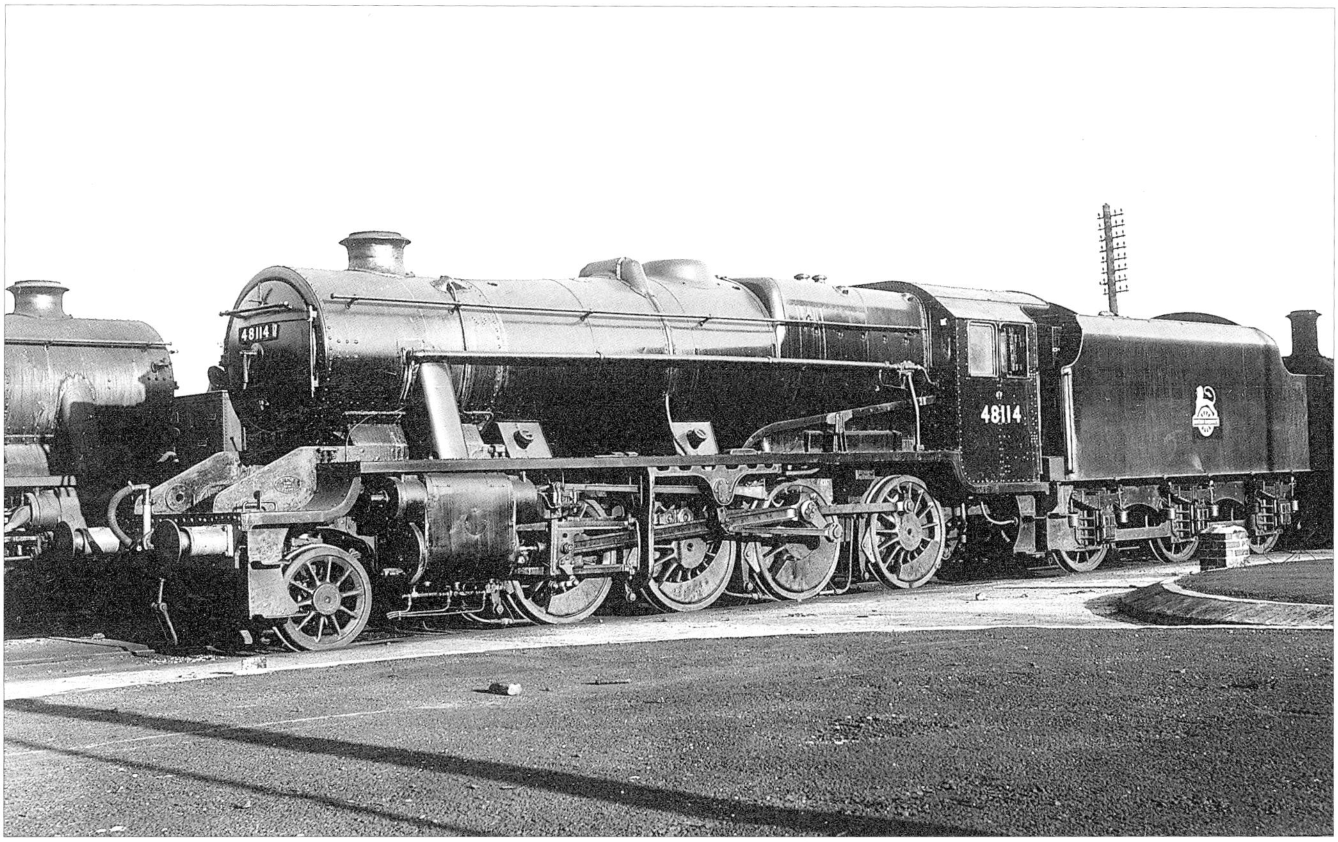

48114 at its Kirkby home (the shed, like Royston, tended to hang on to its 8Fs) on 30 September 1956, after a recent Heavy General at Derby. The tender, as so often happened, did not come back as clean as the loco.

48114 at Crewe South MPD, 18 August 1966. J.L. Stevenson, courtesy Hamish Stevenson.

48115

Built as 8115 at Crewe Works 3rd April 1939
Renumbered 48115 w/e 11/12/48

Improvements and modifications
6/9/52 Removal of sand guns
10/9/61 Fitting AWS

Repairs

28/8/41-27/9/41**HS**	67,550	
5/10/42-30/10/42**LS**	37,782	
4/2/43-10/3/43**LO**	48,809	
13/5/44-14/5/44**TRO**		
22/9/44-20/10/44**HG**	85,423	
17/10/46-20/11/46**LS**	40,626	Crewe
27/10/48-11/12/48**HS**	43,958	Crewe
27/6/50-3/8/50**HI**	32,417	Crewe
19/7/52-30/8/52**LI**	46,764	Horwich
6/1/53-27/1/53**NC[EO]**	8,930	Derby
14/2/55-11/3/55**HG**	44,866	Derby
15/2/58-17/3/58**HI**	61,738	Derby
27/6/61-21/8/61**HG**	78,303	Horwich

Noted at Works: Horwich 12/62; Crewe 9/65

Boilers

No.10434	20/10/44 from	8099
No.11644	11/12/48 from	8352
No.13202	11/3/55	
No.11082	1/8/61	

Tender

LMS 9787	3/4/39

Sheds

Warwick	8/4/39
Northampton	29/4/39
Willesden	27/7/40
Toton	1/11/41
Westhouses	12/6/43
Toton	20/9/58
Newton Heath	8/11/58
Patricroft	5/1/63
Heaton Mersey	27/3/65
Rose Grove	18/5/68

Withdrawn w/e 6/7/68

48115 at York, 23 May 1955. RailOnline

48115 still in excellent condition by the look of it, at Patricroft MPD a decade on in 1964. RailOnline

48116

Built as 8116 at Crewe Works 4th April 1939
Renumbered 48116 w/e 11/9/48

Improvement and modifications
23/2/63 Fitting Automatic Warning System

Repairs

9/8/41-6/9/41**LS**	67,525	
29/5/42-17/6/42**LO**	91,893	
21/8/42-25/9/42**LO**	97,657	
19/12/43-30/12/43**LO**	144,024	
2/4/44-2/5/44**HG**	149,860	
20/3/46-2/5/46**LS**	39,625	
27/10/47-11/11/47**LO**	34,921	Shed
27/7/48-10/9/48**HS**	15,075	Crewe
2/10/50-25/10/50**HI**	44,936	Crewe
7/9/53-30/10/53**HG**	65,013	Derby
13/2/56-5/3/56**LI**	52,797	Derby
14/2/58-19/3/58**HG**	41,696	Crewe
23/7/60-19/10/60**HG**	65,089	Derby

Noted at Works: Horwich 1/63; Crewe 6/65

Boilers

No.10441	2/5/44	from	8106
No.11803	10/9/48	from	8685
No.11818	30/10/53		
No.11353	19/3/58		
No.11681	19/10/60		

Tender
LMS 9788 4/4/39

Sheds

Crewe	8/4/39
Northampton	15/4/39
Toton	11/10/41
Heaton Mersey	1/7/44
Sheffield	1/2/47
Hasland	21/9/57
Nottingham	16/5/64
Leicester	24/4/65
Toton	22/5/65

Withdrawn w/e 19/6/65

Nottingham's 48116 at Cricklewood MPD ready for the return north, on 25 July 1964. It has acquired an unusually prominent flange join on the vacuum ejector pipe. Peter Groom.

48116 at Chinley in the 1950s with a coal train – a simple but glorious composition, perfect to frame an 8F and its train. Norman Preedy.

48117

Built as 8117 at Crewe Works 12th April 1939
Renumbered 48117 w/e 3/7/48

Improvements and modifications
27/1/62 Fitting AWS

Repairs

14/10/41-24/10/41**LS**	70,132	
28/5/43-23/6/43**HG**	125,911	
15/2/45-15/3/45**LS**	42,192	
25/6/46-13/7/46**LO**	79,388	
31/1/47-20/2/47**HS**	92,626	Crewe
9/5/48-19/5/48**LO**	40,870	Shed
4/6/48-30/6/48**HG**	728	Crewe
1/10/49-14/11/49**LI**	42,330	Crewe
24/10/51-8/11/51**LC[EO**]	58,134	Shed
7/4/52-23/5/52**HG**	68,703	Derby
26/11/53-30/12/53**HI**	44,562	Derby
3/4/56-25/4/56**HG**	58,260	Derby
5/1/59-13/2/59**LI**	71,184	Bow
27/2/59-3/3/59**NC[EO]**	289	Bow

Noted at Works: Derby 1/62; Eastleigh 10/64

Boilers

No.9612	23/6/43	from	8067
No.11501	30/6/48	from	8618
No.11506	23/5/52		
No.11864	25/4/56		

Tender

LMS 9789	12/4/39

Sheds

Northampton	15/4/39
Warwick	25/5/40
Shrewsbury	24/5/41
Wellingborough	1/11/41
Toton	8/4/44
Royston	27/5/44
Toton	9/9/44
Nottingham	9/4/55
Wellingborough	25/6/60
Cricklewood	9/7/60
Annesley	22/9/62
Burton	8/8/64
Colwick	10/9/66
Springs Branch	31/12/66
Heaton Mersey	30/12/67

Withdrawn w/e 23/3/68

48117 at Springs Branch MPD, its home for 1967, on 11 June that year. AWS, external pipework to tube cleaning cock, lowered top lamp iron.

48117 with a freight at Duffield, north of Derby, 4 August 1866. R. Siviter, ColourRail

48118

Built as 8118 at Crewe Works 20th April 1939
Renumbered 48118 w/e 30/7/49

Improvements and modifications
8/9/51 New type piston head fastening
25/3/61 Fitting Automatic Warning System

Repairs

1/9/41-24/9/41**LS**	68,383	
5/9/42-15/9/42**LO**	104,150	
30/11/42-16/12/42**LS**	109,701	
6/7/43-16/7/43**LO**	126,855	
7/3/44-23/3/44**HG**	142,452	
26/3/45-3/5/45**HS**	25,120	
28/1/47-1/4/47**HS**	40,641	Crewe
17/6/49-30/7/49**HG**	57,276	Crewe
17/7/51-25/8/51**LI**	42,483	Crewe
29/5/53-25/6/53**LI**	45,066	Horwich
6/6/55-5/7/55**HG**	40,135	Derby
11/1/56-24/1/56**LC[EO]**	12,164	Derby
14/6/58-7/7/58**HI**	65,699	Derby
13/1/61-14/3/61**HG**	68,763	Horwich
14/8/61-19/10/61**LC[EO]**	11,846	Horwich

Noted at Works: Horwich 2/64

Boilers

No.10497	23/3/44	from	8114
No.9616	30/7/49	from	8097
No.11658	5/7/55		
No.11184	14/3/61		

Tender

LMS 9790	20/4/39

Sheds

Northampton	22/4/39
Kirkby[o/l]	4/10/41
Toton	1/11/41
Westhouses	12/6/43
Toton	20/9/58
Leicester	7/3/59
Toton	21/3/59
Northwich	28/4/62

Withdrawn w/e 11/6/66

48118 rounds a curve 'somewhere in England'. The engine carries a Toton plate and was there for spells in 1958-59 so this would be about then, before AWS was fitted in early 1961. S.B. Lee, ColourRail

48119

Built as 8119 at Crewe Works 5th May 1939
Renumbered 48119 w/e 2/10/48

Improvements and modifications
2/10/43 Fitting Griffith laminated springs
8/7/44 Fitting Griffith laminated springs
10/8/57 Providing Metaflex joints to boiler top feed
14/7/62 AWS

Repairs

9/10/41-31/10/41**LS**	72,164	
27/8/43-26/9/43**HG**	125,938	
4/10/44-7/11/44**LS**	24,190	
4/4/46-18/4/46**LO**	65,267	
11/10/46-8/11/46**LS**	75,298	Crewe
31/1/48-15/2/48**LO**	35,346	Shed
26/8/48-2/10/48**HG**	11,480	Crewe
21/3/50-19/4/50**HI**	32,510	Crewe
9/2/51-20/2/51**LC**	15,523	Shed
22/8/51-6/9/51**LC[EO]**	24,700	Shed
26/4/52-11/6/52**HG**	33,649	Derby
28/11/53-4/12/53**LC[EO**]	30,578	Shed
3/5/54-2/6/54**LI**	38,111	Derby
14/3/56-5/4/56**HI**	37,024	Derby
20/6/57-9/8/57**HG**	24,643	Derby
2/1/60-8/3/60**HI**	47,932	Derby

Noted at Works: Derby 6/62; Crewe 5/65

Boilers

No.10500	26/9/43	from	8117
No.11353	2/10/48	from	8163
No.11142	11/6/52		
No.12149	9/8/57		

Tender

LMS 9791	5/5/39

Sheds

Northampton	6/5/39
Leeds	1/11/41
Toton	8/11/41
Staveley	15/1/49
Mansfield	12/3/49
Kirkby	9/4/60
Edge Hill	3/12/66

Withdrawn w/e 2/12/67

48119, at Kirkby from 1960-66, rumbling south with coal north of Wellingborough at the oddly named location Nest Fields, 24 August 1963. 48119 is coasting towards the northern outskirts of the town with an up goods consisting mainly of Nottinghamshire coal, which will almost certainly be signalled into the capacious Neilson's sidings at Finedon Road for examination before continuing its journey to London. The four track section, which extends north to just beyond Kettering, passes under the overbridge locally known as 'The Slips' in the distance, and the photographer is positioned on Nest Fields bridge, so named after a neighbouring farm. Above the locomotive can be seen the long-disused sidings of the Richard Thomas & Baldwin quarrying operation to the north and west of Finedon village, which ceased production shortly after the Second World War, although the track and connection into the northern end of Neilson's sidings remained in place for many years afterwards. ColourRail

48119 later on, at Burton MPD, in good condition from a recent works visit; starred for faster running, lowered lamp iron, AWS. The new Kirkby 16E plate means the period is post-September 1963. RailOnline

48120

Built as 8120 at Crewe Works 22nd May 1939
Renumbered 48120 w/e 22/7/50

Improvements and modifications
1/11/52 Removal of sand guns
1/11/52 New type piston head fastening
8/10/60 AWS

Repairs

22/9/41-23/10/41**LS**	64,378	
11/9/42-18/9/42**LO**	97,851	
23/9/42-2/10/42**LO**	98,259	
13/4/43-29/4/43**LS**	113,193	
1/8/44-21/8/44**HG**	147,575	
24/12/45-19/1/46**LS**	26,334	
6/1/48-11/2/48**LS**	43,948	Crewe
20/6/50-21/7/50**HG**	46,042	Crewe
17/12/51-22/12/51**LC[EO]**	35,032	Shed
4/10/52-28/10/52**HI**	54,592	Crewe
5/2/54-16/2/54**LC[EO]**	34,149	Shed
13/5/54-9/6/54**LI**	39,747	Rugby
17/10/55-10/11/55**HG**	33,479	Crewe
2/8/58-22/8/58**LI**	69,810	Crewe
30/8/60-20/9/60**NC[EO]**	51,039	Crewe
2/12/60-18/1/61**HG**	57,171	Crewe

Boilers

No.10088	21/8/44	from	8035
No.11693	21/7/50	from	8477
No.9835	10/11/55		
No.11483	18/1/61		

Tenders

LMS 9792	22/5/39
No.10412	29/4/63

Sheds

Northampton	27/5/39
Leeds	11/10/41
Staveley	13/6/42
Bury	5/6/48
Newton Heath	21/1/50
Bescot	22/7/50
Birkenhead	2/2/57
Rugby	25/4/59
Oxley	30/1/65
Mold Jct	19/6/65

Withdrawn w/e 15/1/65

48120 in August 1963, near the end of its days as a Rugby (2A) loco.

48121 on 3 August (raining of course) 1963 banking a train at Rugby; this would be the Midland line, north west of the station with the LNW over on the left. RailOnline

48121

Built as 8121 at Crewe Works 23rd May 1939
Renumbered 48121 w/e 17/4/48

Improvements and modifications
30/12/51 Discharge of continuous blowdown into ashpan
29/12/51 Removal of sand guns

Repairs

22/8/41-19/9/41**LS**	64,231	
18/9/42-8/10/42**LS**	97,236	
24/3/44-19/4/44**HG**	15,301	
16/5/45-2/6/45**LO**	40,561	
11/3/46-13/4/46**LS**	65,137	
10/3/48-17/4/48**LS**	60,413	Crewe
26/9/49-17/11/49**HG**	38,409	Crewe
14/11/51-3/12/51**HI**	51,752	Horwich
20/2/53-1/4/53**HI**	31,296	Derby
31/10/55-23/11/55**HG**	58,449	Derby
9/10/58-3/11/58**HI**	67,657	Derby
27/2/61-8/5/61**HG**	51,803	Derby

Noted at Works: Crewe 8/63

Boilers

No.10495	19/4/44 from	8112
No.11014	17/11/49 from	48260
No.13183	23/11/55	
No.9580	8/5/61	

Tender

LMS 9793	23/5/39

Sheds

Northampton	27/5/39
Wellingborough	1/11/41
Coalville	19/6/43
Leeds	10/7/43
Derby	21/2/48
Toton[o/l]	24/2/51
Derby	10/3/51
Woodford Halse	2/2/63
Willesden	19/6/65
Stourbridge	11/9/65
Sutton Oak	16/7/66

Withdrawn w/e 22/4/67

48121 now a Woodford Halse engine, at its home shed alongside 73010 on 18 April 1963. K. Fairey, ColourRail

48121, by chance a native of Derby MPD (17A) stands alongside the roundhouses there on 27 May 1961, having recently emerged from a Heavy General in the adjacent works. D. Forsyth, ColourRail

48122

Built as 8122 at Crewe Works 24th May 1939
Renumbered 48122 w/e 24/5/49

Improvements and modifications
4/10/52 New type piston head fastening
4/10/52 Removal of sand guns and equipment
10/9/60 AWS

Repairs

3/9/41-8/10/41**LS**	56,577	
9/12/42-23/1/43**LS**	110,446	
27/3/43-14/4/43**LO**	110,564	
3/4/44-27/4/44**HG**	133,449	
2/1/46-26/1/46**LS**	40,632	
8/5/47-11/6/47**LS**	69,514	Crewe
27/4/49-12/5/49**HG**	40,439	Crewe
4/5/51-31/5/51**LI**	54,346	Crewe
12/8/52-17/9/52**HI**	33,996	Crewe
24/11/54-17/12/54**HG**	62,609	Crewe
9/1/58-1/2/58**HG**	80,314	Crewe
29/7/60-15/8/60**NC[EO]**	64,686	Crewe
31/10/60-2/12/60**LI**	69,399	Crewe
22/2/61-15/3/61**LC[EO]**	5,578	Crewe

Boilers

No.10440	27/4/44	from	8105
No.12004	12/5/49	from	8367
No.13193	17/12/54		
No.9621	1/2/58		

Tenders

LMS 9794	24/5/39
No.10291	17/12/54

Sheds

Northampton	27/5/39
Wellingborough	1/11/41
Staveley	19/6/43
Northampton	19/6/48
Willesden	8/10/49
Northampton	30/1/60
Rugby	27/1/62
Oswestry	28/11/64
Croes Newydd	30/1/65
Mold Jct	14/8/65
Croes Newydd	11/9/65

Withdrawn w/e 18/2/67

Willesden's 48122, below the street and the 'birdcage', at Leicester MPD; the period is probably about 1957. Norman Preedy.

48122 in a pretty portrait at Northampton on 3 November 1963, reflected in the placid waters of the Brampton arm of the River Nene as it eases towards Northampton Castle station with an up goods. The train is on the Roade to Rugby loop, opened in 1881, and behind the wagons is the junction with the earlier line to Northampton Bridge Street and Blisworth. The area was controlled by the just visible Northampton No.1 signalbox, which was situated at the end of the isolated bay platforms from which branch line services ran to Blisworth, Wellingborough, Peterborough, and Bedford. Tender first working on what was locally known as 'top line' was not all that common, and the train may be the returning daily pick up goods which served the yards at Roade and Castlethorpe before reaching its destination of Wolverton. L. Hanson.

48123

Built as 8123 at Crewe Works 6th June 1939
Renumbered 48123 w/e 3/7/48

Improvements and modifications
5/11/60 AWS

Repairs

14/7/41-21/8/41**LS**	60,609	
24/5/43-20/6/43**LS**	91,548	
9/12/44-30/12/44**HG**	124,289	
6/2/46-13/3/46**HS**	25,379	
2/6/48-3/7/48**LS**	47,403	Crewe
10/10/50-1/11/50**HG**	52,224	Horwich
11/8/52-25/9/52**LI**	45,776	Horwich
19/1/55-19/2/55**LI**	51,044	Horwich
5/1/57-7/2/57**HG**	37,329	Horwich
8/10/58-17/10/58**LC**	36,873	Horwich
19/10/59-4/12/59**LI**	57,279	Horwich
4/11/60**NC**	16,609	Horwich

Noted at Works: Horwich 4/62; Darlington 9/65

Boilers

No.10436	30/12/44 from	8101
No.13228	11/11/50 from	48764
No.10922	7/2/57	

Tender

LMS 9795	6/6/39

Sheds

Northampton	10/6/39
Normanton	11/10/41
Stourton	24/7/48
Normanton	24/7/48

Withdrawn w/e 12/3/67

48123 at Wakefield MPD, 26 February 1961; 2-6-4T 42150 at rear and 8F 48539 in background. AWS, lowered lamp iron. RailOnline

48124

Built as 8124 at Crewe Works 12th June 1939
Renumbered 48124 w/e 1/12/51

Improvement and modifications
1/12/51 New type piston head fastenings
1/12/51 Discharge of continuous blowdown into ashpan

Repairs

22/9/41-25/10/41**LS**	61,840	
10/8/42-3/9/42**LO**	90,497	
17/8/43-11/9/43**LS**	122,461	
18/10/44-2/11/44**LO**	162,510	
26/7/45-14/9/45**LS**	182,653	
6/7/46-17/8/46**TRO**		
21/4/47-20/5/47**HG**	224,016	Crewe
22/6/49-2/8/49**LI**	57,423	Rugby
19/5/51-2/6/51**LC**	44,650	Shed
26/10/51-30/11/51**HG**	53,561	Crewe
30/10/53-3/12/53**HI**	50,077	Derby
7/2/56-5/3/56**HG**	52,673	Derby
30/4/58-18/6/58**LI**	54,305	Bow
12/8/60-4/11/60**HG**	50,216	Derby

Noted at Works: Crewe 4/65

Boilers

No.11258	11/9/43	from	8181
No.11254	20/5/47	from	8177
No.11864	30/11/51		
No.11663	5/3/56		
No.11465	4/11/60		

Tender
LMS 9796 12/6/39

Sheds

Northampton	17/6/39
Wellingborough	1/11/41
Leicester	19/6/43
Leeds	10/7/43
Kingmoor	11/5/46
Kettering	22/11/47
Derby	7/11/59
Westhouses	14/8/65
Kirkby	9/10/65
Edge Hill	3/12/66

Stored serviceable
18/10/65-27/10/65

Withdrawn w/e 4/5/68

48124 has had a Heavy General at Derby and looks resplendent standing in the yard ready to return to work at Derby MPD, 13 November 1960.

48124 on the Midland Kettering-Melton Mowbray line in Rutland, coming south in 1959. The view is north to Oakham, from the down Glendon Junction (Kettering) line platform. The 8F (one of Kettering's finest) has just emerged from Manton tunnel and the load, apart from the first couple of wagons, is probably nutty slack from the Nottinghamshire coalfields to London, or possibly Corby steelworks. The other 8F is in the lay-by at the back of the up platform with northbound empties, probably waiting for a down express to go past. Once upon a time they might both have been Beyer Garratts... Away on the extreme right are the Peterborough lines, Manton being a sort-of triangular station set-up, with the junction and signalbox just behind the train. ColourRail

If 48124 in the previous view was an 'after', here is the loco 'before works attention – ugly duckling to swan, or even vice-versa. Battered, filthy, parked out of use on a siding alongside the roundhouses. D. Forsyth, ColourRail

48125

Built as 8125 at Crewe Works 22nd June 1939
Renumbered 48125 w/e 19/6/48

Improvements and modifications
27/1/52 Removal of sand guns

Repairs

1/8/41-3/9/41**LS**	62,083	
6/6/42-27/6/42**LO**	85,561	
20/2/43-20/3/43**HS**	105,798	
1/8/44-19/8/44**HG**	31,660	
18/3/46-15/4/46**HS**	35,472	
12/5/48-15/6/48**LS**	52,201	Crewe
6/10/49-9/12/49**HG**	30,838	Crewe
1/12/51-4/1/52**LI**	50,282	Horwich
6/10/53-6/11/53**HI**	41,417	Horwich
25/5/55-23/6/55**HG**	40,968	Derby
17/3/58-14/4/58**LI**	68,783	Derby
15/7/60-21/10/60**HG**	60,119	Derby

Boilers

No.10505	19/8/44	from	8122
No.11825	9/12/49	from	8697
No.11527	23/6/55		
No.11072	21/10/60		

Tenders

LMS 9797	22/6/39
No.9869	7/11/53

Sheds

Northampton	24/6/39
Wellingborough	11/10/41
Kettering	16/5/42
Westhouses	7/8/43
Saltley	3/5/52
Westhouses	10/5/52
Wellingborough	6/10/54
Toton	16/7/55
Westhouses	13/8/55
Toton	5/1/57
Hasland	20/7/57
Wellingborough	10/11/62
Toton	6/7/63
Springs Branch	26/12/64

Withdrawn w/e 28/10/67

Finishing with a flourish. 48125 blasts up the Lickey with banker, 2 February 1957. R. Green, ColourRail

8014 delivered brand new at Crewe South, with welded tender, 1 January 1937.

8015 at Royston MPD on 20 February 1938.

3. Foreign Fields

'48013'
Built as 8013 at Crewe Works 1/37
Sheds: Hasland 9/1/37; Toton 8/10/38
Withdrawn from traffic 9/41, to WD 11/41 as 578, shipped to Persia, becomes 41.169; remained there, gone by 1963.

'48014'
Built as 8014 at Crewe Works 1/37
Sheds: Hasland 9/1/37; Wellingborough 9/12/39
Withdrawn from traffic 9/41, to WD 11/41 as 590, shipped to Persia, becomes 41.232; remained there, gone by 1963.

'48015'
Built as 8015 at Crewe Works 1/37
Sheds: Royston 13/2/37; Normanton 17/8/40
Withdrawn from traffic 9/41, to WD 11/41 as 576, shipped to Persia, becomes 41.151, 70373 in 1944. Thence to Egypt/Palestine 1945/46; renumbered 514 in 1952, then 41.153, then Egyptian State Railways in 1956 as 839. Withdrawn 1963.

'48019'
Built as 8019 at Crewe Works 2/37
Sheds: Wellingborough 13/2/37
Withdrawn from traffic 9/41, to WD 11/41 as 574, shipped to Persia, becomes 41.175; thence to Egypt/Palestine 1944, became 70574. Renumbered 510 in 1952, scrapped thereafter.

8015, ex-WD 576 back in Egypt at Suez, and named C/SGT H. McDONALD VC after renumbering 70373. Its exact identity in fact remains in doubt, due to substitutions and so on; whatever, only parts of 8015 seem to been retained in 70373. Even the Master, Peter Rowledge, declares 70373 to be 'particularly difficult to sort out'...

8019 with typical wooden-bodied stock, at Radlett before the War. The loco went new to Wellingborough and was still there when requisitioned in late 1941. It never returned.

8012 went to Persia as 574. It was later shipped to Egypt and as 70574 was blown up by a terrorist bomb at Kantara, in January 1952. It was named CPL LEITCHER VC and as WD 510 (its 1952 number) was finally scrapped in 1954.

Five locos came back to Britain from Egypt, arriving at Derby works in August 1952, the idea being to overhaul and return them; in the event it was clear they were not needed back on the Nile and so, over some years, they were repaired and returned to traffic on WD lines. They never seem to have seen much use and three were eventually sold to BR, in 1957 – as the famous 'final three' 48773, 48774 and 48775. These were WD (new, 1952 numbers) 500, 501 and 512 respectively (original WD 307, 320 and 583). The other two, 508 and 511 (1952 numbers), had begun life as 8021 and 8025 (original WD 508 – by chance – and 575) but this latter pair never came to BR; they too went to military use and by the time the WD was done with them, in 1959, BR was not interested in any more 8Fs so they went for scrap. These are 511 (8021, 575 that was) along with 508, 512 and 501 in the Derby works yard on 18 January 1953. 500 was somewhere else, probably already under repair – certainly it was the first to be dealt with. T. J. Edgington.

8021 was requisitioned as WD 575 and came back as WD 511, as renumbered in 1952. It never ran as a BR loco. Repaired and run in at Derby (after some years – the work was protracted) it was sent to the Cairnryan military railway; here it is on 30 January 1955 at Derby, with the WD tender which was used successively to run in the five 'late arrivals'. Spare Stanier tenders were later purchased from BR, their own ones having remained at Suez. Elaborate style of top feed cover.

'48021'
Built as 8021 at Crewe Works 3/37
Sheds: Burton 13/3/7; Toton 13/8/38; Kirkby 16/3/40
Withdrawn from traffic 9/41, to WD 11/41 as 575, shipped to Persia, becomes 41.152; thence to Egypt/ Palestine 1945/46, became 70575. Renumbered 511 in 1952, returns to UK 1952 repaired and run in at Derby, sent to Cairnryan Military Railway. Scrapped 1959 without entering BR stock.

'48022'
Built as 8022 at Crewe Works 3/37
Sheds: Royston 13/3/37
Withdrawn from traffic 9/41, to WD 11/41 as 580, shipped to Persia, becomes 41.154; remains there, gone by 1963.

'48023'
Built as 8023 at Crewe Works 3/37
Sheds: Royston 10/4/37
Withdrawn from traffic 9/41, to WD 11/41 as 587, shipped to Persia, becomes 41.188; remains there, gone by 1963.

'48028'
Built as 8028 at Vulcan Foundry 7/36
Sheds: Royston 7/1936; Toton 13/6/36
Withdrawn from traffic 10/41, to WD 11/41 as 592, shipped to Persia, becomes 41.191; remains there, gone by 1963.

Not the finest picture but possibly the only one existing of 8022 – 20C shed plate of Royston.

Royston's 8023, welded tender, at Derby on 7 November 1937. Long ago abandoned in Persia as 41.188.

8028 which never came back from Persia –at Pitstone near Cheddington in 1939.

8030 (it too never came back) with a lovely period freight near (it is thought) Hillmorton, a district of Rugby, on 15 August 1938.

Another that never returned, 8031 which became WD 584, with more glorious period wagons, northbound coal empties at Harlington on the Midland main line on 7 June 1939.

8032 on 22 August 1936, days after delivery from Vulcan and the fitting up of its motion, possibly in steam for the first time, at its new home Toton. It ended its days in Italy in 1953.

After its first years at Toton, twenty years on 8034 found itself on the books of the Egyptian State Railways. Here it is in original guise, hauling a freight near Bletchley on 7 June 1939. H.C. Casserley, courtesy R.M. Casserley.

'48030'
Built as 8030 at Vulcan Foundry 8/36
Sheds: Toton 15/8/36; Kirkby 16/3/40
Withdrawn from traffic 9/41, to WD 11/41 as 581, shipped to Persia, becomes 41.173; remains there, gone by 1963.

'48031'
Built as 8031 at Vulcan Foundry 8/36
Sheds: Toton 15/8/36; Kirkby 16/3/40
Withdrawn from traffic 9/41, to WD 11/41 as 584, shipped to Persia, becomes 41.216. Rowledge (Heavy Goods Engines of the War Department Vol.2, Springmead Railway Books, 1977) records that it changed identity with 506 (41.218). Numbered 70584 as well as 506, this came back in 1948, to become 48263. What was 584 remained; it had gone by 1963.

'48032'
Built as 8032 at Vulcan Foundry 8/36
Sheds: Toton 12/9/36; Kirkby 16/3/40
Withdrawn from traffic 9/41, to WD 11/41 as 585, shipped to Persia, becomes 41.162. Thence to Egypt/Palestine 1944 as 9378; sent to Italy, becomes 70575. Withdrawn 1953 as 737.009.

'48034'
Built as 8034 at Vulcan Foundry 8/36
Sheds: Toton 12/9/36
Withdrawn from traffic 9/41, to WD 12/41 as 593, shipped to Persia, becomes 41.199, thence to Egypt/Palestine 1945/46, became 70593. Renumbered 513 in 1952, purchased by Egyptian State Railways 1956.

'48038'
Built as 8038 at Vulcan Foundry 9/36
Sheds: Kirkby 10/10/36
Withdrawn from traffic 10/41, to WD 11/41 as 594, shipped to Persia, becomes 41.182, thence to Egypt/Palestine 1944 as 9370; sent to Italy, becomes 70594. Withdrawn 1953 as 737.011.

'48040'
Built as 8040 at Vulcan Foundry 9/36
Sheds: Wellingborough 12/9/36
Withdrawn from traffic 10/41, to WD 11/41 as 595, shipped to Persia, becomes 41.192, thence to Egypt/Palestine 1944 as 9355; sent to Italy, becomes 70595. Withdrawn 1953 as 737.012.

'48041'
Built as 8041 at Vulcan Foundry 9/36
Sheds: Wellingborough 12/9/36
Withdrawn from traffic 9/41, to WD 11/41 as 572, shipped to Persia, becomes 41.176, thence to Egypt/Palestine 1944 as 9355; becomes 70572. Taken into Israeli stock 1948, withdrawn 1958.

8040 at Toton in June 1937. It had been at Wellingborough since building the year before and would soon pass to the WD, to become 595. Various adventures followed with the 8F winding up in Italy; there was to be no *dolce vita* and the engine was scrapped there about 1953.

8041 ended up in Israel, to be scrapped about 1958. It was at Wellingborough up until its requisitioning as WD 572, working daily on loaded coal up to Brent and, like here, empties down; in this case about to pass through Elstree and Borehamwood. The year of introduction of 8041, 1936, had seen a minor boom in the London coal traffic, such that L&Y 0-6-0s had been sent up to help out. As more (gigantic in comparison) 8Fs arrived the situation eased and the Central Division 0-6-0s drifted back north. The modern building in the background is the recently established fire testing station.

8041 and crew at Toton, 7 November 1936. 'The new C1. 8F 2-8-0s from Vulcan Foundry are frequently to be seen working from Toton to Willesden' *The Railway Observer* reported that year. They were 'painted in the new style' by which they meant the block lettering.

8042 ended up in Israel never to be seen again after about 1958, so it's handy that we have an 'official portrait' of 1936 (though you never quite know what you are looking at with these LMS 'officials' – the authorities were not above substituting numbers...). Boiler top washout plugs in front of firebox, the other pair near the smokebox yet to appear. The reversing reach rod (burnished to an almost unnatural degree) is seen to be in two parts, bolted together, making its removal easier. So there it all is, in perfect clarity – no 'Royal' was ever turned out better...

'48042'
Built as 8042 at Vulcan Foundry 9/36
Sheds: Toton 10/10/36
Withdrawn from traffic 10/41, to WD 12/41 as 596, shipped to Persia, becomes 41.207, thence to Egypt/Palestine 1944 as 9379; becomes 70596. Taken into Israeli stock 1948, withdrawn 1958.

'48043'
Built as 8043 at Vulcan Foundry 9/36
Sheds: Toton 10/10/36
Withdrawn from traffic 10/41, to WD 11/41 as 597, shipped to Persia, becomes 41.193, remains there, gone by 1963.

'48044'
Built as 8044 at Vulcan Foundry 9/36
Sheds: Toton 10/10/36; Heaton Mersey 11/2/39
Withdrawn from traffic 10/41, to WD 12/41 as 598, shipped to Persia, becomes 41.196, thence to Egypt/Palestine 1944 as 9371; sent to Italy, becomes 70598. Withdrawn 1953 as 737.013.

'48047'
Built as 8047 at Vulcan Foundry 9/36
Sheds: Wellingborough 10/10/36
Withdrawn from traffic 9/41, to WD 11/41 as 586, shipped to Persia, becomes 41.161, thence to Egypt/Palestine 1944 as 9377; becomes 70586. Taken into Israeli stock 1948, withdrawn 1958.

'48048'
Built as 8048 at Vulcan Foundry 10/36
Sheds: Wellingborough 10/10/36
Withdrawn from traffic 10/41, to WD 11/41 as 600, shipped to Persia, becomes 41.183, remains there, gone by 1963.

How 8042 looked a year or two later, stabled in the gloom alongside Devons Road Bow MPD, September 1938.

8043 remained in Persia and did not return but we are lucky have two views of it at work in this country – the first at Bourne End on 19 August 1939, days before the outbreak of war and with plans already afoot in the WD concerning the matter of 'war locomotives'. H.C. Casserley, courtesy R.M. Casserley.

Even more remarkably, here it is passing the Casserley residence with a southbound freight at Berkhamsted on 25 July 1940. The number of photographs taken privately actually during wartime are of course vanishingly small. The tarpaulin would be there for the Blackout. H.C. Casserley, courtesy R.M. Casserley.

'48049'

Built as 8049 at Vulcan Foundry 10/36
Sheds: Wellingborough 10/10/36
Withdrawn from traffic 10/41, to WD 12/41 as 610, shipped to Persia, becomes 41.209, remains there, gone by 1963.

'48051'

Built as 8051 at Vulcan Foundry 10/36
Sheds: Wellingborough 10/10/36
Withdrawn from traffic 10/41, to WD 12/41 as 607, shipped to Persia, becomes 41.206, thence to Egypt/Palestine 1944; becomes 70607. Renumbered 502 in 1952, purchased by Egyptian State Railways 1956.

'48052'

Built as 8052 at Vulcan Foundry 10/36
Sheds: Saltley 14/11/36; Staveley 12/12/36
Withdrawn from traffic 10/41, to WD 12/41 as 601, shipped to Persia, becomes 41.194, remains there, gone by 1963.

'48058'

Built as 8058 at Vulcan Foundry 10/36
Sheds: Canklow 14/11/36
Withdrawn from traffic 11/41, to WD 12/41 as 612, shipped to Persia, becomes 41.195, thence to Egypt/Palestine 1944 as 9352; sent to Italy, becomes 70612. Withdrawn 1953 as 737.015.

Toton's 8044, eventually to be withdrawn and disposed of in Italy in 1953, stands at Sheffield Grimesthorpe in 1938. It had gone first to Toton and went on to Heaton Mersey in 1939 before its requisition as 598.

The only picture to be found of 8047, at an unknown shed – date too unknown. Its last resting place was Israel.

8048, by contrast, finished its days somewhere in Persia. Up until its requisition and becoming WD 600 it played its routine part in Midland line freight operations, as here passing Kettering with southbound coal tender first on 27 March 1937. H.F. Wheeler Collection, courtesy R.S. Carpenter.

Working conventionally, 8048 has more southbound coal, at Elstree on 5 June 1937.

Wellingborough's 8051 with an immense train of coal empties returning north at Chiltern Green, 31 May 1939. Requisitioned as WD 607 it was eventually purchased by the Egyptian State Railways.

8052 on arrival at Derby in another Vulcan delivery, along with two others and their 'parts wagons', 11 October 1936. This 8F saw out its days in Persia.

8058 at Cricklewood on 24 September 1938. Before requisition as WD 612, it had been at Canklow; it ended up in Italy about 1953.

'48059'
Built as 8059 at Vulcan Foundry 10/36
Sheds: Canklow 14/11/36; Stourton 10/9/38; Toton 8/10/38
Withdrawn from traffic 11/41, to WD 12/41 as 613, shipped to Persia, becomes 41.205, thence to Egypt/Palestine 1945/46; becomes 70607. Renumbered 515 in 1952, purchased by Egyptian State Railways 1956.

'48066'
Built as 8066 at Vulcan Foundry 11/36
Sheds: Derby 12/12/36; Leicester 9/1/37
Withdrawn from traffic 10/41, to WD 12/41 as 608. Shipped to Persia but LOST: jettisoned when SS PENTRIDGE HALL got in difficulties during a storm. Tender later used with 553.

'48068'
Built as 8068 at Vulcan Foundry 11/36
Sheds: Wellingborough 12/12/36
Withdrawn from traffic 11/41, to WD 12/41 as 622. Shipped to Persia but LOST: jettisoned when SS PENTRIDGE HALL got in difficulties during a storm. Tender later used with 556.

'48071'
Built as 8071 at Vulcan Foundry 12/36
Sheds: Nottingham 12/12/36
Withdrawn from traffic 11/41, to WD 12/41 as 617. Shipped to Persia but LOST: jettisoned when SS PENTRIDGE HALL got in difficulties during a storm. Tender later used with 554.

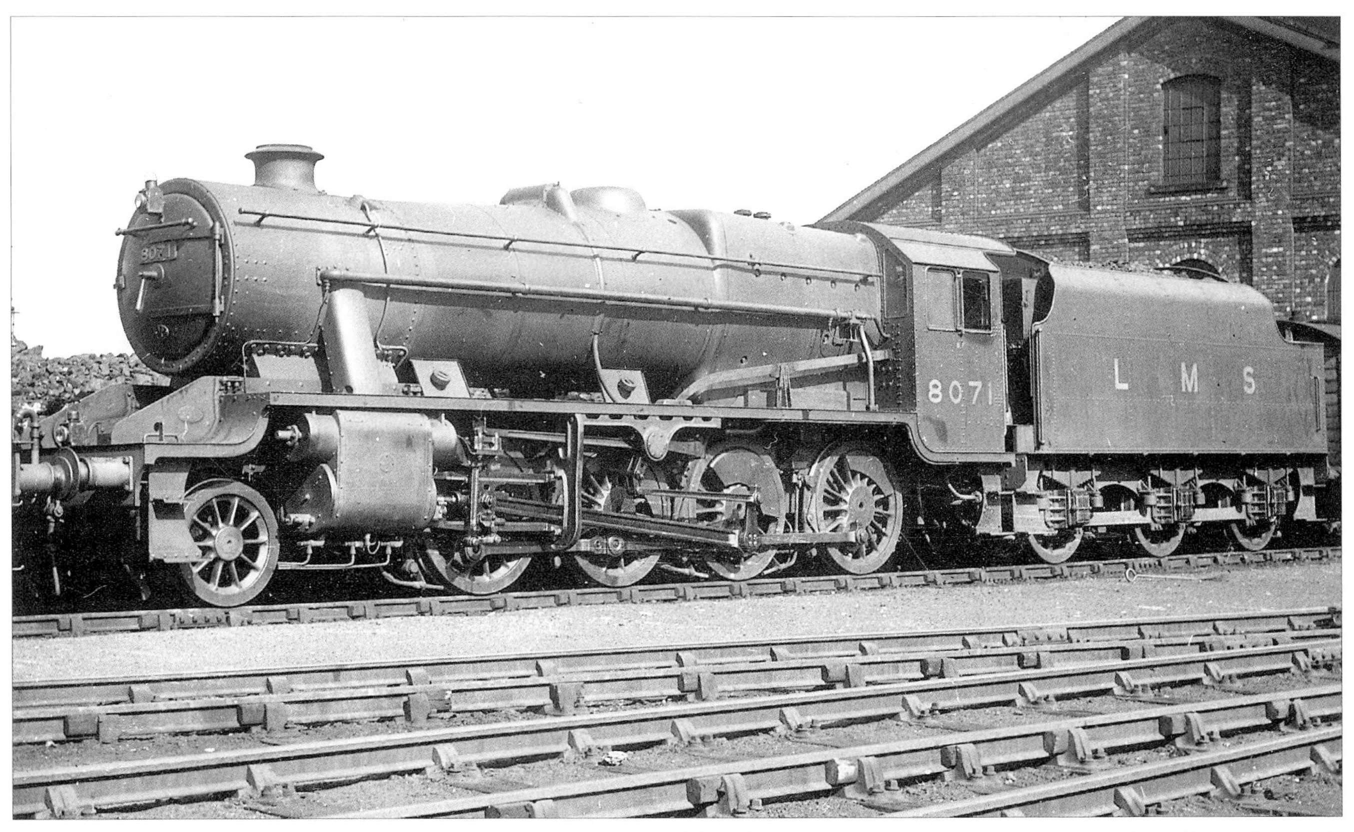

Nottingham's 8071 at Stourton MPD, Leeds, July 1938. Requisitioned as WD 617, 8071 never returned to Britain, though it lies closer to home than most; it was one of the four jettisoned after breaking free (or threatening to do so) when SS PENTRIDGE HALL got into trouble during a storm, leaving Swansea but forced to dock at Glasgow. W. Potter.

'48072'
Built as 8072 at Vulcan Foundry 12/36
Sheds: Nottingham 12/12/36
Withdrawn from traffic 10/41, to WD 12/41 as 609, shipped to Persia, becomes 41.198. Thence to Egypt/Palestine 1944 as 9373; sent to Italy, becomes 70609. Withdrawn 1953 as 737.014.

'48086'
Built as 8086 at Vulcan Foundry 1/37
Sheds: Normanton 13/2/37
Withdrawn from traffic 10/41, to WD 11/41 as 605, shipped to Persia, becomes 41.231, thence to Egypt/Palestine 1944 as 9358; becomes 70605. Taken into Israeli stock 1948, withdrawn 1958.

'48087'
Built as 8087 at Vulcan Foundry 1/37
Sheds: Normanton 13/2/37; Royston 14/1/39; Heaton Mersey 11/2/39
Withdrawn from traffic 11/41, to WD 12/41 as 619. Shipped to Persia but LOST: jettisoned when SS PENTRIDGE HALL got in difficulties during a storm. Tender later used with 555.

'48091'
Built as 8091 at Vulcan Foundry 2/37
Sheds: Kirkby 13/2/37
Withdrawn from traffic 9/41, to WD 11/41 as 589, shipped to Persia, becomes 41.185. Thence to Egypt/Palestine 1944 as 9351; sent to Italy, becomes 70589. Withdrawn 1953 as 737.010.

8072 in Britain, in a rarely (if ever) photographed corner at Nottingham MPD, about 1938. Behind is the former Repair Shop; the corrugated iron structure is the wheel drop building.

Sent to Persia as 609, LMS 8072 ended up in Italy as 70609 and was eventually withdrawn in 1953 as 737.014. In that guise it was out of use at a depot in Naples on 8 September that year.

Kirkby's 8091 before it was requisitioned and shipped abroad as WD 589. It disappeared in Italy in the middle 1950s.

Davy Jones' Locker...